MARKETING IN THE 21ST CENTURY

MARKETING IN THE 21ST CENTURY

Integrated Marketing Communication
Volume 4

Deborah L. Owens and
Douglas R. Hausknecht
Volume Editors

Bruce D. Keillor, General Editor

Praeger Perspectives

Westport, Connecticut
London

Library of Congress Cataloging-in-Publication Data

Marketing in the 21st century / Bruce D. Keillor, general editor.
   p. cm.
  Includes bibliographical references and index.
  ISBN-13: 978–0–275–99275–0 (set : alk. paper)
  ISBN-13: 978–0–275–99276–7 (vol 1 : alk. paper)
  ISBN-13: 978–0–275–99277–4 (vol 2 : alk. paper)
  ISBN-13: 978–0–275–99278–1 (vol 3 : alk. paper)
  ISBN-13: 978–0–275–99279–8 (vol 4 : alk. paper)

  1. Marketing. I. Keillor, Bruce David.
  HF5415.M2194 2007
  658.8—dc22   2007016533

British Library Cataloguing in Publication Data is available.

Library of Congress Catalog Card Number: 2007016533
ISBN-13: 978–0–275–99275–0 (set)
ISBN-13: 978–0–275–99276–7 (vol. 1)
ISBN-13: 978–0–275–99277–4 (vol. 2)
ISBN-13: 978–0–275–99278–1 (vol. 3)
ISBN-13: 978–0–275–99279–8 (vol. 4)

First published in 2007

Praeger Publishers, 88 Post Road West, Westport, CT 06881
An imprint of Greenwood Publishing Group, Inc.
www.praeger.com

Printed in the United States of America

The paper used in this book complies with the
Permanent Paper Standard issued by the National
Information Standards Organization (Z39.48–1984).

10 9 8 7 6 5 4 3 2 1

Contents

SET INTRODUCTION

It is my privilege to introduce this four-volume set, *Marketing in the 21st Century*. Given the myriad changes that have taken place in the area of marketing over the past several years, and the increasingly dynamic nature of marketing as a business discipline, the publication of these volumes is particularly relevant and timely. Each volume deals with an aspect of marketing that is both a fundamental component of marketing in this new century as well as one that requires new perspectives as the marketplace continues to evolve.

The set addresses four of the most compelling areas of marketing, each of which is changing the foundation of how academics and businesspeople approach the marketing tasks necessary for understanding and succeeding in the changing business environment. These areas are global marketing, direct marketing, firm-customer interactions, and marketing communications. By using recognized experts as authors—both academic and business practitioners—the volumes have been specifically compiled to include not just basic academic research, but to speak to business people in terms of how they can translate the information contained in each chapter into long-term success for their firm or organization.

Volume 1, *New World Marketing*, edited by Timothy J. Wilkinson and Andrew R. Thomas, deals with the salient aspects of the global marketplace. More specifically, it focuses on the realities of the 21st-century global market and then moves into how to identify emerging markets of opportunity, operate in these markets successfully from the perspective of the customer, and develop global strategies that are grounded in the concept of constant improvement through the use of value-added strategies. Authors of numerous books and articles related to international marketing, with extensive experience in executive education in international/global marketing, the editors are uniquely qualified to create a cutting-edge volume in their area of expertise.

In Volume 2, *Interactive and Multi-Channel Marketing,* edited by William J. Hauser and Dale M. Lewison, the focus shifts toward the various mechanisms through which firms and organizations can establish a means for direct interaction with their customers, whether individual consumers or other businesses. Using a two-step approach, Volume 2 discusses in great depth issues related to understanding the various direct-marketing options and then moves on to the application of these options to maximize results. As Director and Associate Director, respectively, of the Taylor Institute for Direct Marketing at The University of Akron, the leading institute worldwide for direct marketing, the editors have the ability to draw on the knowledge of the "best and brightest" in this rapidly emerging and influential area of marketing.

Volume 3, *Company and Customer Relations,* edited by Linda M. Orr and Jon M. Hawes, tackles the challenges of not only establishing and maintaining a functioning relationship between company and customer, but also how to sell successfully in the 21st century. Along the way, they deal with thorny issues such as when to disengage customers and where technology fits into what are, typically, personal interactions. Dr. Hawes is a well-recognized expert in building and maintaining customer trust, while Dr. Orr has a wide range of business and academic experience in organizational learning. This combination of perspectives has resulted in a volume that deals head-on with issues of immediate concern for any business organization.

Finally, Volume 4, *Integrated Marketing Communication,* edited by Deborah L. Owens and Douglas R. Hausknecht, addresses the various means of creating a basis for communication between company and customer that goes well beyond the traditional approaches of advertising, public relations, and sales promotion. The volume begins by considering how the new age customer "thinks" in the context of consumer behavior and then segues into methods to construct an interactive communication platform. Both editors are widely recognized in business and academic circles as experts in the field of marketing communication. They are also known for their ability to view traditional marketing communication tools "outside of the box." The result is a volume that puts a truly fresh perspective on communicating with customers.

Each of the volumes in the set presents the most advanced thinking in their respective areas. Collectively, the set is the definitive collection of the necessary new paradigms for marketing success in the 21st century. It has been my pleasure to work with the volume editors, as well as with many of the chapter authors, in bringing this collection to you. I am convinced that, regardless of your area of interest in the field of marketing, you will find *Marketing in the 21st Century* an invaluable and timeless resource.

                                                    Bruce D. Keillor, General Editor

Part I

Consumer Behavior

CHAPTER 1

MARKETING TO CHILDREN: THE FOUNDATION OF CRADLE-TO-GRAVE BRAND RELATIONSHIPS

Anna McAlister

Child consumers are an important target segment to be understood by consumer behavior analysts and marketing strategists. An understanding of this segment can lead to high profitability, since children play an important role in adults' consumption choices. Understanding children is also essential if marketers are to adhere to an ethical code of conduct, since young consumers comprise a vulnerable group whose capacity limitations can easily be violated either intentionally or unintentionally.

This chapter commences with a brief overview of the importance of the child segment, followed by a description of current marketing practices involving children and the influence of these practices on children's attitudes to traditional advertising and marketing messages. Marketing efforts are discussed in terms of their success, particularly with respect to children's recall of information presented, and their consequences, both positive and negative. The chapter concludes with a discussion of guidelines to assist in the development of new promotional campaigns. Concluding comments are provided regarding specific ethical questions that should always be considered when marketing products to children.

IMPORTANCE OF THE CHILD SEGMENT

Research has shown that children play a seminal role in household spending decisions, with estimates that between 30 and 50 percent of annual household expenditure in the United States[1] and Australia[2] is determined by children's demands for particular product purchases. In the United States, this influence equated to $187.7 billion of parents' spending being determined by children's product requests in 1997. In addition to the financial outlay made by parents in response to children's requests, a further $23.4 billion was spent by children (that is, from their own allowance or pocket money) in 1997. This figure has been growing at an unadjusted rate of 15–20 percent per annum[3] and may currently sit at around U.S.$96 billion per year. These figures do not include the annual household or personal spending arising from teenagers as consumers. Teenagers' independent purchases were reported to have amounted to U.S.$55 billion in 1989;[4] however, due to methodological inconsistencies, current figures are not readily available.

Clearly, children constitute a profitable market segment to be targeted by strategists. Recently, academic research has begun to focus on "cradle-to-grave" marketing, acknowledging that brand preferences arising in childhood may pave the way to lifelong relationships between consumers and branded products. Children's requests for specific product purchases begin to emerge at a median age of two years. Typically, these early requests are for products that the child can name by brand and to which they are frequently exposed (such as daily exposure to breakfast cereal).[5] Marketers have realized that there is merit in their brand's name being familiar to children, because as child consumers age they feel bonded to a particular brand. As such, auto and airline companies appeal to children through their advertising in order to position their brand name in the young people's evoked sets and thereby ensure a relationship with a future generation of consumers.[6]

There is currently a great deal of debate surrounding the appropriateness of marketing efforts to shape brand loyalties in children. The prominence of advertisements in children's lives is tremendous. In 2002, approximately $15 billion was spent in the United States on marketing communications specifically directed at children.[7] However, this salience of marketing communications in children's lives is considered by some to be unreasonable. Messages reach children predominantly via television,[8] but also through print media, product placements, Internet games sites, sales promotions, sponsorship efforts, packaging, public relations, and in-school marketing. Elizabeth S. Moore argues that children must possess at least two requisite cognitive skills in order to be capable of processing marketing and advertising communications. Moore explains that first, children must be able to distinguish between commercial and noncommercial content. Second, they must be able to identify the persuasive intent inherent in advertising and use this knowledge to interpret marketing messages. The first of these cognitive capacity requirements is usually evident in children 5 years of age, but the second is typically not achieved until at least 8 years of age[9] (and not employed without prompting from parents or other adults until later than approximately 12 years of age).[10] Therefore, young consumers are considered particularly vulnerable. This conclusion may hold implications for advertising regulations and public policy and will be discussed in further detail toward the end of this chapter.

EXAMPLES OF CURRENT MARKETING PRACTICES TARGETING CHILDREN

This section details two common methods used in marketing to capture the attention of young children. Each of these methods is intended by strategists to increase product recognition and to promote favorable attitudes toward the advertised products. Since both recognition[11] and attitude toward a product[12] have been viewed as predictors of future product use, these techniques may be particularly powerful in building brand relationships to secure a future generation of consumers.

Mere Exposure

"Mere exposure" is a term used to refer to the phenomenon whereby repeated exposure to a stimulus results in an individual's increased positive affect surrounding the stimulus.[13] In the marketing context, mere exposure is used to develop positive affect not only for the specific stimulus to which individuals are exposed, but also for the brand and group of products represented by the stimulus.[14] A popular and universal illustration of the mere exposure effect is the use of the "Golden Arches" that represent McDonald's family restaurants. The "M" is a symbol to which people are frequently exposed (in advertisements, freeway exit signs, and so forth), with the intention that the familiarity of the symbol will create comforting recognition for potential consumers. When traveling, individuals may find that advertisements representing their food choices all seem foreign, with the exception of the familiar M. Thus, the positive feelings induced through mere exposure may result in hungry travelers opting for the familiar M and the restaurant it represents.

In terms of the mere exposure effect, children are not only influenced by company *symbols* such as the Golden Arches. They are also easily targeted to develop positive feelings in response to branded objects, particularly toys, that appear frequently in their environment. Since children are known to be natural collectors, companies can use collectable toys to build a positive effect and as a vehicle to position their brand names within the child's own home, in order to create high brand exposure for the child. Drawing again on the McDonald's restaurant chain as an example, collectable Happy Meal toys exemplify stimuli to which the child is frequently exposed (that is, when playing with the toys within his or her own home) and with which he or she may thereby create a brand relationship.

Trade Characters and Spokes Characters

Trade characters (also referred to as spokes characters) are often employed as "attention grabbers," acting as spokespersons to promote children's products. Trade characters are intended to bond a child to a brand so that the child's brand awareness might form the basis of brand preference either immediately or later in life.[15] A well-known example of this method of marketing to child consumers is the use of three animated characters—"Snap, "Crackle," and "Pop"—who are used to promote Kellogg's Rice Krispies, a popular children's breakfast cereal.

The use of trade characters is reported to be very successful, both in terms of promoting product recognition and also product liking. Using a sample of three- to six-year-old children to conduct an empirical study, Richard Mizerski[16] has reported that accurate recognition of a product advertised via a spokes character is typically around 86 percent (range: 69 percent at three years of age to 96 percent at six years of age). Several other research studies[17] have reported similar results. Children's liking of the advertised product correlated very strongly with recognition, averaging 87 percent for spokes character–advertised products (range: 71 percent at three years of age to 95 percent at six years of age).

Such findings would suggest that spokes characters are an effective means of advertising to children. However, several ethical questions have been raised in relation to this method. For example, there is concern regarding the fact that some adult-oriented products are advertised using spokes characters that have been shown to positively influence children's recognition. Mizerski's study[18] found that three- to six-year-old children's recognition of the Camel cigarette brand was higher than might be expected for an adult product. On average, 52 percent of children recognized the Camel cigarette brand (range: 25 percent at three years of age to 72 percent at six years of age), and this level of recognition was attributed to the use of an attractive cartoon camel as the brand's spokes character. Similar results were found in a 1993 survey conducted for the R.J. Reynolds Tobacco Company; 95 percent of a U.S. sample of 10- to 17-year-olds associated Joe Camel with cigarettes. One saving grace in the case of the young children's recognition of Camel cigarettes is that liking for the product decreased strongly with age (from 41 percent of 3-year-olds to 3 percent of 6-year-olds).[19]

The use of spokes characters has further been criticized by some researchers as being unfair when used to target very young children. Research has shown that preschool children are particularly susceptible to the effects of spokes character advertising because their cognitive capacity is limited and they are not equipped to distinguish between spokes characters and humans. It is typically not until five years of age that a child develops proficiency at distinguishing spokes characters from real people.[20] However, marketers seem reluctant to discontinue the use of spokes characters to target preschool children, since this is the easiest group of children to target; children's levels of interest in spokes character advertisements dwindle with the onset of cognitive developments that empower them to distinguish cartoon characters from humans.[21] Since attention to advertising generally declines with age, marketers appear to be tempted to target to their most attentive audience—in this case, the under-fives.

Marketers are also eager to hold the attention of "tweens" (children who are nearly teens) and are becoming increasingly creative in their attempts to employ spokes characters who are less childish than those traditionally used in spokes character advertising. In the United Kingdom, for example, Quaker Sugar Puffs have traditionally been marketed using a honey monster, but this character has recently adopted a new image as "Sugar Puff Daddy," a rap star. Sugar Puff Daddy has been featured in television advertisements for the breakfast cereal. These commercials were filmed in the style of a rap music video, with the spokes character dressed as a Hollywood rap artist.

CHILDREN'S ATTITUDES TOWARD ADVERTISING

A great deal of research has indicated that children as young as eight years hold skeptical attitudes toward traditional advertising, including television commercials. This section is used to briefly detail children's negative attitudes toward advertising, since an understanding of these attitudes is needed to inform the strategies used to appeal to children.

Creating a Good Advertisement

The success of marketing techniques designed to promote children's products, as well as the effectiveness of parent and child advocate missions, rests on adherence to a simple set of guidelines. Any party wishing to sway the opinions of children needs to first understand that children are fussy, sensitive to criticism (even that which is implicit), and are becoming increasingly savvy consumers. On the basis of intelligence acquired from numerous marketing strategists and research experts, Barrie Gunter and Adrian Furnham[22] have identified four simple guidelines to which one should adhere when designing a marketing campaign to communicate to children:

1. Do not use a condescending tone or message.
2. Be straightforward and sincere.
3. Give young people credit for being motivated by rational values.
4. Be as personal as possible.

Academic researchers Helene Hill and Jennifer Tilley[23] contribute further with the following advice:

Young consumers are very aware of what they want a product to do for them in terms of making them look or feel better or being better accepted within their peer group....

Whichever techniques for reaching child consumers are employed, marketers should always remember the importance of knowing their market. One particularly important feature of the children's market is that its tastes and interests can change very quickly. It is therefore essential for marketers to remain vigilant so that any changes and their marketing implications can be detected almost as soon as they occur.

This advice directs marketers to the importance of advertisements that clearly demonstrate both the instrumental and symbolic performance of the advertised product. Moreover, the desired qualities of a product should not be assumed.

James U. McNeal[24] cautions that a common pitfall when marketing children's products is to assume that children will want the types of products the marketers desired during their own childhoods. Further, McNeal warns, "It is common practice to try to capitalize on the potential of the children's market by producing adult products in kid form—scale them down, make them smaller, lighter, simpler, more fun." Extensive market research, including focus groups and structured child interviews, would be advisable to feed into the design of children's products. Anecdotal evidence suggests that children are eager critics of marketing communications for products that do not represent the current fashion.

The Ad Is Good, but the Kids Do Not Like It!

The aforementioned guidelines are essential to ensure that children of all ages (even the very youngest) are not offended or deterred by the presentation of a marketing message. However, further issues arise when older children are the target segment. Several researchers have indicated that from the age of eight years, children begin to understand the persuasive intention of advertisements and start to appreciate that some advertisements contain content that is misleading or untrue.[25] It is generally agreed that children's developing understanding of persuasive intent is accompanied by an emergence of skepticism and doubt surrounding the validity of marketers' claims.[26]

Traditionally, the skeptical attitudes evident in children aged over 8 years posed a threat to advertisers. Armed with their "cognitive and attitudinal defenses,"[27] children gradually became more resistant to the seductive appeal of advertisements for which they were targets.[28] Between ages 8 and 12 years, children typically required prompting from a parent or other adult in order to utilize these defenses, but by age 12 were generally capable of rejecting advertisements and criticizing marketing messages if they so desired.[29] So even if the advertisement was not offensive as such, it may still have been rejected by older children.

However, marketing strategists have utilized this knowledge of children's attitudes to design new and exciting ways to market to children in the hope that older children's negative attitudes toward traditional advertising will be overcome. Moreover, marketers seem to be aware that it is more difficult to identify the persuasive intent of subtly delivered marketing messages. That is, advertisements that are able to "fly under the radar" when disguised as entertainment are less likely to be detected as deliberate attempts to manipulate an audience and are therefore less likely to evoke the feelings of skepticism that result in cognitive defense.

CREATIVE TECHNIQUES FOR SUBTLE MARKETING

This section outlines a number of techniques commonly used by marketers to communicate messages to children in ways that are subtler than those traditionally used in direct advertising. Each of these methods appears to result in less frequent objections from children. Presumably, this is because children are not as proficient at detecting the persuasive intent of the more subtly delivered messages.

Sponsorship of Children's Web Sites and Online Games

Online gaming is now a popular form of entertainment for children, with estimates that roughly 64 percent of children aged 5 to 14 years visit the Internet regularly for the purpose of playing online games.[30] Advertising is now permitted on the vast majority of children's Web sites (current estimates suggest this proportion may be as high as 98 percent), and more than 60 percent of children's sites source their revenue primarily from advertising and sponsorship.[31]

Sponsored games, known as "advergames," are fun and interactive for children, offering colorful, fast-paced screen movement. Embedded in the games are brand messages that are most likely processed subconsciously while the child focuses its primary attention on game play, but are nevertheless unavoidable since integral game components (including game pieces, prizes, or treasures) bear brand logos or slogans.[32] Children's participation in advergames therefore builds brand awareness, especially since Web site revisiting is likely to occur. Moreover, the subtlety of the brand exposure is unlikely to be objectionable to children, and the pairing of brand images with positive stimuli such as game prizes and rewards conditions children to experience a positive effect in response to the brand alone. Hence, sponsorship of children's Web sites appears to be a successful mechanism by which brand awareness can be enhanced and pitfalls involving children's skepticism can be avoided.

Product Placement

Peter Bartram's research has led to the conclusion that children respond best to marketing messages that reach them in an apparently inadvertent manner by appearing subtly in their surroundings.[33] Increasingly often, marketers are using product placement to achieve this goal. Product placement occurs when branded products are seen or referred to in the media, including movies, video games, and film clips. Product placement is all about the products being seen and used, where endorsement is implied.

Notable examples of product placement include the use of a "Big Boy" shaped spacecraft in the original *Austin Powers* movie (that is, promotion of the Big Boy Restaurants International chain) and the use of Ray-Ban sunglasses by Tom Cruise in the *Top Gun* movie. Research findings indicate that recall of product placement items a day after viewing is higher than next-day recall of products viewed in traditional television commercials. Although product placement recall varies according to factors such as the prominence of the product within the entertainment medium and the duration of its appearance, the average next-day recall of product placement items by teenagers is reported to be around 38 percent.[34]

The effects of product placement are not only seen in terms of recall. Children also show remarkable behavioral changes in response to having watched a movie that incorporates product placement. For example, in a study of children aged 6 to 12 years, a control group of children who viewed a scene from *Home Alone* that showed no branded products was found to be significantly less likely to choose Pepsi over Coke, compared to a matched group of children who had seen a similar clip from the movie that involved a clearly labeled Pepsi drink being spilled at the dinner table.[35] This finding suggests that the children who viewed the clip incorporating a Pepsi product placement were positively influenced to respond to offerings of the Pepsi drink. The study involved good empirical controls to rule out alternative interpretations of the findings. Interestingly, the children's recall for the drink in that study was higher than average product placement recall. Sixty-seven percent of children aged 11 to 12 years accurately recalled the product from the movie clip, as did 50 percent of children aged between 6 and 7 years.[36]

A final note on product placement is that it is considered by many to be a relatively underhanded manner of promoting a brand or product. In the United States, as well as several other countries, television advertising of certain products is banned, and limits are enforced regarding the appropriateness of marketing certain products to "vulnerable" segments. However, product placement provides a forum for marketers to promote their products without violating the bans that pertain to direct advertising methods.

To illustrate, although cigarette and alcohol companies are banned from advertising to children directly, in theory they could pay for product placement opportunities to promote their brand and products to whomever they like.

Promotional Offers

According to the Promotional Products Association International, "promotional products marketing" may be defined as "[t]he advertising or promotional medium or method that uses promotional products, such as ad specialties, premiums, business gifts, awards, prizes, or commemoratives."[37] Typical items used in promotional efforts targeting children include T-shirts, watches, wallets, kites, balls, puzzles, stuffed animals, and figurines.

Promotional offers are used by companies to achieve any number of purposes, such as thanking customers for their patronage, ensuring the company name is salient in the consumer's environment, reinforcing the name of an existing company, product, or service, or introducing new products (for example, pairing a sample of a new product with the purchase of a product that is currently used by the consumer).[38] Children are known to be very responsive to reward and reinforcement. Subsequently, they are particularly receptive to the effects of promotional marketing efforts because of the reward associated with receiving a "gift" with their purchase.

Children may also be strongly influenced by promotional offers because they typically lack the cognitive capacity to appraise a promotion and become skeptical of its offerings in the same way that adults do. Adults may develop feelings of skepticism toward promotions because they are dubious of the *value* of the offer, or they may doubt the *quality* of the products involved.

According to the developmental stages described by child psychologist Jean Piaget, the ability of children to compare numbers and values of things does not emerge until the concrete operational stage (that is, 7 to 11 years of age), and children cannot reason about abstract concepts or think hypothetically until the formal operational period (that is, 11 years onward).[39] A great deal of research evidence has shown support for Piaget's stages of development; therefore, it is concluded that children are not capable of properly evaluating the value of promotional offers until the "tween" years.

Similarly, children typically do not question the *quality* of promotional product offerings. Again, Piaget's stages of development provide an understanding of children's developmental limitations that are relevant to understanding their responses to promotional offers. Even in the concrete operational period (that is, 7 to 11 years), children are learning to think logically and rationally, but are typically not capable of thinking beyond problems that are physically present. Therefore, until 11 years of age, children are unlikely to foresee problems with product performance. Children are likely to be overcome by the symbolic performance of the promotional products (for example, feeling overly excited about how much fun and entertainment a toy will provide or how "cool" a promotional clothing item will look) and are less likely (due to their lack of cognitive ability) to foresee potential problems with a product's instrumental performance. Moreover, simply due to a lack of consumer experience, children are less likely than adults to have experienced prior feelings of disappointment with product performance and may therefore be less likely to anticipate problems with product quality.

HOW MARKETING SHAPES CHILDREN'S BEHAVIOR BEYOND THE CONSUMER CONTEXT

So far, this chapter has discussed a number of techniques that are used to encourage children to purchase particular products. However, mere exposure, spokes characters, Web site sponsorship, advergames, product placement, and promotional offers each have the potential to influence the child's behavior not only in terms of actual or intended purchasing, but also with respect to various other behavioral outcomes. This section describes how child-oriented marketing techniques have the potential to impact nonpurchase behavioral outcomes in children, including overeating, collecting, family relationships, and illegal activities including underage drinking and smoking.

Overeating

Several research papers have linked food advertising to overeating and obesity in children. For example, a U.K. study has reported a significant positive relationship between children's recognition of television food advertisements and amount of food consumed when children were instructed that they could eat as little or as much as they wanted with no time constraint.[40] Among the group of 42 nine- to eleven-year-old children, those who were obese recognized significantly more food advertisements than those who were not obese; however, there was no difference between the two groups with respect to their recognition of nonfood advertisements.

The researchers concluded that exposure to food advertisements promotes excessive consumption. It is important to note that little is understood about the direction of causality in this relationship. It is implied that exposure to food advertising "causes" children to overeat and subsequently be obese; however, it may be the case that children who are already experiencing weight problems for other reasons (for example, genetic predisposition or poor parenting) may be more likely to attend to food advertisements. Therefore, it should not be concluded that food advertising necessarily leads to overeating. What is fair to conclude is that food advertising clearly does not assist children to learn to control their food consumption.

The burden of responsibility, in terms of whether marketers should stop targeting their food advertisements at children, governments should restrict food advertising, parents should control their children's eating, or children need to be taught self-discipline, is discussed at the end of this chapter. Clearly, obesity is an increasingly concerning societal problem,[41] and, whatever the role food advertising plays (whether it is causal or merely exacerbatory of a preexisting condition), it should be considered as a factor that may contribute to children's overeating. Currently food advertising is very prominent in children's lives; during the screening of children's television shows, 37 percent of U.S. advertisements and 49 percent of U.K.

advertisements are for food products. Snack foods are the most commonly advertised products on children's television, followed by breakfast cereals and fast food.[42]

Children's overeating may also be influenced by marketing of food products via mechanisms other than traditional television advertising. Because children are very easily manipulated by reward and reinforcement, situations in which food consumption is associated with positive affect may result in a propensity for children to eat more than what is necessary. The attractiveness of spokes characters may be responsible for children being conditioned to find eating "fun" and entertaining. Therefore, children may become tempted to eat beyond the point of satiation.

Similarly, product placement of food products in movies or other media that links the consumption of a certain food or beverages to a cool image or a fun experience may lead children to not only want to try the product, but to continue to consume the product in order to prolong the positive experience with which it is associated. Using again the Pepsi example of product placement in the *Home Alone* movie, children may see Pepsi consumption as a fun activity because it appeared in a fun scene in the movie. However, if children drink Pepsi and continue to drink several cups of the drink after their thirst has been quenched, the excessive consumption effectively results in unnecessary sugar and caffeine intake, both of which are undesirable for children (as well as adults, for that matter).

Product pairing, such as that which occurs in promotional offers, may also play a role in the overeating behavior of children. It seems likely that there would be times when a child demands that the parent purchase a food product (such as a packet of chips) purely to obtain the promotional item that accompanies the food product (such as a Tazo or playing card), despite the fact that the child is not necessarily hungry. In instances where a child consumes a food product in order to collect a specialty item and not because the food fulfilled a hunger, overeating has occurred.

Although current estimates are not available to illustrate how frequently children's requests for paired food and specialty items are requested when the child is not hungry, it could be argued that the frequency of such occurrences would be reduced if the specialty items were not "addictive." Many promotional offers used to target children involve specialty items that are members of collectable sets. For example, McDonald's Happy Meal toys, which are sold with children's meals, typically belong to a set, as do Tazos and trading cards, which are often paired with packets of chips. Hence, children feel compelled to acquire numerous objects to complete their collectable set, and they often want to do so quickly in order for the growth of their collection to remain competitive with that of friends or siblings.

Collecting

As outlined above, the nature of many promotional offers encourages children to pursue collecting a *set* of available items. Thus, collecting is a behavioral response that frequently occurs as a result of children's exposure to promotional marketing efforts. Statistics indicate that, in the United States, 91 percent of six- to ten-year-old children own at least one collection.[43]

Collecting behavior has been associated with positive and negative outcomes for children, both of which are discussed briefly here. In terms of positive effects, collecting allows children to feel good about acquiring a number of belongings; whereas accumulation of numerous belongings would typically be viewed as greedy or selfish, collecting is a socially acceptable behavior, encouraged by many parents.[44] The social acceptability of children's collecting may be attributable to the fact that collections are associated with active goal setting and planned behavior, both of which are desirable developmental achievements for children to accomplish.

Self-extension is another positive outcome that results from children's collecting. According to Russell W. Belk and colleagues, "self-extension" describes the symbolic fulfilment of self that occurs when a collection is completed.[45] Thus, some credit is given to the notion that collections provide a very valuable educational opportunity for children to learn to set goals and work toward them and to find that achievement of goals results in positive feelings of self-worth.

Further educational opportunities arise when children collect merchandised items. Typically, different members of a set of children's collectables have different values attributed to them. For example, rare Tazos or collectable playing cards may be worth much more than the common collectable items when children decide to swap and barter their collectables. Thus, collectables of this nature allow children to learn to share and trade in hypothetical economies.

Anecdotal evidence suggests that children's awareness of collectable sets of items may also result in negative experiences, such as feeling anxious or frustrated about the uncertainty of completing their collections. Often when a child receives a collectable item and becomes aware of the existence of a set to which that item belongs, the child will be instinctively driven to achieving set completion. Although there seems to be a lack of research evidence to qualify precisely what cognitive and affective processes lead to these outcomes, a possible explanation is offered here.

James J. Kellaris's *cognitive itch theory*[46] may be applied to children's collecting behavior to explain why set completion is necessary to resolve a "brain itch," that is, a transient mental state that causes feelings of frustration. Typically, cognitive itch theory is used to explain an individual's need to complete a song (either by singing it aloud, humming the tune, or listening to a recording) in order to diffuse pent-up frustration when a song becomes "stuck" in one's head. Kellaris argues that when having heard an incomplete song frustrates an individual, the only solution is to complete the song; distraction by substitution (that is, by listening to a different song) will not bring relief. Applied to children's collecting, the concept of a brain itch would explain why children typically remain frustrated about an incomplete collection and cannot be pacified by distractions such as the availability of other toys that are not constituent members of the collectable set.

Family Relationships

Anecdotal evidence suggests that child-oriented marketing results in an increase in children's awareness of available products, which in turn may lead to parent-child conflict and sibling rivalry. While relatively little research has investigated this phenomenon, evidence of the effect is everywhere. Anyday, at anytime, a trip to the supermarket will provide scenes of children at checkouts demanding point-of-purchase display items. In the juice aisle, children beg for the juice poppers (that is, the Tetra Paks) that feature cartoon characters on the packaging, while parents may be seen assessing the nutritional information. Children feel the urge to collect Tazos and playing cards and subsequently insist on a particular brand of chips that may not always meet with parental approval. Sibling rivalry sets in when one child has a better collection of Kinder Surprise toys or owns a greater number of rare Tazos.

Traditionally, research has focused on the *intentional* effects of marketing to children (for example, purchase requests, recall, recognition, and so forth) However, one recent study has examined the unintentional impact that families experience in response to children's increased consumer socialization experiences. Moniek Buijzen and Patti M. Valkenburg reported negative effects on family relationships having arisen in response to children's purchase requests. The authors interviewed 360 parent-child dyads in the Netherlands. The child participants in these dyads were aged 8 to 12 years. The authors report that children's purchase requests showed significant positive relationships with measures of family conflict, children's disappointment, and life dissatisfaction.[47] These results provide evidence to support the claim that "pester power"—a child's insistent demands for the purchase of a particular product—can lead to relationship denigration within families.

Alcohol and Tobacco Consumption

Older children, particularly those aged over ten years, are susceptible to taking part in activities that involve alcohol and tobacco consumption. Developmental psychologists agree that it is normal for older children and young teenagers to want to experiment with drinking and smoking and that their curiosity regarding these behaviors may stem from a number of factors, including the desire to emulate adult behavior, to fit in with a peer group, to portray a particular image to others, as well as the fact that alcohol and tobacco are not classified as illicit drugs (and are therefore considered "safe" drugs with which to experiment).[48]

Direct advertising, as well as less direct promotion of alcohol and tobacco products, can be argued as making each of these predictive risk factors more salient to children. For example, by viewing a sports event in which alcoholic beverages are subtly promoted through logos on clothing or other memorabilia, children learn to recognize the different alcohol brands and to associate those brands with sporting heroes or other adults (for example, sports coaches, umpires, and so forth) whom they may admire. Similarly, children may view a movie in which product placement of a particular brand of cigarettes occurs. Wanting to portray an image similar to that of their heroes, children may then consume the relevant brand of cigarettes.

The example linking children's smoking to *product placement* was intentionally chosen, as this seems to be a very powerful marketing tool to promote tobacco products to children. For more than a decade, cigarette advertising (that is, traditional direct advertising such as television commercials) and, to some extent, sponsorship (that is, displaying the logo of a tobacco company at a popular event) have been tightly controlled in many countries throughout the world.[49] However, evidence shows that tobacco companies exploit loopholes in policies and continue to market their products to children via the use of subtle marketing techniques, such as product placement, that do not violate such bans.

Children provide a "good" target segment for tobacco and alcohol companies since the products they promote are addictive; therefore, early indoctrination of users ensures a steady flow of future consumers. T. Bettina Cornwell's 1997 paper detailing international public policy issues in tobacco promotion reported that confidential documents seized from tobacco companies by the U.S. Federal Trade Commission were self-incriminating in terms of revealing a clear intent to get children "hooked."[50] Cornwell quotes advice that an advertising research agency provided to the tobacco industry to succeed at marketing to children. The advice items are detailed below and clearly indicate intent to exploit the risk factors previously described above as preempting children to experiment with underage smoking.

> An attempt to reach young smokers, starters, should be based...on the following major parameters:
>
> • Present the cigarette as one of a few initiations into the adult world.
>
> • In your ads create a situation taken from the day-to-day life of the young smoker but in an elegant manner have the situation touch on the basic symbols of the growing-up, maturity process.
>
> • To the best of your ability (considering some legal restraints) relate the cigarette to "pot," wine, beer, sex, etc.

As outlined above, subtle forms of product promotion are intentionally used by alcohol and tobacco companies to increase the likelihood that children will commence experimentation with drinking and smoking. These efforts on behalf of alcohol and tobacco companies may explain the documented relationships between marketing techniques and children's adoption of these behaviors.

A U.S. study of 260 teens aged 12 to 18 years (M = 14.79) has linked alcohol promotional clothing items to underage experimentation with alcohol.[51] It reports that 76.3 percent of the sample of teens had tried drinking alcohol, and more than 36 percent owned an item of clothing that promotes alcohol. Further, those whose parents gave them an alcohol promotional clothing item were more likely than others to perceive that their parents approve of underage drinking. These findings illustrate that, through the use of promotional clothing items (mostly T-shirts and hats), alcohol companies are influential in encouraging young people to take up drinking.

Research investigating the effects of cigarette promotion has reported that the relationship between brand promotion and brand choice is significantly stronger among teenagers than among adults.[52] The ability to recognize a brand is a particularly important prerequisite to young teenagers' decisions to purchase a particular brand of cigarettes.[53] Anecdotal evidence suggests that the importance of brand recognition may occur because the underage consumers are struggling to appear mature and confident in their decisions and to not be recognized as underage.

In countries where cigarette sponsorship is still permissible, sponsorship is used to enhance a brand's image, thereby increasing the probability of brand recognition. It has been argued that cigarette sponsorship is incredibly powerful in terms of extending a brand's identity by aligning with particular sports and experiences. For example, Timothy Dewhirst and Robert Sparks argue that, through its sponsorship of Formula One and Indy Car racing, the Philip Morris Marlboro brand extends its long-standing "lone cowboy" image to encompass contemporary portrayals of individualism and self-sufficiency.[54] This image enhancement may assist potential youth consumers to recognize the Marlboro brand and therefore choose it over competing brands.

Disturbing figures reflect the success of tobacco companies' sponsorship efforts. For example, a U.K. study of 726 children found that by late primary school, the majority of children are aware of sponsorship efforts. Further, more than half of the secondary school children could successfully name cigarette brands and the sporting events for which those brands were sponsors.[55]

REDIRECTION OF MARKETING EFFORTS

In the previous section, we saw that marketing can impact children's behavior to encourage overeating, collecting, and consumption of alcohol and tobacco products, while possibly being harmful to family relationships. We also saw that many of these behavioral outcomes can be detrimental to children's physical and mental health. The following section details various ways in which the potential harmful effects of marketing may be avoided. Ideally, marketing strategists would be willing to incorporate child-friendly advice into the design of future marketing campaigns. However, assuming that marketing messages continue to emerge in much the same way as they presently do, recommendations are also presented to be used by parents and child advocates to negate the unfavorable effects of marketing toward children.

Manipulation of the Polarization Effect

Empirical research has found that the effectiveness of exposure techniques can, in fact, result in an increased *negative* effect if a brand or product is originally viewed by the consumer as unfavorable.[56] Known as the "polarization effect," the consumer holds a preexisting negative attitude toward the brand or product, which is exacerbated with repeated exposure to the brand or product. It has also been suggested that polarization can occur in response to spokes character advertisements if children's preexisting attitude to the spokes character's product is negative.[57]

Armed with the knowledge that polarization can occur in response to mere exposure and spokes character marketing attempts, parents and other child advocates may be equipped to manipulate marketing attempts to their advantage. In theory, it should be possible to create in children a negative attitude toward certain products by describing those products as "bad," "dangerous," or "naughty." Exposure to the products and their spokes characters should then polarize the children's feelings toward those products to be even more negative. Clearly, though, the first step in this process can be difficult to achieve and would best be undertaken with the guidance of a child behavior expert.

Parental Involvement

A further factor that has been found to be successful in negating the messages children receive from marketers is the messages they receive from "sources of socialization," including parents.[58] Although few researchers specify exactly how the negation of marketing influences can be achieved, several have argued that children of parents who assist with interpretation of advertising, monitor and restrict television viewing, or attempt to induce in their children feelings of skepticism toward media advertising are less vulnerable to persuasion.[59]

Parents are reminded that children learn primarily through modeling (that is, by mimicking the behavior of those around them). Therefore, children's consumer behavior can be shaped by the example set by their parents. Parents who provide well-rounded good examples to their child demonstrate congruence between their behaviors and their attitudes. Most parents are aware of the need to demonstrate desired behaviors (for example, purchasing a fruit bar instead of a chocolate bar); however, many may overlook the need to demonstrate the preferred attitudes. By way of illustration, it is important for a parent to not only model the purchase of healthy food, but to also expressly communicate beliefs about the various options (for example, that the unhealthy option only looks good in the packaging, but will not help to keep the body healthy).

Not only is active involvement from parents likely to result in children's mimicking of desired behaviors, but other advantageous outcomes are also likely to occur. By following the above example of providing a model of cognitions as well as a model of actual enacted behavior, parents are forced to communicate with their children regarding decision-making processes. A great deal of evidence from the developmental psychology literature indicates that a parenting style that engages children in decision-making processes (that is, an authoritative parenting style) is more beneficial than one in which parents do not communicate about their thought processes.[60] Benefits to the child include superior academic performance, higher self-esteem, greater social competence, and fewer behavior problems. Therefore, by providing a good model of behaviors *and* cognitions, the parental influence may result not only in the reduction of negative marketing outcomes such as overeating and excessive consumption, but may also benefit family relationships (via increased social competence) and thereby reduce the frequency of pester power tantrums and the intensity of sibling rivalry.

Responsible Marketing

A further factor that can act against product promotion is "anti" campaigns or awareness appeals. Research has shown that it is possible to create a negative attitude toward a brand or product by repeatedly presenting such stimuli in a negative context. For example, repeat broadcasts of an anti-junk-food campaign, in which the packaging of particular food products is clearly depicted, can lead child viewers to feel negatively about those foods.[61] This finding suggests that marketing of potentially harmful products to children (including marketing messages that are intended for adults, but reach children) may be reversed or thwarted by campaigns designed to demote those products and their usage. Here the responsibility would lie with government and community groups to foil the efforts of marketing and advertising companies.

Ethical Considerations and the Future of Children's Marketing

This chapter has uncovered a number of potential negative outcomes resulting from marketing efforts that target children. Even marketing toward adults may impact children in a negative manner. Whether the negative effects are intentional (as in some marketers' efforts to create cigarette addiction in young people) or unintentional is not always clear. Therefore, it can be difficult to assert that marketers have a responsibility to alter the ways in which they market children's products. Perhaps the persuasive and manipulative nature of children's marketing cannot be eliminated. However, there may, in fact, be many benefits to children when they are exposed to manipulative, targeted messages. It is inevitable that *adults* will receive very targeted and persuasive messages from marketers and advertisers; therefore, exposure to messages of that nature during childhood provides a valuable socialization experience.

Consumer socialization—the process by which children acquire the skills needed to function in the marketplace as consumers—is a very important component of child development. As part of this process, children must learn how to plan a shopping trip, where to acquire various goods and services, and must also develop an understanding of the value of money and the costing system. In addition to these clearly identifiable achievement goals, children must also learn more subtle consumer skills. They must learn to become self-disciplined, to question the quality of products, and to consider the extent to which they really need a coveted product. With these developmental goals in mind, children's marketing may be viewed as an opportunity for parents to teach their children important life skills. In the absence of children's marketing, the consumer environment would effectively exclude children, making the task of consumer socialization much more difficult. Without proper consumer socialization, children would grow to be young adults entering a consumer environment without the requisite skills to function adaptively.

NOTES

1. Foxman, Ellen R., Patriay S. Tansuhaj, and Karin M. Ekstrom (1989), "Family Members' Perceptions of Adolescents' Influence in Family Decision-Making," Journal of Consumer Research, 15 (March), 433–441.

2. Australian Professional Marketing (1995), "Born to Shop," June, p. 10.

3. McNeal, James U. (1999), "The Kids Market: Myths and Realities," Paramount Market Publishing, Ithaca, NY.

4. Sellers, Patricia (1989), "The ABC's of Marketing to Kids," Fortune, May 8, 114–117.

5. McNeal, James U., and Chyon-Hwa Yeh (1993), "Stages of Consumer Socialization in Childhood," Proceedings of the Social Statistics Section, American Statistical Association, Alexandria, VA, pp. 856–860.

6. Horovitz, B. (1997), "Retailers in Search of Customers for Life", USA Today, December 18, pp. 1–2A.

7. Center for Science in the Public Interest (2003), "Pestering Parents: How Food Companies Market Obesity to Children," Washington, DC.

8. Lindstrom, Martin, and Patricia B. Seybold (2003), "Brand Child," Kogan Page, London.

9. Moore, Elizabeth S. (2004), "Children and the Changing World of Advertising," Journal of Business Ethics, 52 (June), 161–167.

10. Brucks, Merrie, Gary M. Armstrong, and Marvin E. Goldberg (1988), "Children's Use of Cognitive Defenses against Television Advertising: A Cognitive Response Approach," Journal of Consumer Research 14 (March), 471–482.

11. Fischer, Paul M., Meyer D. Schwartz, John W. Richards, Adam O. Goldstein, and Tina H. Rojas (1991), "Brand Logo Recognition by Children Aged 3 to 6 Years," Journal of the American Medical Association, 266 (22), 3145–3148.

12. McNeal, James (1987), "Children as Consumers: Insight and Implications," Lexington Books, Lexington, KY.

13. Zajonc, Robert (1968), "Attitudinal Effects of Mere Exposure," Journal of Personality and Social Psychology Monographs, 9 (2), 1–27.

14. Mizerski, Richard (1995), "The Relationship between Cartoon Trade Character Recognition and Attitude toward Product Category in Young Children," Journal of Marketing, 59 (October), 58–70.

15. Fischer et al., "Brand Logo Recognition by Children Aged 3 to 6 Years."

16. Mizerski, "The Relationship between Cartoon Trade Character Recognition and Attitude toward Product Category in Young Children."

17. Fischer et al., "Brand Logo Recognition by Children Aged 3 to 6 Years."

18. Mizerski, "The Relationship between Cartoon Trade Character Recognition and Attitude toward Product Category in Young Children."

19. Ibid.

20. Raju, P.S., and Subhash C. Lonial (1990), "Advertising to Children: Findings and Implications," in Current Issues and Research in Advertising, Vol. 12, James Leigh and Claude Martin, eds. Ann Arbor, University of Michigan, MI, 231–274.

21. Ward, Scott (1972), "Children's Reactions to Commercials," Journal of Advertising Research, 12 (April), 37–45.

22. Gunter, Barrie, and Adrian Furnham (1999), "Children as Consumers: A Psychological Analysis of the Young People's Market," Routledge, London.

23. Hill, Helene, and Jennifer Tilley (2002), "Packaging of Children's Breakfast Cereal: Manufacturers versus Children," British Food Journal, 104 (9), 766–777.

24. McNeal, James U. (1992), "Kids as Customers: A Handbook of Marketing to Children," Lexington Books, NY.

25. Macklin, M. Carole (1987), "Preschoolers' Understanding of the Informational Function of Television Advertising," Journal of Consumer Research, 14 (September), 229–239; Roberts, D. F. (1982), "Children, and Commercials: Issues, Evidence and Interventions," Prevention in Human Services, 2, 19–35; Roedder-John, Deborah (1999), "Consumer Socialization of Children: A Retrospective Look at Twenty-Five Years of Research," Journal of Consumer Research, 26 (3), 183–213.

26. Federal Trade Commission (1978), "FTC Staff Report on Television Advertising to Children," U.S. Government Printing Office, Washington, DC; Rossiter, John R., and Thomas S. Robertson (1974), "Children's TV Commercials: Testing the Defenses," Journal of Communication, 24 (4), 137–144.

27. Moore, "Children and the Changing World of Advertising."

28. Federal Trade Commission, "FTC Staff Report on Television Advertising to Children"; Rossiter and Robertson, "Children's TV Commercials."

29. Brucks, Armstrong, and Goldberg, "Children's Use of Cognitive Defenses against Television Advertising."

30. U.S. Department of Education (2003), "Computer and Internet Use by Children and Adolescents in 2001," National Center for Education Statistics, NCES 2004-2014.

31. Neuborne, E. (2001), "For Kids on the Web, It's an Ad, Ad, Ad, Ad World," Business Week, no. 3475, August 13, 108–109.

32. Moore, "Children and the Changing World of Advertising."

33. Bartram, Peter (2001), "Child's Play," Director, 54 (February), 64–67.

34. Gupta, Pola B., and Kenneth R. Lord (1988), "Product Placement in Movies: The Effect of Prominence and Mode on Audience Recall," Journal of Current Issues and Research in Advertising, 20 (1, Spring), 1–29.

35. Auty, Susan, and Charlie Lewis (2004), "Exploring Children's Choice: The Reminder Effect of Product Placement," Psychology and Marketing, 21 (9, September), 697–713.

36. Ibid.

37. Promotional Products Association International (Irving, TX), 1996, as cited in Belch, George E., and Michael A. Belch (2001), *Advertising and Promotion: An Integrated Marketing Communications Perspective, 5th edition,* McGraw-Hill/Irwin: MA, p. 450.

38. Belch, George E., and Michael A. Belch (2001), "Advertising and Promotion: An Integrated Marketing Communications Perspective," 5th ed. McGraw-Hill/Irwin, MA.

39. Piaget, Jean (1983), Piaget's Theory. In P.H. Mussen (Ed.), "Handbook of Child Psychology" (4th ed., Vol. 1, pp. 103–128), Wiley, NY.

40. Halford, Jason C.G., Jane Gillespie, Victoria Brown, Eleanor E. Pontin, and Terence M. Dovey (2004), "Effect of Television Advertisements for Foods on Food Consumption in Children," Appetite, 42 (2, April), 221–225.

41. Ibid.

42. Furnham, Adrian, Staci Abramsky, and Barrie Gunter (1997), "A Cross-Cultural Content Analysis of Children's Television Advertisements," Sex Roles, 37, 91–99.

43. Baker, Stacey Menzel, and James W. Gentry (1996), "Kids as Collectors: A Phenomenological Study of First and Fifth Graders," Advances in Consumer Research, 23, 132–137.

44. Belk, Russell W., Melanie Wallendorf, John F. Sherry, and Morris Holbrook (1991), "Collecting in a Consumer Culture," In Russell W. Belk (Ed.), Highways and Buyways (pp. 178–211), Association for Consumer Research, UT.

45. Ibid.

46. Kellaris, James J. (2003), "Dissecting Earworms: Further Evidence on the Song-Stuck-in-Your-Head Phenomenon." In C. Page & S. Posavac (Eds.), Proceedings of the Society for Consumer Psychology Winter 2003 Conference (pp. 220–222). American Psychological Society, New Orleans, LA.

47. Buijzen, Moniek, and Patti M. Valkenburg (2003), "The Unintended Effects of Television Advertising," Communication Research, 30 (5, October), 483–503.

48. Gelfand, Donna M., William R. Jenson, and Clifford J. Drew (1997), "Understanding Child Behavior Disorders," 3rd Ed. Harcourt Brace College Publishers, NY; Workman, Jane E. (2003), "Alcohol Promotional Clothing Items and Alcohol Use by

Underage Consumers," Family and Consumer Sciences Research Journal, 31 (3, March), 331–354.

49. Cornwell, T. Bettina (1997), "The Use of Sponsorship-Linked Marketing by Tobacco Firms: International Public Policy Issues," The Journal of Consumer Affairs, 31 (2), 238–254.

50. Ibid.

51. Workman, Jane E. (2003), "Alcohol Promotional Clothing Items and Alcohol Use by Underage Consumers," Family and Consumer Sciences Research Journal, 31 (3), 331–354.

52. Pollay, Richard, S. Siddarth, Michael Siegel, Anne Haddix, Robert K. Merritt, Gary A. Giovino, and Michael P. Eriksen (1996), "The Last Straw? Cigarette Advertising and Realized Market Shares Among Youths and Adults, 1979–1993," Journal of Marketing, 60 (April), 1–16.

53. Aitken, P.P., D.S. Leathar, and S.I. Squair, (1986), "Children's Awareness of Cigarette Brand Sponsorship of Sports and Games in the U.K.," Health Education Research: Theory and Practice, 1 (3), 203–211.

54. Dewhirst, Timothy, and Robert Sparks (2003), "Intertextuality, Tobacco Sponsorship of Sports, and Adolescent Male Smoking Culture," Journal of Sport & Social Issues, 27 (4, November), 372–398.

55. Aitken, Leathar, and Squair, "Children's Awareness of Cigarette Brand Sponsorship of Sports and Games in the U.K."

56. Schindler, Robert, Morris Holbrook, and Eric Greenleaf (1989), "Using Connoisseurs to Predict Mass Tastes," Marketing Letters, 1 (1), 47–54.

57. Mizerski, "The Relationship between Cartoon Trade Character Recognition and Attitude toward Product Category in Young Children."

58. Goldberg, Marvin E., and Gerald J. Gorn (1978), "Some Unintended Consequences of TV Advertising to Children," Journal of Consumer Research, 5 (June), 22–29.

59. Barkin, Shari, Edward Ip, Irma Richardson, Sara Klinepeter, Stacia Finch, and Marina Kremar (2006), "Parental Media Mediation Styles for Children Aged 2 to 11 Years," Archives of Pediatrics and Adolescent Medicine, 160 (April), 395–401; Brucks, Armstrong, and Goldberg, "Children's Use of Cognitive Defenses against Television Advertising."

60. Baumrind, Diana (1991), "The Influence of Parenting Style on Adolescent Competence and Substance Use," Journal of Early Adolescence, 11 (1), 56–95; Miller, Nancy B., Philip A. Cowan, Carolyn Pape Cowan, and E. Mavis Hetherington (1993), "Externalizing in Preschoolers and Early Adolescents: A Cross-Study Replication of a Family Model," Developmental Psychology, 29 (1), 3–18; Weiss, Laura H., and J. Conrad Schwarz (1996), "The Relationship Between Parenting Types and Older Adolescents' Personality, Academic Achievement, Adjustment, and Substance Use," Child Development, 67 (5), 2101–2114.

61. Goldberg, Marvin E., Gerald J. Gorn, and Wayne Gibson (1978), "TV Messages for Snack and Breakfast Foods: Do They Influence Children's Preferences?" Journal of Consumer Research, 5 (September), 73–81.

CHAPTER 2

YOUR TEAM IS MY TEAM: A SOCIAL NETWORK APPROACH TO SPORT MARKETING

Catherine Quatman, Annemarie Farrell, Heidi Parker, and Janet Fink

Imagine that you are a new college graduate. Your dream throughout your undergraduate years was to land a job in the sport industry upon graduation. You are elated to discover that you have made the final round of interviews for a position as an Assistant Director of Marketing for a relocated WNBA (Women's National Basketball Association) team.

The team was relocated from Utah to San Antonio, Texas, a city of about 1.3 million, in 2003. San Antonio is home to only one other major professional sport franchise, the NBA's San Antonio Spurs, but is also home to a minor league baseball team and a minor league hockey team. Last year, 9 of 13 WNBA teams posted poorer attendance records from the previous year, and 5 of those teams had double-digit declines. Midway through the current season, it appears that the majority of WNBA franchises will again suffer attendance declines. The San Antonio Silver Stars have endured a similar fate. Attendance was 10,300 in 2003, dropped to 8,395 in 2004, and decreased to 7,944 in 2005.[1] As a result, management is looking for someone who has fresh ideas for capturing more fans.

COMPETITION FOR SPORT CONSUMERS

The individual hired in the above scenario will not have an easy job. According to D.R. Howard and J.L. Crompton, there are currently more than 800 professional sport teams at all levels throughout North America. This proliferation in sports entertainment options, along with slowed growth of consumer spending on entertainment in general, has created fierce competition for sports consumers' patronage. As Howard and Crompton (2004) note, "It is evident that sport managers face more competition from both within and outside the sports industry than ever before. Finding ways to attract new, and retain existing, customers in an increasingly saturated marketplace is a formidable challenge."[2]

Typically, sport marketers have relied upon demographics (for example, age, gender, and race) to target consumers and market sports teams. Somewhat less frequently, sport marketers have assessed individual attributes of sport fans (for example, motives for attendance and fan identification levels) and used these attributes to group existing and potential fans as target markets. While these strategies are helpful to sport marketers, we contend that there is a vital piece of information missing from these strategies to build sport fandom—the influence of others.

Thus, this chapter aims to fill that void by introducing the reader to a different type of strategy that incorporates the idea of social influence called a *social network approach*. The chapter begins with an overview of some of the typical approaches toward sport marketing and highlights a few limitations of these approaches. Next, the chapter provides a basic introduction to some of the general principles of a social network approach. Finally, the chapter provides the reader with concrete examples of how a social network approach can be used by sport marketers.

TYPICAL SPORT MARKETING EFFORTS

Much like marketers of other products or services, sport marketers rely heavily on demographics to locate target markets. While generalization across sport is difficult, males still outnumber females as fans, and typically, these men are younger, more educated, and more affluent than the men in the general population.[3] Further, sport marketers have come to realize that the demographic profiles of fans of various sports differ substantially. For instance, three out of five teens regularly watch the X Games on television; in the 2001 Summer X Games, 219,000 kids between the ages of 12 and 17 watched the games and nearly 330,000 males between the ages of 18 and 34 tuned in. The median age for baseball viewers, in contrast, was 46.4.[4]

Thus, if a sport marketer for the San Antonio Silver Stars were to use demographics to target fans, she might obtain demographic information about the current fans of the team, fans of other WNBA teams, or fans of women's basketball in general to streamline the marketing campaign. The strengths of this method are that demographic information is easy to obtain and can provide quick, useful data regarding particular sport fans. The weakness of this method, however, is that not all members of a demographic group have similar interests. Further, by narrowing our focus to only current fans of a sport or team, we may be missing strong, viable markets.

For example, if the demographic information of the current Silver Stars fans led us to believe that the people most likely to become fans of the team are women between the ages of 16 and 43, we might focus our efforts on trying to get more local women that fall into this segment to come to games. However, just because a woman falls into this category, does that necessarily mean she is likely to become a fan of the San Antonio Silver Stars? Likewise, if a person does not fall into the category of females between the ages of 16 and 43, does that mean she is less likely to become a fan of the Silver Stars? Hence, by limiting our lens of marketing segments to demographic categories derived from current fans, we may fail to attract potential consumers who might choose to attend games for reasons entirely unrelated to their demographic attributes.

In addition to viewing sport fans as always adhering to certain demographic norms, sport marketers have also relied upon individual attributes to target fans such as motives for attendance,[5] team loyalty,[6] fan identification,[7] and D. F. Mahony, R. Madrigal, and D. Howard's concept of psychological commitment to team (PCT),[8] to name a few. Using this type of strategy, a sport marketer would assess specific individual attributes of current fans, fans of other WNBA teams, or fans of women's basketball in general and then utilize the findings to create advertising and promotional materials.

For example, imagine that as a marketer, you choose to use the Mahony et al. PCT scale to assess WNBA fans' psychological commitment toward the Silver Stars. The PCT score relegates fans into one of four loyalty segments—high, spurious, latent, or low. Each segment requires different types of marketing strategies to best satisfy, and increase, levels of fan attachment. Thus, you could then use different strategies to target the groups of fans falling into the different segments.

However, like the demographic approach, relying upon individual attributes as a strategy also incurs a number of limitations. The strength of this method is that individual attributes can be quite strong and these attributes cross over different demographic groups. The weakness of the strategy is that sport fans are viewed as acting in complete isolation of one another. In other words, using an approach based upon the individual attributes that a person possesses does not account for the fact that the person may choose to consume a game simply because a friend or family member is a fan or consuming the game.

Additionally, in this strategy, the individual sport fan's characteristics are viewed as unchanging, or static. While somewhat of an exaggeration, it is almost as if the traditional approaches infer that a person is born with or simply wakes up one morning with an affinity for a particular team. That is, the traditional approaches assume that an individual either possesses the characteristic or does not, leaving no room for creation, or fluctuation, of the characteristic over time.

ADDRESSING THE LIMITATIONS OF TYPICAL SPORT MARKETING STRATEGIES THROUGH A SOCIAL NETWORK APPROACH

While the use of demographics and individual attributes has undoubtedly assisted sport marketers, researchers in sport marketing have called for new methods to address the above-mentioned limitations. As D. C. Funk and J. D. James expressed, "The complexity of attitude formation requires a framework that allows for the systematic study of how, when and why individuals develop evaluative responses related to sport events."[9] In order to embrace such ideas, however, it is first necessary to step outside the assumptions of traditional approaches and find a way to overcome the static and individualistic views the traditional methods invoke.

One approach that provides the ability to do just that is based upon some of the foundations of a field of study called social network theory and analysis. A social network approach is a unique way of looking at the world in which dynamic processes and the social relationships between people are points of emphasis. Traditionally, marketers tend to look for similarities in the attributes of people who think and act in similar ways (for example, attend the games and are fans of a certain team) to explain consumption behavior. In contrast, using a social network approach, marketers look at the actual social relationships between people first and then similarities between attributes secondarily. It is then assumed that these social relationships exert an influence on a person's decision to consume a product that is as powerful, or in many cases, more powerful than a person's personal attributes.

This difference in emphasis is very important as it allows us to incorporate the idea that the reasons people attend can be socially related in addition to their personal attributes and demographic characteristics. For these reasons, applying a social network approach to sport consumer behavior alleviates many of the limitations of other strategies as it encourages marketers to view fandom as dynamic in nature and a process that is socially influenced.

To clarify these ideas, consider Figure 2.1, which uses small stars to represent individuals who are fans of the team, circles to represent individuals who would not be classified as fans of the team, and a large star to represent the team itself. In traditional sport marketing strategies, sport fandom is viewed as a static characteristic. Figure 2.1 illustrates this view by showing that people are simply viewed as either being fans or non-fans in the population. In addition, individuals in the population are all assumed to be unassociated with anyone else in the population. That is, individuals' interactions with others in the population are assumed to be random and one-time occurrences.

However, intuitively we know that people are neither born nor suddenly wake up one day as fans of a particular sport team. Nor do people operate in social or

Figure 2.1
Sport Fandom as a Static Characteristic

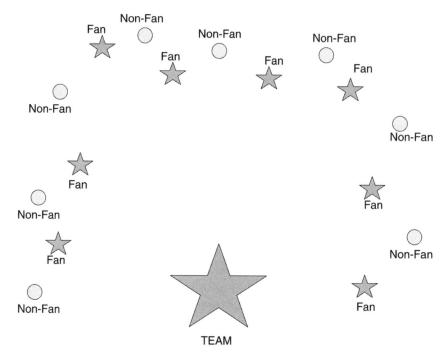

environmental vacuums. Think about your favorite sport team. How did you first become interested in that team? Why did you become a fan? Perhaps your fandom began when you were a child and you were first introduced to a sport team by a parent or friend. Or, maybe you moved to a new city and were introduced to a local team by your new friends or co-workers. Nonetheless, time and repeated exposure to a sport team by individuals with whom we have a positive relationship can influence us to adopt a team and become a fan.

Becoming a fan is a dynamic, evolving process and is likely influenced by our social relationships with other people. Consequently, we contend that a social network approach can be used to incorporate the dynamic and social process of becoming a fan. To do so, we first use a social network approach to diagram the relationships that develop between individuals and a team over time.

Figures 2.2(a), 2.2(b), and 2.2(c) illustrate the dynamic elements a social network approach emphasizes. In the dynamic view, all individuals in the population start out as non-fans as shown in Figure 2.2(a). Figure 2.2(b), then, incorporates dotted lines to indicate that *over time,* in some way, non-fans somehow become aware of the team. Finally, Figure 2.2(c) shows that over time, for some reason, several non-fans become fans of the team while others remain non-fans.

Figure 2.2(a)
Social Network Approach: Stage One

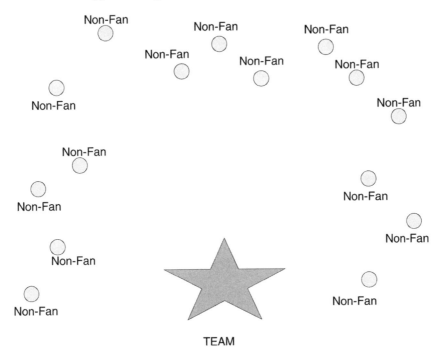

TEAM

Beyond what the diagrams convey, it is also important to understand that someone who becomes a fan does not necessarily remain a fan and someone who is a non-fan does not necessarily remain a non-fan. That is, non-fans can become even further distanced from the team or can be enticed to attend more games over time. Existing fans can also change as they may become more loyal or more distant fans as time passes.

In addition to viewing individuals in a population as either static fans or non-fans, marketers have traditionally viewed the consumer-team relationship as individualistic in nature. In other words, it is assumed that people become fans based solely upon their personal attributes such as interest in the sport or that they feel a sense of achievement when the team does well. As such, it could be said that, at best, marketers have considered consumption behaviors only from the perspective of a relationship between only two parties—the consumer and the team. In many cases, the relationship is reciprocal in that both parties get something in return for what they receive. Figure 2.3 illustrates this point. A consumer becomes a fan of a particular team, and in exchange for his or her loyalty, the team provides the consumer with intangibles such as a means of escape from daily hassles, increased self-esteem, or a sense of belonging.

Figure 2.2(b)
Social Network Approach: Stage Two

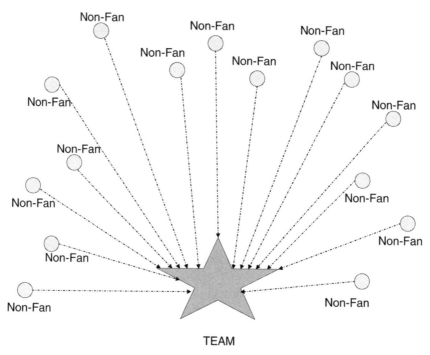

TEAM

MOVING BEYOND THE TWO-PARTY VIEW OF CONSUMER-TEAM RELATIONSHIPS

In contrast to the traditional strategies, a social network approach expands the idea of a simple consumer-team relationship to a view that incorporates social relationships between not only a consumer and a team, but a consumer, a team, and other people in a population. To make this leap, scholars often use F. Heider's balance theory to explain the process of social influence.[10]

The balance theory suggests that individuals strive to maintain a sense of balance in their lives, and their actions and judgments are influenced by the need to preserve such balance. In general, it is useful to discuss the balance theory using diagrams representing social relationships among three parties such as the ones shown in Figure 2.4.

In essence, the adages "your friends are my friends" and "the enemy of my enemy is my friend" neatly summarize the principles of the balance theory. For example, consider the relationships among Kris, Jamie, and Alex in the first triangle of Figure 2.4. As the diagram shows, Kris has a positive relationship with Alex as well as a positive relationship with Jamie. The balance theory suggests that

Figure 2.2(c)
Social Network Approach: Stage Three

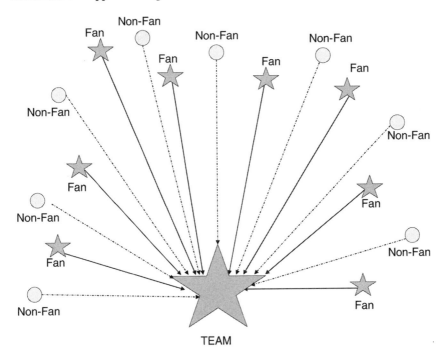

TEAM

if Kris has positive relationships with both Alex and Jamie, it is likely that Alex and Jamie know and like each other as well.

Likewise, as depicted in the second triangle of Figure 2.4, if Kris dislikes Jamie but has a positive relationship with Alex, then it seems reasonable to assume that Alex may also dislike Jamie. However, as depicted in the third triangle, if Kris has a positive relationship with Jamie and a negative relationship with Alex, but Jamie and Alex have a positive relationship, then the triad is unbalanced. In other words, it is somewhat unsettling for two foes to share a common friend.

The very same principles of the balance theory in terms of friendships and enemies can also be applied to our vignette about the Silver Stars. In other words, we can use Heider's balance theory to move beyond the traditional dyadic consumer-team relationship toward considering a triadic consumer-team-other relationship. To clarify, Figure 2.5(a) depicts the vignette examples to the approach suggested by Heider's balance theory. Notice that in Figure 2.5(a), the reciprocal two-way relationship between team and consumer still exists. However, by adding a third party into the relationship we must consider how this "other" individual will impact or be impacted by the consumer-team relationship already in existence.

Figure 2.3
Fan-Team Relationship

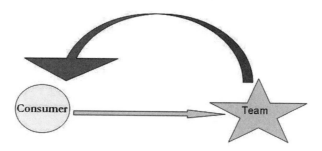

What motivates consumer to follow team?

- Personal Interest?
- Attitude?
- Team Identification?
- Gender?
- Race?

What does following the team provide consumer?

- Self-esteem?
- Means of escape?
- Opportunity to interact with others?

Put more simply, we must then consider how a social relationship between two individuals might impact each individual's relationship with a team.

According to Heider's balance theory the relationships presented in Figure 2.5 (a) would be unbalanced, at least initially. Thus, it is likely that over time the triad would gravitate toward a balanced state in which either the non-fan would become a fan of the team, too, or the fan would become a non-fan. For clarification purposes, it is useful to combine the dynamic process of becoming a fan discussed earlier and the social influence process suggested by the balance theory into a single series of diagrams. Figure 2.5(b) provides a dynamic illustration of Heider's balance theory and the dynamic and social process of becoming a fan as it applies to the vignette we have used throughout the chapter.

The picture suggests the following:

- Two friends (as indicated by the reciprocal tie between them), Jamie (J) and Kris (K), initially are not fans of the Silver Stars (as indicated by the absence of the ties between Jamie and the team and Kris and the team).
- At some point in time, Jamie becomes interested in the Silver Stars and starts to devote a little time and attention toward following the team.
- Over time, Jamie finds that following the team provides something back to him, creating a positive reciprocal team-consumer relationship and establishing him as a fan.
- As a result of her friendship with Jamie, then Kris becomes interested in the Silver Stars as well.

Figure 2.4
An Example of Balance Theory

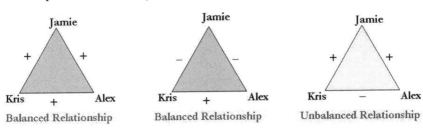

- Ultimately, Kris becomes a fan of the Silver Stars at least in part due to the relationship between Jamie and the team and her relationship with Jamie reinforcing her new relationship with the team.

Incidentally, a social network approach takes this process one step beyond a party of three and suggests considering an entire population consisting of networks of relationships. Simplistically, you might consider the fact that Jamie is likely to have a number of people in his life that he can potentially influence into becoming fans. Figure 2.5(c) provides a visual image of this process.

A social network approach would further encourage us to

Figure 2.5(a)
Sport Marketing Application of Heider's Balance Theory

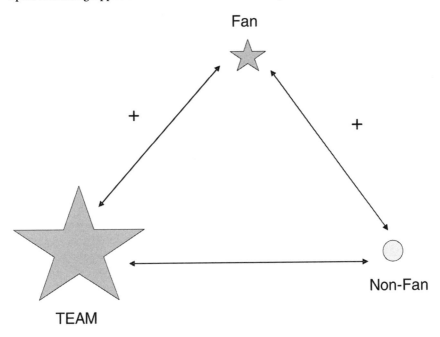

Figure 2.5(b)
Dynamic Social Network Approach Combined with Heider's Balance Theory

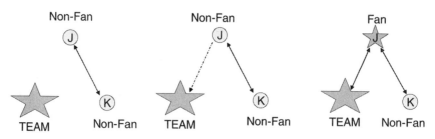

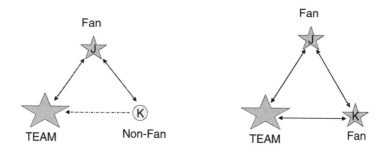

- Imagine Jamie and Kris as being members of a larger population as depicted in Figure 2.5(d).

- Although there are personal attributes that can lead a person to become a fan, using a social network approach, we should first consider the relationships between the individuals in the population as part of a dynamic process of social influence for consumption behaviors as Figure 2.5(e) illustrates.

- Conceivably, then, as Figures 2.5(f), 2.5(g), and 2.5(h) demonstrate, other people within the population in addition to Kris and Jamie have the opportunity to influence individuals in their social networks to become fans of the Silver Stars.

SOCIAL CONTAGION

Ultimately, Heider's[11] balance theory used in conjunction with a social network approach demonstrates how social influence can impact consumers and fans of a sport team. It also provides the foundation for understanding how social influence can impact an entire community or population: a process commonly referred to as *social contagion*.

While the word "contagion" is often used when talking about infectious diseases, an interesting connection can be drawn between the phenomena of disease

Figure 2.5(c)
The Combined Model

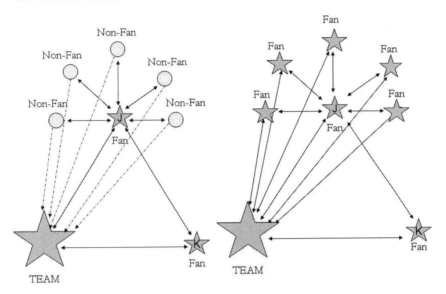

spread and social influence. In fact, Malcolm Gladwell published a National Best Seller in 2000 called *The Tipping Point* in which he linked principles of disease contagion to colorful examples of how social epidemics such as fashion trends and innovation adoption disseminate through a population.[12] Over the last 15 years or so, scholars in a number of fields have embraced the idea that social behavior can easily be tied to many of the same principles used to explain the spread of diseases.[13]

Intuitively, we can make an argument for how social influence and sport fan behavior is similar to the spread of infectious diseases. To make this connection, we draw upon the classic SIR (susceptible infectious removed) model of disease contagion as it relates to this vignette.

The SIR model is the basic framework around which most disease models are constructed. SIR stands for the three primary classifications individuals are grouped into relative to a disease:

- Susceptible—an individual who is vulnerable to infection (in our case, a non-fan who has the potential to become a fan of the Silver Stars);

- Infectious—an individual who is not only infected, but can also infect others (an individual who is already a fan of the Silver Stars); and

- Removed—an individual who is either immune or ceases to pose any greater threat (a non-fan who will never become a fan of the Silver Stars—for example, a fan of the Silver Stars' rival or someone who hates all sports).

Figure 2.5(d)
Application: Jamie and Kris as Members of the Population

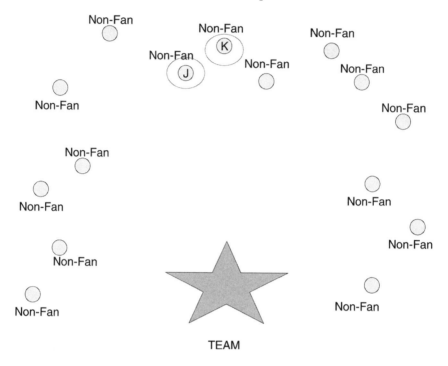

TEAM

According to the classic SIR model, disease can spread only when an infected individual comes into direct contact with a susceptible individual. Further, the SIR model suggests three stages of growth through which a disease can be spread to a population.

- Slow-growth stage where the infected population is small and the interaction between infected and susceptibles is low (slow infection rate);
- Explosive stage where lots of infected individuals interact with lots of susceptible individuals (rapid infection rate);
- Systemic burn-out stage in which susceptibles are hard to find because most people in the population are either already infected or are immune to the infection (infection rate is extremely slow if the disease continues to spread at all).

Thus, in essence, the whole key to spreading anything, whether it be a disease or fandom, is for individuals who are infected to come into contact with individuals who are susceptible to infection. Even so, there are a number of other considerations that can significantly impact the social spread of phenomena throughout a population. Many of these considerations are directly related to several of the ideas suggested by a social network approach.

Figure 2.5(e)
Application of Social Network Approach Combined with Heider's Balance Theory: Stage One

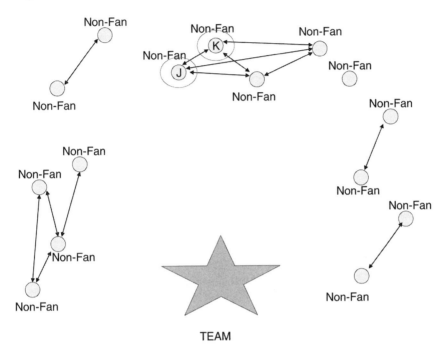

TEAM

As noted before, traditional approaches to sport marketing assume that social interactions are random and simply one-time occurrences. A social network perspective, on the other hand, suggests that more often than not, our interactions with one another are not random nor are they one-time occurrences. This difference in assumptions is very important because interaction frequency (how often people come into contact with one another), intimacy (the level or intensity of interaction), and diversity (the range of different people with whom individuals interact) can produce very different outcomes in terms of the social contagion that takes place across a population of actors.

For example, let us say that a grandfather who rarely leaves the house and interacts only with his eight-year-old granddaughter on a regular basis comes down with a cold. Given the limited amount of interaction he has with other people outside of his house, it is likely that the only person he will have the opportunity to pass the cold on to would be his granddaughter. However, if instead, the granddaughter were the one with a cold, she could not only potentially pass the cold on to her grandfather, but could also pass it on to all of the children in her class or even school. So, while the grandfather, as an infected individual exposes only

Figure 2.5(f)
Application of Social Network Approach Combined with Heider's Balance Theory: Stage Two

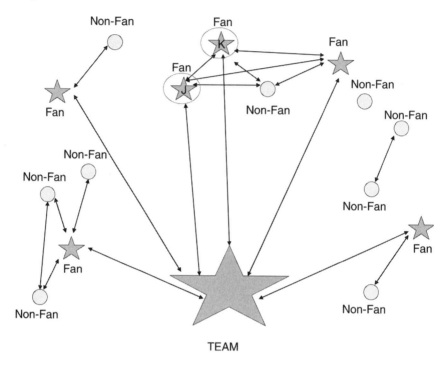

TEAM

one susceptible to the virus, the grandchild has a greater potential of exposing a larger portion of the population to the infection.

Similarly, the strength of social connections plays a part in the transfer of disease. For instance, if your best friend or a member of your immediate family became infected with a disease, you would be more likely to catch the disease from your friend or family member than a complete stranger whom you pass on campus, if you caught it at all. Why is this so? The strength of our relationships with our best friends and family members often leads us to interact with them more frequently and more intimately than with other people with whom we may come into contact.

Furthermore, the number of people we are close to who are infected also impacts the likelihood of becoming infected ourselves. That is to say, if two of the people in our lives to whom we are close are infected, as compared to only one, we are much more likely to catch the disease than if only one of them was an infected individual.

Tying these examples back to the vignette, let us say that being a fan of the Silver Stars implies that an individual is "infected" with a "disease." It seems logical

Figure 2.5(g)
Application of Social Network Approach Combined with Heider's Balance Theory: Stage Three

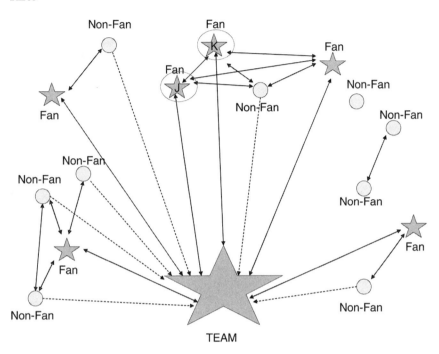

to assume that a child may be more likely to become a fan of the Silver Stars if say her father is a fan of the team. Likewise, the more often the child interacts with her father in a context that engages his fandom, the more likely the child is to become a fan of the team. Furthermore, if both the child's father and mother were fans of the team, the likelihood also increases that the child would become a fan of the team as well.

FACILITATING SOCIAL CONTAGION

Given the ideas presented in this chapter, we contend that a social network approach can be effectively used for proactively marketing a sport team. Let us suppose marketers of the Silver Stars are trying to create an epidemic of fandom in the San Antonio community. According to the SIR model, the Silver Stars would currently be positioned in the slow growth phase where there is little interaction between the infected individuals (fans) and the susceptibles (non-fans). Therefore, to move the "fandom" disease to the explosive growth stage, there has to be more interaction between the infected fans and susceptible non-fans.

Figure 2.5(h)
Application of Social Network Approach Combined with Heider's Balance Theory: Stage Four

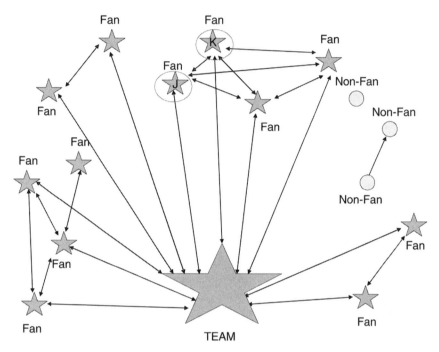

In a general sense (as suggested in the example of the grandfather and his grand-daughter), there are potentially some people who are more connected or have stronger ties with a greater number of individuals in the community. Individuals who are indeed more socially connected offer a unique opportunity for sport marketers because they are located in positions that increase their likelihood of catching and ultimately spreading the "disease" (that is, fandom).

To illustrate this phenomenon, consider the implications suggested by Figure 2.6. Imagine that Figure 2.6 represents a concrete map of the social structure of individuals in the San Antonio community. The points represent the individuals and the lines between them indicate a type of strong relationship such as a friendship, a family member, or co-worker. Looking at the structure, if you wanted to trigger an epidemic of Silver Stars fandom, which individuals would you target?

Individuals C, N, O, X, and P are all connected to the greatest number of people and therefore are likely to be in the best positions to become "infected" as well as "infect" others. Targeting these individuals would likely be the most advantageous strategy in terms of getting the "infection" to spread across the entire population at the fastest rate.

Figure 2.6
Social Structure of Individuals in the San Antonio Community

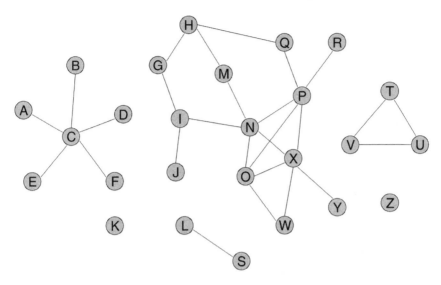

To further facilitate the social contagion process, you might try to find ways to motivate these individuals to interact with their social contacts more frequently and more intimately. Implementing such strategies would increase the opportunities for these highly connected individuals to socially influence their contacts to become fans of the Silver Stars.

While the ideas of this chapter provide an interesting theoretical and conceptual overview of a social network approach to sport marketing, it should be noted that real-life sport marketers and managers have already begun to use social networking as a marketing tool. For instance, Brett Yormark, President and CEO of Nets Sports & Entertainment, which is the parent company of the NBA's New Jersey Nets, has found a way to target the individuals he perceives to be the most socially influential fans of the New Jersey Nets.

Yormark offers to throw a party, complete with appearances from Net's players and coaches, at the home of any season ticket holder who can assure 20 to 30 potential customers will be in attendance. He calls this unique marketing strategy the Influencer and has noted that each Influencer party has resulted in, on average, $75,000 in new ticket sales.[14]

SUMMARY AND CONCLUSIONS

The purpose of this chapter was to introduce a social network approach as an advantageous strategy toward the marketing of sport. With the examples presented in this chapter, we demonstrated that it is vital to view fans and potential fans as dynamic and social beings. We also introduced how to use a social network approach in conjunction with the classic models of disease contagion, as a means of triggering an "epidemic" of fandom. In doing so, we contended that a social network approach allows us to streamline marketing efforts and target potential consumers from an entirely new angle.

While this chapter is geared toward the marketing of a sport team, the aspects of the social network approach that we covered can be utilized to market any product or service. Nevertheless, using a social network approach is especially powerful for products or services that are experiential, that is, simultaneously produced and consumed, and those often consumed with other people, that is, socially consumed. As such, a social network approach toward fandom is both a unique and useful strategy for sport marketers to embrace to increase their customer base, and ultimately enhance revenue.

NOTES

1. Bailey, W.S. (2006, July 3). New silver stars chief plans to reverse attendance trend. *San Antonio Business Journal*. Retrieved July 2, 2006 from http://sanantonio.bizjournals.com/sanantonio/stories/2006/07/03/story6.html.

2. Howard, D.R., and Crompton, J.L. (2004). *Financing Sport*. (Second Edition). Morgantown, WV: Fitness Information Technology, Inc.

3. Shank, M.D. (2002). *Sports marketing: A strategic perspective*. (Second Edition). Upper Saddle River, NJ: Pearson Education, Inc.

4. Raymond, J. (2002). Going to extremes—marketing and extreme sports. *American Demographics*. Retrieved July 13, 2006 from http://www.findarticles.com/p/articles/mi_m4021/is_2001_June_1/ai_76579404.

5. Funk, D.C., Mahony, D.F., and Ridinger, L.L. (2002). Characterizing consumer motivation as individual difference factors: Augmenting the sport interest inventory (SII) to explain level of spectator support. *Sport Marketing Quarterly, 11 (1)*, 33–43. Trail, G., Anderson, D., and Fink, J.S. (2003). Sport spectator consumer behavior. *Sport Marketing Quarterly, 12 (1)*, 8–17

6. Funk, D.C., and James, J.D. (2004). The fan attitude network (FAN) model: Exploring attitude formation and change among sport consumers. *Sport Management Review, 7 (1)*, 1–26.

7. Madrigal, R. (1995). Cognitive and affective determinants of fan satisfaction. *Journal of Leisure Research, 27 (3)*, 205–227. Wann, D.L., and Branscombe, N.R. (1993). Sports fans: Measuring degree of identification with their team. *International Journal of Sport Psychology. 24 (1)*, 1–17.

8. Mahony, D.F., Madrigal, R., and Howard, D. (2000). Using the psychological commitment to team scale to segment sport consumers based on loyalty. *Sport Marketing Quarterly, 9 (1)*, 15–25.

9. Funk and James, The fan attitude network (FAN) model, p. 19.

10. Heider, F. (1958). *The Psychology of Interpersonal Relations*. New York: John Wiley & Sons.

11. Ibid.

12. Gladwell, M. (2002). *The Tipping Point: How Little Things Can Make a Big Difference*. New York: Little Brown and Company.

13. Watts, D.J. (2003). *Six Degrees: The Science of the Connected Age*. New York: W.W. Norton & Company; Rogers, E.M. (2003). *Diffusion of Innovations*. New York: Free Press.

14. Lidz, F. (2005, December 13). The turnaround twins. *SI Extra*. Retrieved May 16, 2006 from http://premium.si.cnn.com.

CHAPTER 3

FADS, FASHIONS, AND FAST-BREAK PRODUCT LIFE CYCLES: AN INTEGRATED APPROACH

Vincent Tallepied

How can you compare the popularity of a movie like *Batman Begins* with *The Blair Witch Project*? One movie was produced by Warner Brothers Entertainment, Inc., while the other was created by a group of college students and released by Artisan Entertainment. One movie was heavily publicized in different media, whereas the other's popularity came from word-of-mouth advertising. The answer: the study of consumer diffusion and the product life cycle.

The study of consumer diffusion and the product life cycle (PLC) is a theory within marketing and communications. Diffusion is the process by which ideas, products, cultures, and values spread. Diffusion theory is useful in explaining the spread of new ideas, new practices, and new products according to Hubert Gatignon and Thomas S. Robertson.[1] Robertson said, "It is the integration of this [diffusion] framework with the traditional marketing framework that may advance our understanding of how new products disseminate and gain consumer acceptance and which may advance our understanding of how new products disseminate and gain consumer acceptance and which may suggest means of improvement in new marketing strategies."[2]

Product life cycle research takes on additional significance in today's rapidly changing global economy. Increased competition and technological advances have resulted in an increased focus on speed to market. Today speed is king. The combination of higher expectations for new products coupled with shorter product life cycles has placed increased pressure on managers. This pressure to get results and get them quickly is not the exclusive domain of the high-tech computer or pharmaceutical industries. The pressure to produce profitable new products and show results faster impacts all industries. From manufactured goods to leisure pursuits, product managers are facing the "need for speed." This chapter focuses on fads, fashions, and fast-break product life cycles in light of new product diffusion, past research, and by means of an integrated framework for conceptualizing, understanding, and managing this unique subset of new products.

LIMITATIONS OF PAST RESEARCH

The diffusion process has generally been modeled as the traditional S-shaped (sigmoid) pattern. While this normal noncumulative shaped bell curve may not actually parallel the time of adoption for a particular product or service, it has served as an excellent tool for guiding the discussion of marketing strategy options and for discussing the various characteristics of new product adopters within the social system. Past research has investigated the applicability of the general diffusion curve to different industries and product categories. Research in product life cycles has advanced considerably since its roots in studying agricultural practices, hybrid corn seed, political candidates, and dispensing of prescription drugs.[3]

The main focus of most research has been in mass market acceptance of household products, consumer durable goods, high-technology goods, and industrial innovations.[4] Although leisure products and fashions make up 36 percent (percentage for France includes cloth, 5 percent; furniture, 6 percent; cars, 11 percent; personal care, 5 percent; and entertainment, 9 percent) of the gross domestic product, their product life cycles are not as widely researched or understood.[5] While clothing is perhaps the most widely discussed product in this category, fashions and fads are found in consumer choices ranging from food, music, movies, and books, to name a few.

PRODUCT DIFFUSION THEORY AND THE TRADITIONAL PRODUCT LIFE CYCLE

The study of new product diffusion was integrated into the consumer behavior literature in the mid 1960s as companies sought to better understand how to successfully disseminate new products, services, technologies, and public policies.[6] With the increasingly complex, competitive, and fast-paced nature of today's technology-driven global marketplace, the role of new product introduction has taken on additional significance.[7] An understanding of the product life cycle patterns puts the manager in a more advantageous position to plan marketing strategies regarding promotion, pricing, and distribution. As noted by Peter N.

Golder and Gerard Tellis, predicting the "turning points of takeoff and slowdown are essential to avoid premature withdrawal or excessive investments."[8]

As originally set forth, the diffusion paradigm has several conceptual foundations including the following: "The main elements in the diffusion of new ideas are: an *innovation* that is *communicated* through certain *channels* over *time* among members of a *social system.*"[9] It is important to note that as defined within the diffusion literature, the term innovation has many different interpretations. Newness may be defined in terms of function, technology, or fashion.[10] Inherent within each of these is the critical notion that a new product must impact established patterns of consumption behavior.[11] In any case, effective new product introductions require an understanding of the market segment, the timing of promotions, appropriate selection of media, and the general shape, slope, and speed of the diffusion process. Past research has "uncovered many shapes, durations, and sequences. These efforts have not been matched by systematic research into the reasons for the difference between shapes."[12] It is this last area, the general shape, slope, and speed of the diffusion process that this research addresses, and specifically fad, fashion, and fast-break product life cycles.

After discussing the general shape of the traditional product life cycle, this chapter investigates the nature and behavior of three distinct forms of product life cycles: fad, fashion, and fast-break product life cycles. The next section develops an integrated mathematical framework for analyzing these three unique short PLC curves. The final section of this chapter will propose research propositions for further analysis of fad, fashion, and fast-break product life cycles, as well as discuss management recommendations for marketing strategy.

The S-Shaped Diffusion Process

The diffusion process can be charted as sales over time (referred to as a "Product Life Cycle Graph") or as cumulative sales over time shown as a diffusion curve. Previous research has investigated the general shape of the traditional product life cycle curve.[13] As described in nearly all marketing textbooks, the traditional product life cycle curve is traditionally shown as a symmetrical bell-shaped curve, with time on the X axis and unit sales, or dollar sales, on the Y axis (Figure 3.1). The cumulative diffusion curve is typically shown in the traditional "S" shape, or logistic pattern, again with time on the X axis and the cumulative number of sales units, or dollar value, on the Y axis (Figure 3.2).

Much past research has substantiated these traditional patterns of a normal shaped noncumulative diffusion pattern that results in the S-shaped cumulative diffusion curve. This sigmoid pattern is expected under conditions of high risk, as characterized by conditions of high switching costs, a learning hierarchy process, and high uncertainty.[14]

Figure 3.1
The Diffusion Process

Traditional Product
Life Cycle Curve

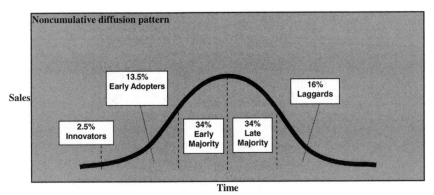

The Social System

Diffusion occurs within a social system in which the actions of consumers are influenced by marketing actions, competitive actions, and others within the social system. Research has also documented that the traditional S-shaped diffusion curve is expected under conditions of high social influence and a "unimodal distribution of initial beliefs toward the innovation within the social system."[15] As outlined below, within this social framework various names have been assigned to each specific category to characterize the different segments of consumers that purchase during this stage of the product life cycle.

Innovators, the first to try new products, make up 2.5 percent of the population. They are adventuresome, independent personalities who are generally younger, better educated, and have higher incomes than the average consumer.[16] These risk-loving individuals enjoy the status of being the first to own a new computer technology, see a movie on opening night, or try a new Indian restaurant. *Innovators* are not influenced by others within their social network, but may be influenced by marketer-controlled information, often having access to specialty publications that narrowly target specific market niches. As the first to try new things, innovators are critical to the success of new products and ideas. "The marketer must attract a substantial group of early buyers in order to insure the survival of a new product."[17] It is this innovator group who through their actions and word-of-mouth advertising are critical to the potential success of a new product, a new service, or a new idea.

Early Adopters, who make up about 13.5 percent of the population, are critical to the continued diffusion of the product within the social system. The Early

Figure 3.2
Cumulative Diffusion Curve

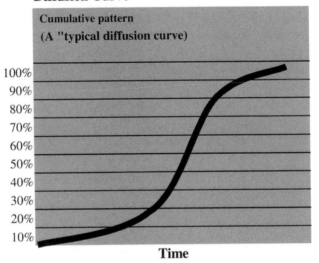

Adopters are similar to the Innovators in terms of income, age, and education, but are much more socially integrated, read more, and are more visible within the social community. Early Adopters are critical to the success of new products because their status as opinion leaders within their social networks makes them an excellent conduit to the Early Majority that contains the large numbers of consumers necessary for a commercial success. The Early Majority and the Late Majority are those that are within one standard deviation of the mean time for adoption, while those labeled Laggards are two standard deviations to the right of the mean year of adoption. These later adopters take a wait-and-see approach, consistent with their risk-adverse natures.

Bass Diffusion Model

The bell-shaped product life cycle, or the S-shaped diffusion model, when cumulated, is the cornerstone of the vast majority of the diffusion literature.[18] Most notable within this sector is the Bass diffusion model that also triggers the S-shaped diffusion curve.[19] The Bass model has a concise mathematical equation that is both theoretically and conceptually sound. It implies that consumers adopt an innovation based on the coefficient of innovation (p), which may be most influenced by the media, and through a coefficient of imitation (q), which is primarily influenced by observation and interpersonal communication channels. With this model, management must then estimate only three parameters: Q, the total number of potential adopters, and the primary parameters of p and q, which can be estimated for further forecasting. The primary focus of the Bass model is the direct impact between those who may adopt by those who have already adopted. As such the Bass model categorizes consumers as either adopters, made up of both the innovators and the early adopters, and those who have yet to adopt.

The more extensive adopter categories led to the five-stage model previously discussed (Innovators, Early Adopters, Early Majority, Late Majority, and Laggards). However, the Bass model does not drive to normality even though the distribution has an S shape when cumulated. The Bass model assumes that growth rate starts off slowly, grows rapidly, peaks, and then significantly declines.

NONTRADITIONAL DIFFUSION MODELS

Research has suggested that certain product categories such as industrial products diffuse very slowly,[20] while other product categories such as fashion and leisure-enhancing products may diffuse very quickly.[21] While the diffusion research stream has analyzed the general applicability of the PLC curve across industries as diverse as farming, pharmaceutical, electronics, and communications, it has not adequately analyzed models of diffusion that may differ from the traditional shaped diffusion curve.[22] Unfortunately, there has been very little research into other potential patterns of the PLC and their impact on the market mix and on competitive strategy.[23] One exception to this is the research on informational cascades of fads, fashion, customs, and cultural change by Suchil Bikhchandani, David Hirshleifer, and Ivo Welch and applied by Golder and Tellis that sought to broaden the theory of the PLC and further explain unique market characteristics using the concept of informational cascades, which may significantly influence the shape of the diffusion curve.[24]

In practice there are many products that do not take on the shape of the traditional bell-shaped PLC curve. Two of the most notable are fads and fashion products. Most marketing principles texts include only a short reference to the PLCs of fashion or fad products. Early in the diffusion literature stream researchers acknowledged the unique nature, issues, and strategy problems inherent with fad and fashion products according to Robertson, but additional work in this area has remained very limited.[25] The distinct nature of the life cycles of fads and fashion products can also be extended to other leisure product categories that may exhibit nontraditional life cycles that are quite different than consumer durables or high-technology products that make up the vast majority of diffusion studies.[26]

For example, in the marketplace we observe some products that experience huge sales volumes in their introductions, followed by gradual decline and death.

These products are referred to as "fast-break products." These products may not be commercial failures, but rather a unique subset of product categories that potentially share unique attributes while indeed being a commercial success from a sales and profitability perspective.

This chapter presents an integrated framework for exploring nontraditional PLCs associated with fad, fashion, craze, or fast-break life cycles and analyzes their general patterns of diffusion, their unique characteristics, as well as establishes propositions for further research and implications for their marketing strategy. We first investigate the product categories that fit this general shape and identify their common structures, markets, and marketing strategies. In the first section, the chapter discusses fashion and fad products and then introduces numerous time series that have fast-break patterns from industries as diverse as movies, music, and books.

EXPONENTIAL DIFFUSION MODELS

While not as widely studied, research has also documented an exponential diffusion curve.[27] Research has suggested that an exponential curve is expected under lower risk conditions, as exhibited with lower involvement products, lower uncertainty, and lower switching costs.[28] The exponential diffusion curve is also more likely to occur when interpersonal social influence is low, the risk of trial is low, and there is a uniform pattern of beliefs within the social system.[29]

As noted earlier, many leisure and clothing products do not fit the traditional bell-shaped product life cycle curve. Consumer selections of books, movies, shoes, DVDs, and even baby names may not fit the traditional model. Instead each of these categories has examples of new products that do not represent the traditional normal shaped diffusion curve, but many fit with the lognormal model well. The data suggest that each of these can be modeled using a lognormal distribution. The lognormal distribution is the law of multiplicative effects, and, as such, there is an underlying multiplicative or social imitation process in the adoption and diffusion of the products that may have a good empirical fit with the lognormal distribution.

Fashion Products

As noted by past scholars analyzing fashion life cycles, "the very survival of the fashion industry depends on regular style changes."[30] Fashion products, such as mini-skirts, baggy pants, feminine peasant blouses, and slim ties for men may experience a wave action PLC curve, which represents the cyclical nature of these product categories. As early as 1904, sociologist Georg Simmel noted that the distinguishing characteristic of this product category was in the perceived newness of the product rather than relative functional advantage over current product offerings.[31] Simmel emphasized that as fashion spreads, it goes to its doom.[32] "As soon as the social consciousness attains to the highest point designated by fashion, it marks the beginning of the end for the latter."[33]

Noting the role that fashion innovators play in the life cycle of fashion, Charles W. King noted that "innovator's early selections and reactions to the fashion inventory often give certain styles legitimacy in the mass market."[34] Fashion has enlarged its original realm of clothes and ornaments to now encompass cosmetics, cultural products like movies, music, TV series, and books, as well as other leisure pursuits like travel, restaurant offerings, furnishing trends, and decorations, to name a few.

The very nature of fashion products suggests a highly symbolic social display value whether related to status or other measures of group identity. In the modern consumer society where identity builds through consumption, it is hypothesized that more products will tend to go through fashion cycles. Past scholars have recognized fashion as "a generalized phenomenon of human behavior."[35]

Fast-Break PLCs

The fast-break PLC is one that does not follow the traditional path of slow introduction, rapid growth, a flat plateau, and then rapid decline. Indeed fast-break PLCs reach their peak very quickly after introduction and then proceed to a rapid decline. Fast-break PLCs are often commercial successes despite their rapid decline in the marketplace. In the marketplace, we observe some products that experience huge sales volumes in introduction followed by gradual decline and death. These products may not be commercial failures, but rather a unique subset of product categories that potentially share unique attributes while indeed being a commercial success from a sales and profitability perspective. Declining life cycles have been neglected by marketing research because under the traditional model rapid decline is considered a lack of success.

Examples: Fast-Break PLCs in Movies

For example, the revenue over time for *Harry Potter and the Goblet of Fire* (shown in Figure 3.3 and Table 3.1) is one of those products that does not show the traditional textbook bell-shaped PLC curve. The movie's marketing and promotional budget was an amazing $150 million. Three days after the show's premiere, the film had grossed $102 million in the United States, the highest first week of the series. The film earned $290 million in its entire life span in the U.S. market and made $892 million worldwide, the best box-office performance in 2005 and the eighth highest grossing worldwide film of the movie industry. The DVD has been the fastest selling DVD of all time. Well, that is business success. However, the movie *Harry Potter and the Goblet of Fire* shows a rapidly decaying pattern.

Figure 3.3
Box Office Gross for *Harry Potter Goblet of Fire*

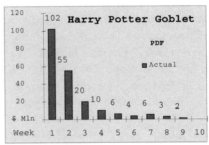

The remainder of this chapter identifies the unique nature of the subset of PLCs that exhibit one of three patterns: (1) fashion, (2) fad, or (3) fast break. It provides an integrated framework for their general patterns of diffusion and establishes propositions for further research as well as discusses implications for their marketing strategy. It is important to establish that all three of these patterns have one thing in common: they have a lognormal diffusion pattern. As noted earlier, the lognormal distribution is the law of multiplicative effects, and, as such, there is an underlying multiplicative process in the adoption and diffusion of the products that were empirically found lognormal. In fact, sociologists have regarded fashion as a multiplicative process.

AN INTEGRATED FRAMEWORK: THE LOGNORMAL DISTRIBUTION

Movies Exhibiting Fast-Break PLCs

The movies charted in Table 3.1 represent the top movies released during the two-year period 2004–2005.[36] Not all of them generated the same amount of revenue. Some made more than $100 million during their premiere week, while others did not make that number in their entire life span. Some benefited from a huge marketing budget. Others did not. They are different genres: animation, fantasy, children, and science fiction. However, all of them show the same declining pattern. None of them display bell curves or S shapes.

Typology of Fast-Break PLCs

The lognormal distribution is a two-parameter distribution. It has a scale parameter and a shape parameter. Computation of both parameters is rather tedious. It is much easier to characterize the lognormal distribution with M°, as the geometric mean, or size parameter, and S°, as the contagion parameter, also known as the shape parameter. This is summarized as follows:

- $M° = \exp(\mu)$, where μ is the mean of the log-transform normal distribution. $M°$ is the scaling factor.
- $S° = \exp(s)$, where s is the standard deviation of the log-transformed normal distribution. $S°$ is the shaping factor as the distribution gets more skewed when the parameter rises.

When mathematically analyzed and plotted, all exhibit an excellent fit with the lognormal approximation as demonstrated by the regression coefficient, shown as R-square in Table 3.1. R-square is the correlation coefficient. If the coefficient equals 1, then the time series has a perfect fit with the lognormal distribution; if $R°$ equals 0, there is no correlation, and when it equals −1, a series has inversed

Table 3.1
Top 20 Movies of 2004–2005: Lognormal Representations of Fast-Break PLCs

Rank by Revenue	Movie	Box Office Sales in Millions ($)	M°	S°	R-Square
1	Stars Wars: Episode III—Return of the Sith	230.1	1.80	1.92	0.8
2	Harry Potter and the Goblet of Fire	207.4	1.71	1.86	0.98
3	Lord of the Rings	179.7	2.09	1.90	0.98
4	Harry Potter and the Prisoner of Azkaban	173.1	1.68	1.88	0.96
5	The Chronicles of Narnia	169.2	2.07	1.92	0.83
6	War of the Worlds	132.2	1.74	1.86	0.97
7	Charlie and the Chocolate Factory	129.8	1.93	1.95	0.96
8	Mr. & Mrs. Smith	124.2	2.04	1,99	0.96
9	Chicken Little	108.0	1.94	1.82	0.99
10	Robots	96.4	2.15	2.04	0.97
11	The Pacifier	86.6	2.26	2.09	0.97
12	Walk the Line	68.8	2.20	1.97	0.98
13	Flightplan	68.6	2.15	1.97	0.96
14	Saw II	65.7	1.68	1.76	0.98
15	Ray	54.0	2.01	1.8	0.98
16	Yours, Mine & Ours	35.2	1.65	1.72	0.95
17	Derailed	27.2	1.76	1.76	0.96
18	Syriana	26.9	1.86	1.83	0.85
19	Just Friends	21.0	1.72	1.69	0.96
20	Get Rich or Die Tryin'	19.9	1.44	1.63	0.98

correlation. As shown all R-square values range from a low of 0.83 to a high of 0.98 with an average of 0.95. Since all R-square coefficients are close to 1, this demonstrates that movie box-office revenue can be appropriately fitted with the lognormal model.

Lognormal Representations of Fast-Break PLCs

In addition graphical representations of the top four grossing films are shown in Figure 3.4, plotting the gross box-office weekly revenues against time. The general shape of the noncumulative diffusion function does not look like a bell curve, but rather has a fast-break shape in which sales start out at a high level and then slowly dissipate. The general shape of the cumulated density function is not an S shape; instead it is rather Pareto-like. It should be noted that the lognormal path is plotted in a plain line on the charts.

MOVIES THAT EXHIBIT A TRADITIONAL PRODUCT LIFE CYCLE PATTERN

Not all movies follow this fast-break PLC. Indeed some movies represent the more traditional normal-shaped life cycle. What have these films in common? No stars. No mega production budget. No mega promotion budget. Were they a commercial success? Very much so. They gained public acclaim and a large audience in a less hyperbolic way than the fast-break group.

In many cases these were niche films designed to appeal to a narrower target market. For example, *March of the Penguins* is a documentary about how the emperor penguins travel hundreds of miles and take on incredible weather and tasks just to bring new life into the world. The production budget was a very low $3 million. It opened in just 695 theaters nationwide. This film raised its fame through word-of-mouth advertising by raising controversy on evolutionist matters. Though it was first released in artsy, big-city theaters, it eventually moved to suburban popular movie theaters and with its G rating brought in families that were not regular moviegoers. It eventually hit 2,506 theaters at its peak, and grossed $77 million in its U.S. run.

The Blair Witch Project is a film documentary about three young filmmakers who get lost in an eerie woodland steeped in legend. The film was shot with rough and shaky techniques, much like an amateur would shoot it. It opened in college towns rather than regular theaters and quickly acquired a small cult-like following as rumors circulated that the young filmmakers really died making the film. The film's cost was just $35,000, while it grossed $140 million. No other film in the history of Hollywood has made such a multiple.

My Big Fat Greek Wedding is a kind of sitcom with a relatively low budget of $5.5 million. Originally the film critics hated it, but the public thought otherwise.

Figure 3.4
Fast-Break PLC Curves

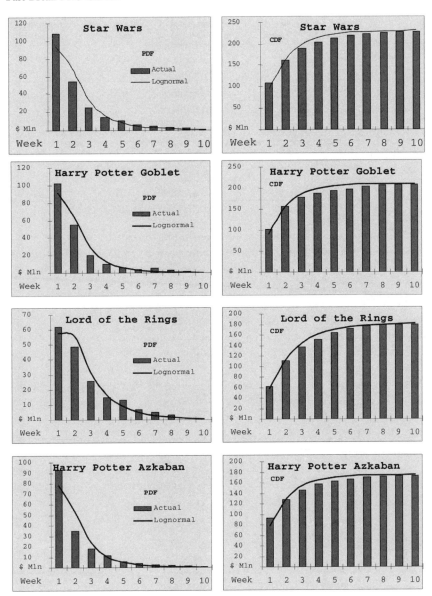

It started in just 108 theaters. The public, it appears, bought a good laugh, and a contagious laugh at that. The movie ran for almost a year and eventually grossed $267 million (see Table 3.2).

Table 3.2
A Comparison of Movie Performance

	March of the Penguins	*The Blair Witch Project*	*My Big Fat Greek Wedding*	*Brokeback Mountain*
Production $ (Millions)	3.0	0.350	5.5	14
Opening Screens	695	College Preview	108	5
Gross $ (Millions)	78.8	167.7	266.7	83
Lead time	15 weeks	15 weeks	49 weeks	20 weeks
S° Shape parameter	1.56	1.48	1.18	1.66
M° Scale parameter	7	4	22	7
R-Square	0.96	0.98	0.90	0.92

Brokeback Mountain opened in only five theaters originally. With a nontraditional plot, about gay cowboys, the film, which cost $14 million, was considered a high-risk venture. The movie was an economic success, running for 20 weeks and grossing $83 million in its U.S. run.

While the promotional budgets of these four movies are undisclosed, one can assume that by Hollywood standards their budgets were extremely low. A good indication they are low is that they opened in so few theaters, ranging from 4 to 700. A more traditional large budget Hollywood production would open in 2,500 theaters.

Not surprisingly, these four movies share a very different pattern than the previous films we have surveyed. They do not show the fast-break pattern. As shown in Figure 3.5, we observe a relatively gradual increase in attendance and fat tails. Indeed they look like skewed bells. They also model really well with the lognormal distribution. The coefficients of correlation are 0.98, 0.96, 0.92, and 0.90, respectively, for *The Blair Witch Project, March of the Penguins, Brokeback Mountain,* and *My Big Fat Greek Wedding*. Their shape coefficients S° are lower than those of the fast-break movies discussed previously.

SUMMARY

This chapter demonstrates that some successful products do not follow the traditional bell-shaped diffusion curve. While movies were the product category used, it is likely that many other leisure products exhibit what the author has called a "fast-break product life cycle pattern." Furthermore, it was shown that the lognormal distribution can be used to portray a wide variety of diffusion patterns. Time series taken from businesses as diverse as movies, music, and the automotive industry appear to fit the lognormal model. This is due to the

Figure 3.5
Movies That Exhibit a More Traditional Product Life Cycle Pattern

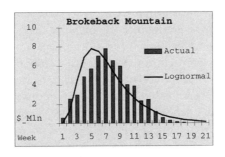

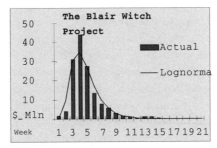

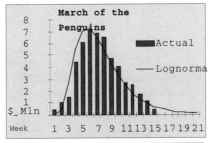

underlying impact of informational cascades, and imitation as a social norm in many cultures.

As discussed, a very important aspect of the lognormal distribution is its ability to accommodate more than one shape. It can adapt to a rapidly decaying, fast-break pattern, or a skewed bell-shaped curve. It appears from these data that movies with high promotion budgets, as suggested by a large number of opening screens, exhibit the fast-break lognormal decaying pattern of eagerly wanted products. Movies that rely more significantly on word-of-mouth communication exhibit a more traditional lognormal skewed bell shape.

Thanks to a unique property of the lognormal distribution, fashion cycles can take three shapes: fast break, craze, or traditional. Eagerly wanted products have the profile of the fast break. In 2002, there was a serious pandemic. It struck millions of children around the world, mostly boys from the age of 7 to 10. This virus was virulent. It came from East Asia, as is common. Children had a short incubation period and would then fall into a sort of depressive melancholy. Soon, the virus was coined the "Beyblade mania." The Beyblade is a spinning top, a rather mind-numbing toy. Takara Co., the Beyblade's marketing company, sold 100 million units. In 2002, Beyblades were so eagerly wanted that all retailers were short of the toys to the great disappointment of the children and their parents. The point is that today's children live in the exponential time. The consumption mode for many products is of the fast-break cycle. When they become grown-ups this fast-break generation will likely retain these fast-break patterns. Tomorrow's consumers of movies, music, travel, and other leisure pursuits will not likely follow the traditional normal shaped diffusion pattern. They will keep the consuming habits of their childhood. Marketers should get ready.

NOTES

1. Gatignon, Hubert, and Thomas S. Robertson, "A Propositional Inventory for New Diffusion Research," *Journal of Consumer Research*, Vol. 11 (1985).

2. Gatignon and Robertson, p. 21.

3. Gatignon and Robertson.

4. Bayus, Barry L., "Are Product Life Cycles Really Getting Shorter?" *Journal of Product Innovation Management*, Vol. 11 (1994), 300–308; Higgins, Susan H., and William Shanklin, "Seeking Mass Market Acceptance for High Technology Consumer Products," *The Journal of Consumer Marketing*, Vol. 9 (1992), 5–14; Vesey, Joseph T., "The New Competitors: They Think in Terms of 'Speed-to-Market,'" *Academy of Management Executive*, Vol. 5, (1991), 23–33.

5. Golder Peter N., and Gerard Tellis, "Growing, Growing Gone: Cascades, Diffusion and Turning Points in the Product Life Cycle," *Marketing Science*, Vol. 23, No. 2 (2004), 207–218.

6. Arndt, Johan, "Role of Product Related Conversations in the Diffusion of a New Product," *Journal of Marketing Research*, Vol. 4 (1967), 201–295.

7. Calantone, Roger J., and Kim E. Schatzel, "Strategic Foretelling: Communication-Based Antecedents of a Firm's Propensity to Preannounce," *Journal of Marketing*, Vol. 64 (2000) 17–30.

8. Golder and Tellis, p. 207.

9. Everett Rogers, *Diffusion of Innovations,* Free Press, 5th ed. (1995), p. 272.

10. Golder and Tellis.

11. Robertson, Thomas S., *Innovative Behavior and Communication,* New York: Holt, Rinehart and Winston (1971).

12. Day, George S., "The Product Life Cycle: Analysis and Application Issues," *Journal of Marketing,* Vol. 45 (1981), p. 61.

13. Day.

14. Gatignon and Robertson.

15. Gatignon and Robertson.

16. Summers, John O., "Media Exposure Patterns of Consumer Innovators," *Journal of Marketing,* Vol. 36 (1972), 43–49.

17. Summers, p. 43.

18. Rogers.

19. Bass, Frank, "A New Product Growth Model for Consumer Durables," *Management Science,* Vol. 15 (1969), 215–217.

20. Zaltman, Gerald, and Ronald Stiff, "Theories of Discussion," in *Customer Behavior: Theoretical Sources,* eds. Scott Ward and Thomas S. Robertson, Englewood Cliffs, NJ: Prentice-Hall (1973), 416–468.

21. Golder and Tellis.

22. Johnson, William C., and Keith Bratteir, "Technological Substitution in Mobile Communictions," *Journal of Business and Industrial Marketing,* Vol. 12 (1997), 8–15.

23. Golder and Tellis.

24. Bikhchandani, Suchil, David Hirshleifer, and Ivo Welch, "A Theory of Fads, Fashion, Custom, and Cultural Change as Informational Cascades," *Journal of Political Economy,* Vol. 100 (1992), 99–1026.

25. Robertson.

26. Golder and Tellis.

27. Cox, William E., Jr., "Product Life Cycles as Marketing Models," *Journal of Business,* Vol. 40 (1967), 375–384.

28. Fourt, Louis A., and Joseph W. Woodlock, "Early Prediction of Market Success for New Grocery Products," *Journal of Marketing,* Vol. 25 (1960), 31–38.

29. Gatignon and Robertson.

30. Sproles, George B., "Analyzing Fashion Life Cycles—Principles and Perspectives," *Journal of Marketing,* Vol. 45 (1981), 118.

31. Georg Simmel, "Fashion" (1904), reprinted in *Fashion Foundations: Early Writings on Fashion and Dress,* eds. Kim K.P. Johnson, Susan J. Torntore, and Joanne B. Eicher, Oxfordshire, UK: Berg (2003), 104–106.

32. Simmel.

33. Simmel.

34. King, Charles W., Jr., "Fashion Adoption: A Rebuttal to the 'Trickle Down Theory,'" in *Proceedings of the American Marketing Association,* ed. Stephen A. Greyser, Chicago: American Marketing Association, 1964, p. 125.

35. Sproles, p. 116.

36. IMDB—Internet Movie Database, http://www.imdb.com/title/tt0388795/.

REFERENCES

Arndt, Johan (1967), "Role of Product Related Conversations in the Diffusion of a New Product," Journal of Marketing Research, 4 (August), 201–295.

Bayus, Barry L. (1994), "Are Product Life Cycles Really Getting Shorter?", Journal of Product Innovation Management, 11 (September) pp. 300–308.

Bass, Frank (1969), "A New Product Growth Model for Consumer Durables," Management Science, vol. 15, pp. 215–217.

Bikhchandani, Suchil, David Hirshleifer, and Ivo Welch (1992), "A Theory of Fads, Fashion, Custom, and Cultural Change as Informational Cascades," Journal of Political Economy, vol. 100, 99–1026.

Calantone, Roger J., Schatzel, Kim E. (2000), "Strategic Foretelling: Communication-Based Antecedents of a Firm's Propensity to Preannounce," Journal of Marketing, January, vol. 64, no. 1, pp. 17–30.

Cox, William E., Jr., (1967) "Product Life Cycles as Marketing Models," Journal of Business, Vol. 40, 375–384.

Day, George S. (1981), "The Product Life Cycle: Analysis and Application Issues," Journal of Marketing 45 (Fall) 60–67.

Fourt, Louis A., and Joseph W. Woodlock (1960), "Early Prediction of Market Success for New Grocery Products," Journal of Marketing, Vol. 25, 31–38.

Gatignon, Hubert, and Thomas S. Robertson (1985), "A Propositional Inventory for New Diffusion Research," Journal of Consumer Research vol. 11, March.

Golder, Peter N., and Gerard Tellis (2004), "Growing, Growing Gone: Cascades, Diffusion and Turning Points in the Product Life Cycle," Marketing Science, vol. 23, no. 2, Spring, pp. 207–218.

Higgins, Susan H., and William Shanklin (1992), "Seeking Mass Market Acceptance for High Technology Consumer Products," The Journal of Consumer Marketing, vol. 9, Winter, pp. 5–14.

IMDB—Internet Movie Database, http://www.imdb.com/title/tt0388795/.

Johnson, William C., and Keith Bratteir (1997), "Technological Substitution in Mobile Communictions," Journal of Business and Industrial Marketing, vol. 12, no. 6, pp. 8–15.

King, Charles W., Jr. (1964), "Fashion Adoption: A Rebuttal to the 'Trickle Down Theory,'" in Proceedings of the American Marketing Association, ed. Stephen A. Greyser, Chicago: American Marketing Association, 108–125.

Robertson, Thomas (1967), "Determinants of Innovative Behavior," in Proceedings of the American Marketing Association, ed. Reed Moyer, Chicago: American Marketing Association, 328–332.

Robertson, Thomas S. (1971), Innovative Behavior and Communication, New York: Holt, Rinehart and Winston.

Rogers, Everett (1995), Diffusion of Innovations, Free Press, 5th ed., p. 272.

Simmel, Georg (1904) as found in Robertson (1971).

Simmel, Georg (1904), "Fashion," in Fashion Foundations: Early Writings on Fashion and Dress, Oxford, England: Berg.

Sproles, George B. (1981), "Analyzing Fashion Life Cycles—Principles and Perspectives," Journal of Marketing, Fall, pp. 116–124.

Summers John O. (1972), "Media Exposure Patterns of Consumer Innovators," Journal of Marketing, January, vol. 36, pp. 43–49.

Vesey, Joseph T. (1991), "The New Competitors: They Think in Terms of 'Speed-to-Market,'" Academy of Management Executive, May, vol. 5, no. 2, pp. 23–33.

Wiedmann Klaus-Peter, Gianfranco Walsh, and Vincent-Wyane Mitchel (2001), "The Mannmaven: An Agent for Diffusing Market Information," Journal of Marketing Communications, December, vol. 7, no. 4, pp. 195–212. (7)

Zaltman, Gerald, and Ronald Stiff (1973), "Theories of Discussion," in Customer Behavior: Theoretical Sources, eds. Scott Ward and Thomas S. Robertson, Englewood Cliffs, NJ: Prentice-Hall, 416–468.

CHAPTER 4

FUTURING: ANTICIPATING THE EMERGING VOICE OF THE CUSTOMER

Stephen M. Millett

THE CHALLENGE

The cardinal rule of marketing has been, "Listen to the customer." The theory is that to be responsive to customer demand, marketers need to pay attention to what customers say they want. But what if they cannot express what they want? Sometimes, waiting for customers to state their needs results in being too slow and not sufficiently competitive to respond to customer demand. In still other cases customers may not be able to envision or articulate what they want. For example, Henry Ford allegedly asserted, "If I'd only listened to customers, I'd have developed faster horses."[1]

Traditional market research methods have proven to be very effective, even predictive, of identifying short-term and well-articulated customer wishes. Focus groups, interviews, and surveys have been invaluable when customers can see and react to the proposed new product or service. They can react to the tangible. The shorter the time frame, the more predictive the voice of the customer is. Yet, these same market research tools typically fail when more abstract concepts and longer time periods are presented to customers. Customers generally find themselves unable to articulate what they will want in the extended future or whether or not they would buy at a specific price point until they can see and feel a product prototype.

What is an enterprise to do when the length of time it will take to bring a product or service to market is three years or more into the future? How can we know that a new product will sell when it reaches the market? How do we know what customers are willing to spend?

These questions pose a particularly troubling challenge to companies that pride themselves on innovation, original research and development (R&D), and being the first to market with new products and services. They must accurately anticipate customer demand in the future as well as respond to present customer demands without the information to make accurate assessments.

Futuring is emerging as a new tool for identifying likely consumer preferences and demands in the extended future when customers themselves cannot say what they will want. It employs a number of methods to explore likely states of customer behavior and needs yet unknown to customers themselves.

The purpose of this chapter is to explore the substance, methods, and applications of futuring as a potentially vital approach to marketing in the 21st century.

THE SUBSTANCE OF FUTURING

Futuring is the systematic study of long-term consumer trends and patterns of behavior in place of short-term consumer-articulated research. While straight trend extrapolations can be misleading, an understanding of how consumers have behaved in the past provides foresight into how they are likely to behave in the future.

One very important and often studied consumer trend is the composition of the consumer population, or demographics. An understanding of age, gender, ethnic origin, and other population characteristics has long been a part of market segmentation research. Futuring, however, extends the time horizon of market segmentation research to anticipate how people are likely to behave, under certain circumstances, in the future. A few examples illustrating the point follow.

In 1991, William Strauss and Neil Howe published a book in which they asserted that there had always been four basic types of generational cohorts in American history and that the generations followed predictable patterns of behavior.[2] By studying generational types, one could anticipate the predilections and preferences of generations. This principle could also be applied to consumer behavior. In an independent study, Yankelovich Partners, Inc. built a database and provided an analysis of three generations in the 20th century: Matures, Boomers, and Gen X.[3] It claims to have established patterns of behavior that could be used to explain and anticipate how each generation would likely behave while passing through the stages of life. This analysis provided insights into new product and service development as well as marketing strategies. While generational trend analysis remained controversial into the 21st century, the concept of age as a demographic indicator of future consumer behavior is now widely accepted and practiced.

Generational analysis by itself, however, is not as robust as when it is combined with other demographic trends. One is life-stage analysis, which was popularized by the best-selling book authored by Gail Sheehy in the 1970s.[4] Her adherents placed a heavy emphasis on life stage rather than generation cohort as the primary driver of consumer behavior. The emerging theory is that all generations have their own peculiar attitudes and preferences based on shared cultural and historical experiences, especially those of their youth. But all individuals and generations pass through stages of life, such as adolescence, marriage and early family raising, careers, midlife, retirement, and old age. Generational analysis tells us that all age groups do not act exactly the same way as they move through different life stages, but that life stages set up the aspirations, achievements, and frustrations that are common to everyone.

By way of illustrations, Matures, or the World War II generation, typically accepted authority, worked very hard, and retired with occasional but rarely regular postcareer employment. They tended to have single marriages and careers. With fresh memories of the Great Depression, Matures tended to spend within their financial means and saved money for their futures. The Baby Boomers, who were born between 1946 and 1964, however, developed great skepticism about authority from their experiences of the Vietnam War, Watergate, and corporate layoffs. Their generation experienced higher divorce rates than in the past, and many Boomers have had multiple marriages, families, and careers. Boomers have consistently been heavy spenders and light savers. How they will behave in retirement is now a major question. The expectation is that they will continue working, at least part-time, well into their 80s, with many Boomers starting their own businesses relatively late in life.

While insightful, generation cohort behavior is not sufficient by itself to anticipate future behavior. One also has to understand life stage. At certain life stages, people face similar challenges, such as gaining an education, marrying and raising a family, pursuing a career, entering middle age, retirement, and so forth. Originally it was believed that one needed only to understand life stage to predict consumer behavior. This is not true, because different generations have different styles based on their common life and historical experiences and respond differently to the challenges of various life stages. As mentioned above, the World War II generation, due to their military experiences, approached family life and their career-building challenges in the 1950s very differently than the Baby Boomer generation did in the 1980s. Accordingly, the Boomers' style of retirement may prove to be very different.

By understanding generational and life-stage behaviors, one can anticipate at least in general terms how certain consumers are likely to act and what they are likely to buy in the future even when the customers may not be able to articulate their wants and needs. Yet, futuring must take into account additional demographic and economic trends.

While generation and age are important demographic indicators of the future, so is ethnic identity, especially in an era of heavy immigration into the United States. Of primary importance are Hispanics who are entering the United States from Mexico, Central America, South America, and the Caribbean, both legally and illegally. Counted as a distinct group, irrespective of country of origin, Hispanics are now the single largest minority group in the United States. While their presence is well known in the border states of Texas, New Mexico, Arizona, and California, they also represent a significant social group in such other states as Nevada (23 percent), Florida (19 percent), and New York (16 percent).[5]

Is Hispanic consumer behavior in the United States the same as that of other Americans? Are the types of homes and neighborhoods in which they live reflective of their ethnic tastes, their economic strata, or some other factors? What evidence exists indicates that given sufficient income, Hispanic consumers have a hunger for many of the same life-styles and consumer products favored by American consumers? Oddly, we still do not fully know the answers to these and similar questions. It is assumed that Hispanic Baby Boomers, whether born in the United States or not, but living and working in the United States, behave generally the same as American-born Baby Boomers. However, we do not have the studies to confirm this.

Observations also tell us that while Hispanics may patronize Hispanic businesses, they will also shop extensively in the mainstream American marketplace. Therefore, most consumer products and large retail chains will offer information in both English and Spanish.

Asians, who are a rapidly growing minority with approximately more than 4 percent of the total U.S. population, are another significant minority in the United States. Their life-styles and spending patterns are noticeably different from both Americans and Hispanics. They tend to have a very strong sense of Asian and family identity and will adhere to Asian ways to the greatest possible extent. They will shop largely within their own community for products ranging from groceries to financial services. This may be due to language problems, but it may also be due to cultural preferences and an associated trust of similar Asians with a corresponding distrust of native Americans. The historical pattern, however, is that second- and third-generation Asians born in the United States acculturate as quickly as any other ethnic group in American history.

Gender is another important demographic factor. The United States has slightly more females than males, and in many consumer niches, women are more likely to be the consumers as well as the primary decision makers. For example, it has been well known for years that women buy more men's clothes than men do. Yet, so many men's clothing stores appeal to masculine rather than feminine tastes. Women are also the primary buyers of health care services. Yet, again, so many doctors, clinics, and hospitals are male rather than female in language, behavior, and culture. In still other cases, women have an increasingly major influence on the purchases of large ticket purchases, such as homes (primary and resort), cars, and travel.

Futuring considers all of these demographic trends and sorts them out as to what outcomes are most likely to occur by what designated date in the future.

Demographics, as contextual as they are, do not tell the whole story of consumer behavior. One has to consider economics and technology as well. Economic forecasting, however, is notoriously difficult to do and mostly inaccurate. That is not for a lack of data or sophisticated modeling and simulation; it is due primarily to the dynamics of so many variables interacting with each other, which make prediction difficult. For example, the events of September 11, which greatly impacted the American economy, were not predictable.

At the macroscopic level, with only a few years as exceptions, the U.S. economy has shown consistent positive annual growth since World War II. The average annual growth of the largest economy in the world is not likely to sustain more than 5-percent growth in the gross domestic product (GDP). The United States is not likely to have the kind of hypergrowth rates of China and India. More importantly, however, is the real GDP or the growth rate normalized into constant dollars. More important still are average household income and disposable income. These economics touch the lives of everyday consumers. While the data are readily available for household income, household wealth (now represented primarily by savings, investments, 401(k) accounts, and pensions) is very difficult to estimate.

The trend has been that average American household incomes have remained remarkably stable for nearly ten years and that household wealth, which is difficult to measure, may actually be declining. Many of the apparent gains in income must be discounted by inflation (especially in the staples of housing, energy, and food). Household wealth has been increasing due to the rapid inflation of real estate prices in the last decade or so. If the real estate market were to cool, then household wealth in real estate assets may plateau and even decline. More troubling is the decline in pension wealth as a long-term household resource. Many corporations have eliminated or reduced their pension plans. On the other hand, while household finances have changed in the last 20 years, technologies have continuously improved the general quality of life with many products and services declining in prices due to technological advancements.

Health care insurance is also critically important. While many Americans are employed, they may be underemployed (meaning that their levels of responsibilities and their incomes may not be parallel with their education and past work experience) and have little or no health care insurance. It is estimated that nearly 50 million Americans have no health insurance at all at a time in history when a visit to the emergency room could cost $5,000 or more.

When thinking about the future of consumer behavior, one has to consider beyond income the matter of net household wealth. This takes into account debt versus wealth. With rising consumer debt, declining real estate prices, rising energy costs, and rising interest rates, net assets may begin falling rather than rising more several years into the future. Such a trend would have potentially devastating impacts on the Baby Boomer generation as it enters its retirement years.

Futuring must also consider emerging technologies. Everyone has seen the enormous impacts on life-styles, employment, productivity, and consuming caused by the personal computer and the Internet within just the last 20 years. What will be the next Internet? Computers will likely range in size and bandwidth like TVs and telephones. Beyond the information technologies, there are the potentially important new energy technologies and biotechnologies. Breakthroughs in both could be as revolutionary in the marketplace as the personal computer was in the early 1980s and the Internet was in the late 1990s.

THE METHODS

All futuring methods generally fall into three categories: trend analysis, expert judgment, and alternative futures, or multi-options analysis.[6] A brief overview of each follows.

Trends

Some of the leading indicators of future consumer behavior have already been identified above. These are trends or patterns of behavior over time (as opposed to discrete events, which are very difficult, if not impossible, to predict).

Trend extrapolation continues to be the most frequently used method to make forecasts. All forecasters use trend data, because data exist only for the past and the present. No one has data from the future. Trend analysis can be very reliable in some cases, but it can only anticipate continuity. It cannot predict discontinuities.

I was asked once how many data points were required to draw a trend line. I thought the questioner was kidding me, so I said that I liked at least two, but prefer three. He looked at me with a straight face and said that was odd, because at his company typically only one was used. Obviously predicting a trend for the future based on only one data point is risky business.

A common assumption is that additional data leads to better predictions. This may not be true. Indeed it may be the opposite, as past data may emphasize certain events, or recent past events, more than they should. Trends within an industry may be used to develop projections for shifts in purchase behaviors, due to changes in culture, tastes, fashion, or technology. Trend data are often collected and disseminated by associations or trade groups. For example, recent trend data published by the International Association of Culinary Professionals are shown in Table 4.1, which shows several key trends, such as a trend toward life-style simplicity, that will likely impact consumer eating habits and purchases in the future.

The theoretical problem with trend data, however, is not merely the amount of it or even its accuracy. The problem is the variability of the phenomena for which we gather data. In cases where the data are extensive and accurate and the

Table 4.1
Key Consumer Food Trends

The focus is on healthy living

- People continue to cook, but want to take advantage of quick preparation time and convenience while taking advantage of healthy, fresh ingredients
- Focus on holistic health, including the mind, body, and waistline

Lifestyles are more casual

- Focus on simplicity and sharing
- More interest in local and regionally grown foods
- Slow cookers, aka crock pots, are experiencing a comeback

Ethnic Foods

- Italian and Mexican foods are no longer considered ethnic, but mainstream
- New ethnic trends are Thai, South American, and Mediterranean

Kids want food to be fun

- Enjoy a surprise element

Source: McLain, Cathy, *Forum Offers Food Marketers Trends Snapshot,* "The Hungry Mind," Quarterly Joint Publication of the Marketing Communicators Section of the International Association of Culinary Professionals and the Food and Beverage Section of the Public Relations Society of America (IACP and PRSA), Second Quarter 2004, p. 4.

phenomena are very stable, then trend analysis can be very accurate. Trend projections do work on many occasions, especially in the short term and for things known to vary little over time. One very interesting trend is the shift in work in the United States over the past century. In 1900, over 40 percent of American working men were engaged in farming, fishing, and mining. By 2000, the proportion had dropped to about 4 percent. In the same 100 years, the proportion of professionals and retail male employees rose from 21 to 58 percent. Workers in production facilities, like mills and factories, and transportation rose from 38 percent in 1900 to a peak of about 50 percent by 1950, and then declined back to 38 percent by the end of the century.[7]

These trends reflect the economic shift from agriculture to manufacturing to retail and the "knowledge economy." However, even over long periods of time, will these trend lines be linear projections in the future? It is hard to imagine that agriculture will drop further, although a decline to 1 to 2 percent of the working population is certainly possible. Will manufacturing jobs in the future drop like agricultural jobs have? Considering trends in technology, especially information and communications technologies, it seems likely that the proportion of manufacturing jobs may fall to 20 percent, but not to 2 percent, of the work force in the United States by the year 2010.

Trend analysis, however, breaks down when the data are not sufficient, are inconsistent in accuracy, or the phenomena display a potential for great variability (or instability). The more complexity that exists in the phenomena (such as a large number of variables that are highly interactive with each other) and the longer the time horizon, the more there will be variability, risk, and uncertainty. For example, trend analysis is not very helpful in predicting fashion trends such as skirt length, tie widths, or baby names.

Trend analysis is another form of pattern recognition. In the many worlds of pattern recognition, there are fundamentally three categories of pattern recognition problems:

- Type I: *Background Pattern Recognition.* The first type occurs when the background pattern is the principal focus of interest. It establishes what is the norm and the baseline of continuity. When the background is well understood, one looks for deviations ("signal") from the background to detect changes. One theory is that patterns of human living exist for long periods of time; the routines of everyday life endure despite periodic (and thankfully rare) great events of history.[8] In this context, the patterns have great stability, even though there may be relatively small deviations from time to time—and occasionally (but rarely) major disruptive events. One is impressed more with the continuities than the momentary exceptions. In this situation, trend analysis would generally be predictive.

- Type II: *Signal Pattern Recognition.* The second type occurs when an event or a thing, called the signal, is the focus of interest rather than the background. One watches for the presence of the signal with little or no regard to the background (which may only be clutter confounding the detection of the signal). This perspective is the opposite of Type I; one is interested in the great events or discontinuities rather than the background, long-term patterns. Discontinuities do happen for all sorts of reasons, some of which are beyond the powers of mankind to control. Type II pattern recognition cannot be predicted from Type I analysis, although Type I trends are necessary to provide the context for understanding the significance of Type II pattern recognition.

- Type III: *Emerging Pattern Recognition.* In the third type, neither the background nor the pattern is known, so one collects data and searches for the pattern in them. Here is where both historians and futurists imagine all kinds of possibilities. The most favored Type III trend analysis is linear projections, even when complicated repression analysis has to be used to even find a line. It is possible that lines do exist, so a Type III analysis may lead to something that would fall into Type I. Another very popular pattern is cycles, whereby the analyst sees a consistent pattern of up and down curves.[9] A variation of cycles, called S curves, has been developed to forecast the development of new technologies.[10] Cycles are very popular in all kinds of forecasting, but the periodicity of them and the exact replication of the curves over and over again is rarely achieved. The theory has great attraction, but the applications can be very messy.

In a true inductive style, one would need a great deal of data to be sure that the pattern would be repeatable over long periods of time. The pattern might be very irregular and have no similarity to either a line or a cycle. If the pattern did emerge, then Type III analysis would be a very effective way or discovering new Type I patterns.

Expert Judgment

Expert judgment is a form of intuitive forecasting. It is the only way, in most cases, to anticipate the discontinuities that cannot be predicted by trend analysis. In the ancient world, the experts with extraordinary predictive powers were called prophets, oracles, and soothsayers. Ultimately, in this historical context most of the predictions of such people came from their gods. Today, the experts are called analysts, professors, and consultants. Their inspirations come largely from their study of history, existing data, stringent logic, and the mental "black box" called intuition.

All expert judgments suffer from two major liabilities. One is the fact that no expert, contrary to what he or she may proclaim, can possibly know everything. The other is that all experts have their own biases. Therefore, the best expert judgment methods involve many experts to fill in the gaps and smooth out the biases.

Expert judgment methods include interviews, questionnaires, surveys (both actual and virtual over the Internet), and group dynamics (such as brainstorming, variations on idea generation, and the Nominal Group Technique).[11]

Expert focus groups and expert judgment methods in general are used in ways very similar to the methods of short-term market research where the "experts" are the consumers themselves. The techniques for extracting judgments are about the same. The difference is largely in the pool of experts and the time frame of the questions. Whereas customers cannot articulate what they will likely do in the future, the experts who know about customers can make predictions based on their studies and their intuition. They may know more about the behavior patterns of customers than the customers know about themselves.

It should be noted in passing that all forms of modeling, even the most complex and quantitative, begin with expert judgment. Someone has to ask the focus question and select the variables that will be included and excluded from the model. Too often when futuring, there is no direct acknowledgment of this. In many cases the expert judgment, typically called assumption, is invisible in the construction of econometric and financial models. For example, assume we are interested in developing a model for predicting the number of students that would be available to attend state universities sometime in the future. We may include data on the number of high school students within the state, the present rate of college attendance, and the expected increase in tuition. Should this model also include students from outside the state, and what about students from other nations? What if we assume that the in-state tuition rate is extended to out-of-state students? Will this impact our results? What if the bias of the authors is that only legal residents should be able to attend the state university? Would this impact the result?

Alternative Futures

Alternative futures provide multiple possible futures. In trend analysis, there is an underlying assumption that there will be a single, most likely, if not predetermined, future because of the momentum of the phenomena behind the trend data. There is a future and it is knowable. In expert judgment, there may be either singular or multiple predictions for the future. In alternative futures, the assumption is that there are multiple possible, even likely, futures and each requires examination. The most popular form of alternative futures today is scenario writing, although this category of methods also includes paths, trees, matrix analysis, and real options analysis.

The contemporary use of scenarios may be traced back to the RAND Corporation and the planning scenarios done for the U.S. Air Force in the 1950s. These scenarios were hypothetical, not predictive, sequences of cause-and-effect actions leading to a logically consistent end state. The RAND scenario method was adapted, with the help of Herman Kahn, by both General Electric Company (GE) and Shell Oil Company in the early 1970s with a significantly different twist. In the applications of GE and Shell, scenarios became alternative end states with logically consistent components (trends, issues, factors, and so forth), but without a presumed sequence of events. The Shell variation became highly publicized and the model for most scenario projects today.[12]

Depending upon their purposes and techniques, scenarios can be generated both intuitively, as a variation on expert judgment in a group setting with a potential for multiple (typically two to four) outcomes, and analytically using both expert judgment and trends analysis combined with probabilities, cross-impact analysis, and computer-based modeling and simulation.

Scenarios can be used a variety of ways just as they can be created in different ways. One use is contingency planning as just used by Kahn for the U.S. Air Force. The point of thinking about multiple endings (alternative futures) was to encourage the consideration of plans beyond the main one. For every Plan A there must be Plan B, C, D, and so forth to cover possible alternative outcomes once a sequence of actions is put into motion. The military has been rigorous about contingency planning (at least at the tactical level), but businesses have not proven to be as flexible in their thinking and their actions as the military.

Another use of scenarios is the learning process itself. The scenarios are neither plans nor predictions, but rather a method for simulations of various complexity. Scenarios in the business context are similar to war games in the military sense.

They are hypothetical rehearsals of alternative, hypothetical futures. The benefits of the scenarios are derived from the insights gained in the process rather than the scenarios themselves. A secondary value is the team building that also comes from the process involving the social dynamics of the same people who will be responsible for the implementation of strategies that emerge from the scenario exercise.

A third application of scenarios is forecasting, but in a different way than in statistical, financial, and economic forecasting. Scenarios, at least analytical rather than intuitive scenarios, can be generated by modeling and simulation with or without a computer software program. As practiced by Battelle for over 20 years using the Interactive Futures Simulation (IFS) software program, scenarios begin with a topical question of importance to a client. The answers to the topical question will be used to make a decision in the near future about investments or strategies that will likely lead to desired outcomes in the long-term future. Expert judgment is used to identify the most important descriptors (trends, issues, factors, or variables) relative to the topical question. Trend analysis is performed for each descriptor. Then each descriptor is assigned alternative outcomes with *a priori* probabilities of occurrence by a target date.

While the software program provides the structure for cross-impact analysis of all the descriptors and their alternative outcomes with each other, the software program, using the judgments entered, also calculates adjusted probabilities of descriptor outcomes and arranges them in alternative sets (scenarios). The scenarios with the highest adjusted probabilities of occurrence are the scenarios that are most likely to occur given current information about trends. Desired scenarios may be included in the sets, although they may have low probabilities of occurrence. The desired scenarios provide foresights into what would need to occur, or what investments and strategies would have to be put in place in order to achieve desired outcomes (which provides more rigor and direction than just wishful thinking).[13]

CASE HISTORIES OF FUTURING

Three case histories are offered to illustrate how futuring can be used to anticipate future consumer demand and to identify the emerging but yet unarticulated voices of customers. Two come from the experience of Battelle, a large independent technology development, management, and commercialization firm headquartered in Columbus, Ohio. The third is an example of intuitive scenarios generated by the State Board of Education in Ohio for long-term strategic planning for the consumers of public education.

The Case of the Intuitive Champion

The quotation by Henry Ford in the beginning of this chapter reflects the futuring of a new product champion, or one who sees the future with opportunities that few others do. It is the futuring of successful inventors and entrepreneurs. The first case history presented here tells the story of the origins of the Xerox machine when the intuitive futuring of the champion proved to be successful despite the flawed predictions of traditional market research.

In 1944 a patent lawyer from Battelle in Columbus, Ohio, met another patent lawyer in New York who was also an amateur inventor named Chester Carlson. Carlson had a patent of his own invention for a dry, electrostatic copying machine. It was a revolutionary concept, but Carlson did not have the resources or the scope of complex technical knowledge to make it work beyond a bench top model. So he joined forces with Battelle, which undertook at its own expense the development of an operational and commercially viable dry copying machine. Battelle's effort took 14 years! After many disappointments, the first commercially successful machine (called "Xerox") was offered on the market in 1960. It proved to be huge success and emerged as one of the great technological innovations of its era.[14]

During the development of the Xerox process, Battelle and its partners commissioned a market research study. The study interviewed many potential customers and concluded that there was no market pull for a dry process copier. But Carlson, acting like a true new product champion, thought otherwise. He had his own view of the future. As a patent attorney, he knew from experience that there was no good process for him to make multiple copies of legal documents already in his possession. He personally knew trends in the law, government, and business. He knew that there would be a potential demand for offices to have their own copying capabilities. The people at Battelle and the Xerox Corporation agreed with him.

Why was the market study wrong in light of the later huge success of Xerox during the 1960s? The apparent reason was that the market study asked the wrong set of customers, who in turn could not verbalize their reactions to a totally unfamiliar product concept.

The market researchers went to secretaries, printers, and other people who generated copies. These people said they already had the tools that they needed, and they did not see a role for a dry copier (which they apparently had a very difficult time visualizing in the framework of their normal work routines). When the Xerox machine was introduced and when people saw it and worked it, they came to see benefits not visualized or articulated before. It turned out that the customer base they had used was people who received, not generated, material. The original market research study had asked the wrong questions of the wrong potential customers and failed to anticipate several trends toward the explosion in business, legal, and academic paperwork.

Another point is that the Xerox Corporation was very clever to introduce a new business model for commercializing a new product. It was not only that the Xerox machine was a "better mousetrap" or that the Xerox Corporation was a better "mousetrap company," but that the business model for the new product was also a "better mousetrap value proposition." A major lesson here is that typically a new technology, especially a very novel one, requires a new business model.

The lesson of this case history is that, as asserted earlier, traditional market research methods fail when they ask prospective customers what they would buy in the future, especially when the product concept is not clearly developed, understood, or presented. Perhaps the market research went to the wrong target market (which frequently occurs), or it went to the right target market but asked the wrong questions (which also commonly happens). The point remains that the traditional market research came up with the wrong answer, which was ignored by the new product champion, who proved to be correct.

An important lesson is to understand that the customer of tomorrow may not be the customer of today. Who would have predicted 20 years ago that teenagers would be making the primary purchase decision for household telephones, for example? In this case, the expert judgment of Chester Carlson and his Battelle allies carried the day over the market research. Admittedly, they took huge technical and financial risks, but they were successful in implementing their vision of the future.

The Case of the Predictive Scenarios

The second case history also comes from Battelle, and it is one in which this author was involved intimately. A consumer product company with a well-known corporate and brand name and with a common household product came to Battelle for futuring. The concept was to use futuring as a frame of reference for developing new products leveraged from existing capabilities. We used the IFS scenario method and supporting software program. The topic question concerned the future of American households and expectations for household cleaning. We conducted two expert focus groups (expert judgment), one with Battelle experts and one with corporate experts, from which we derived a number of demographic, social, economic, and technological descriptors. The core team, consisting of both Battelle and client project principals, performed trend analysis on the descriptors and projected the most likely alternative outcomes for each descriptor. The alternative outcomes (comprehensive, mutually exclusive, and numbering two to four for each descriptor) were assigned *a priori* probabilities of occurrence in the future based on trend analysis and expert judgment with peer review. Cross-impact analysis was performed with the IFS software program.

A large number of scenarios were generated by the software program. Most of them could easily be combined into five principal scenarios. With the scenarios giving us views to the future, we held yet another expert focus group at Battelle to derive product concepts from the scenarios. A materials engineer concluded that if people wanted cleaner homes, meaning more hygienic and free from illness-causing bacteria and viruses, but if people wanted to spend less time cleaning, then there was a potential market for a disposal wipe that would be impregnated with an antimicrobial substance. The product would be highly effective, easy to use, easy to throw away, and affordable.

The scenarios had stimulated a process of creating new product concepts. The client took the scenarios and their implications back to its R&D center, where it supplemented the scenarios with its own research and idea generation processes. The result was that within two years the corporation introduced a home cleaning disposable wipe that became very popular as soon as consumers saw and tried the wipes.

When the scenarios were generated, we used a ten-year planning horizon. We asked the question in a way that gave a long-range perspective, but we never said that we had to wait ten years to launch a new product. The client company introduced its wipe about three years after we began the scenario project. It made a likely future happen faster by being proactive rather than reactive to already existing and known consumer needs. Therefore the company seized all the competitive advantages of being first to market with an innovative product that captured people's imagination and store shelf space.

Futuring, particularly scenario analysis, proved to be the engine of innovation in new product development. It identified a potential consumer need in the future that had not been previously articulated in any meaningful way by traditional market research.

The Case of the Farsighted Board

The third case history illustrates how futuring, specifically intuitive scenarios, can be used to frame policy through the consensus of a group. The group was the 19-member State Board of Education in Ohio, which met in June 2006 for a three-day retreat to formulate broad and long-term policies for public education. Both the present author and one of the editors (Dr. Deborah L. Owens), as members of the State Board of Education, participated in this exercise.

We began with the topic question, "What are or will be the most important trends or issues determining student achievement in Ohio from 2006 to 2026?" We used unstructured brainstorming and generated a list of 67 trends or issues in response to the topic question. The board members were then asked to vote on three from the list that they thought were both the most important and the most uncertain. The two trends or issues that received the most votes were "expectations for educational achievement" (those of the federal No Child Left Behind Act of 2001, state law, standards set by the State Board of Education, and the broader expectations of society) and "globalization" (meaning the extent and impacts of the new global economy, both as stimulants of growth and as negative impacts of outsourcing of manufacturing, services, and investment capital on the State of Ohio).

We then set up a quadrant of high and low expectations and high and low impacts of the new global economy (see Figure 4.1). The four quadrants were (1) high impact and low expectations, (2) high impact and high expectations, (3) low impact and low expectations, and (4) high impact and low expectations. We then divided the board members into four discussion groups, one for each quadrant (scenario). They were asked to define their terms and to make up a story about the level of student achievement in each scenario and why. They were also asked to work in as many of the 67 trends as they could.

The members of the board enthusiastically responded to the challenges of the exercise. We took just an hour to hear all four scenarios, and the discussion and questions were at a very high level of critical judgment. From the discussion of

Figure 4.1
Scenarios for Public Education in Ohio by 2016

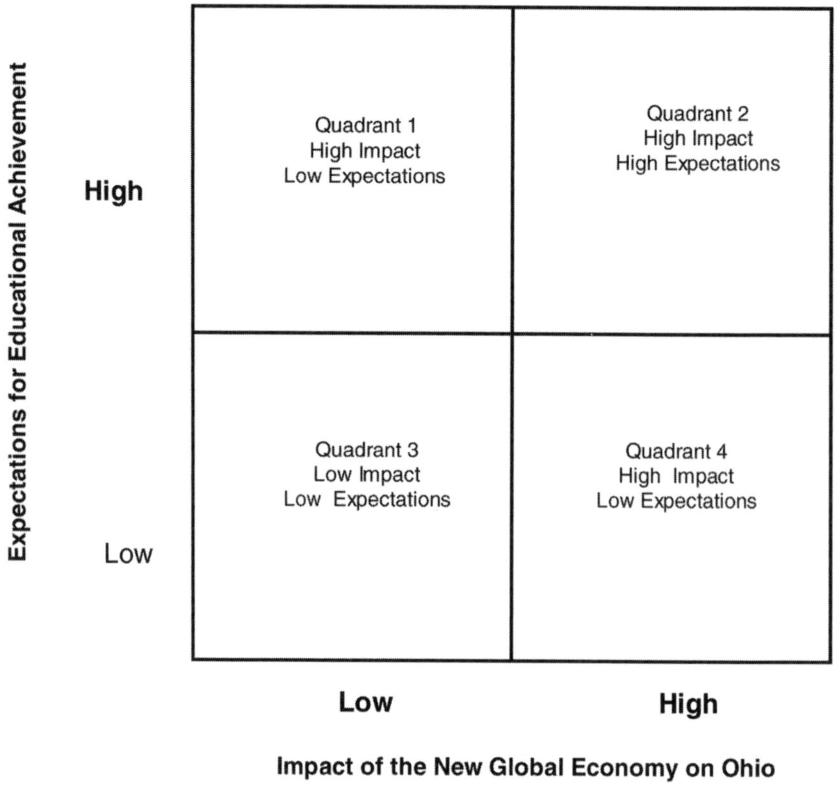

all four scenarios, the board drew seven general implications for the future of public education in Ohio:

1. Expectations, and the accountability that goes with them, are indeed a major driver of future student performance.

2. The New Global Economy is perhaps the single most important driver of the future economic health of Ohio, and in turn the resource base and societal needs of this state.

3. Leadership is vital for linking the potential opportunities of the new global economy with high achievement in education.

4. People generally "don't get it"—many people cannot see what is happening to the economy of Ohio and do not see the impact of industrial outsourcing, competition, failed businesses, and Ohio still has folks who expect the large steel mills of northeastern Ohio to reopen someday.

5. We need a strong sense of community in this state. Community means shared values, strong relationships, and mutual cooperation to achieve educational goals.

6. Economic growth must increase at a faster rate than it has in the last ten years or Ohio will likely continue to fall behind the rate of growth in other leading states and become an international backwash.

7. Alignment of the educational system with the "real world," meaning that we have to revise the curriculum and teaching to make content more relevant to the needs of employers and postsecondary education.

Next, we did a Nominal Group Exercise on the topic question "Considering all four scenarios, what can the State Board of Education do to contribute the most to student achievement in Ohio from 2006 to 2016?" We generated 41 ideas in response and voted on them. The top ten ideas were, in rank order, as follows:

1. Create high educational expectations for Ohioans in light of a globally competitive economy.

2. Establish an effective early childhood education system.

3. Continue working closely with institutions of higher education to ensure better teacher preparation.

4. Reassess the redesign of academic standards to build more relevance to globalization and "the real world."

5. Engage business and government in strategic conversations and collaborative initiatives about Ohio's future and the role of education in Ohio's economic future.

6. Develop standards and best practices for a process of individualized student instruction.

7. Expand and promote data availability and analysis to guide the improvement of student achievement.

8. Implement models for differentiated educator/teacher roles and performance-based pay.

9. The State Board of Education must take a thought leadership role on globalization and the changing economy in Ohio.

10. There must be accountability with rewards and penalties for meeting or not meeting expectations.

We broke into two discussion groups to compare this top ten list with last year's board priorities and with the recommended priorities of the Ohio Department of Education (which operates under the authority of the State Board of Education). The two groups came up with remarkably similar results, such that we had to talk through only one priority in order to reach a consensus. The final six priorities were as follows:

1. Identify the causes of and develop remedies for low academic performance.

2. Build relevance into the content and standards, especially for high achieving middle and high schools.

3. Enhance teacher development and preparation programs.

4. Modernize school funding and resource management.

5. Provide leadership in early childhood learning (a new priority).

6. Engage the business community and political leadership in strategic conversations about the New Global Economy and the role of education in it.

The State Board reviewed these priorities and officially passed them at the subsequent regular board meeting. To implement these priorities, the Ohio Department of Education set up a schedule of briefings and began to frame the programs for each and every meeting of the State Board of Education for the following year.

THE APPLICATIONS OF FUTURING

Looking into the future, four obvious applications of futuring come to mind, as follows:

R&D Investments and Portfolio Management

R&D organizations have the dilemma of developing technologies for future products with little or no direction on what consumers of the future will want. Some R&D organizations will conduct their own consumer research, but rarely market research. In too many companies, there is too little practical guidance from marketing. (In most companies there is a tension between marketing, which says to R&D, "Why can't you make what I can sell?" and R&D says to marketing, "Why can't you sell what I can make?") While the typical horizon of marketing organizations and traditional market research may be up to one year, the time horizon of R&D can be as far as ten years into the future. Therefore, R&D is turning to futuring as its long-term perspective on what technologies it should invest in and pursue.

Product Development

Both case histories above concerned futuring as the engine of innovation in new product development. In the past, new product development occurred primarily within R&D, but more recently new product development may be a separate function. Sometimes it falls under marketing rather than R&D. Some organizations will even have an innovation group and process separate from R&D and marketing. Whatever the structure, the question remains—What is the inspiration of innovation? Thinking about the future of customers, markets, and competitors provides an excellent avenue to stimulate innovation toward practical and successful new products and services.

Strategic Marketing

Marketing organizations need to do long-term thinking just as R&D groups must. Strategic marketing for the future addresses the issues of changing customers, shifting value propositions, and evolving market positioning of products and services. Skillful long-term marketing facilitates and reduces the costs of short-term selling.

Thought Leadership

Thought leadership occurs when a company takes ideas to its customers and shapes their very thinking. The object of thought leadership is mindshare, which in the future of virtual networks, will be like the shelf space of the future. It is the telling of a compelling story about the future to customers who are looking for answers they themselves do not have. Particularly in business-to-business relationships, buyers often look to their suppliers and partners to come up with new ideas for the future.

Policy Making

As illustrated by the case history of intuitive scenarios used by the State Board of Education in Ohio, futuring provides an external frame of reference for policy making, whether it be private or public policy. It places the focus on external challenges before considering internal resources and desires.

CONCLUSIONS

The purpose of this chapter was to explore the substance, methods, and applications of futuring as an emerging method for both companies and organizations to estimate the emerging, unarticulated voices of customers when customers themselves cannot say what they will want or buy in the future. "Customers" may be literally consumers or they may be stakeholders and constituents. It is important to remember that customers cannot always articulate what they will want in the future. Futuring is a way to anticipate the unarticulated voice of the customer based on various trends, including patterns of customer behavior. These patterns turn out to be better predictors of the future than what customers may say. In addition, futuring not only identifies potential new opportunities with existing customers, it may likely foresee new customers and growth opportunities.

NOTES

1. Thomas Goldbrunner, Richard Hauser, Georg List, and Steven Veldhoen, The Four Dimensions of Intelligent Innovation. Winning the Race for Profitable Growth. Booz Allen Hamilton, 2005 (www.boozallen.com), p. 4.

2. William Strauss and Neil Howe, *Generations: The History of America's Future, 1584 to 2069*. New York: Morrow, 1991.

3. J. Walker Smith and Ann Clurman, *Rocking the Ages: The Yankelovich Report on Generational Marketing*. New York: Harper Business, 1997.

4. Gail Sheehy, *Passages: Predictable Crises of Adult Life*. New York: E.P. Dutton, 1976.

5. U.S. Census Bureau, *Statistical Abstract of the United States: 2004–2005*. 124th edition. Washington: U.S. Government Printing Office, 2004, p. 24.

6. Stephen M. Millett and Edward J. Honton, *A Manager's Guide to Technology Forecasting and Strategy Analysis Methods*. Columbus, OH: Battelle Press, 1991.

7. Theodore Caplow, Louis Hicks, and Ben J. Wattenberg, *The First Measured Century: An Illustrated Guide to Trends in America, 1900–2000*. Washington: The AEI Press, 2001, pp. 24–49.

8. Fernand Braudel, *The Structures of Everyday Life: The Limits of the Possible. Civilization and Capitalism, 15th–18th Century, Vol. I*. Translated and revised by Sian Reynolds. Berkeley, CA: University of California Press, 1992 (1979).

9. Strauss and Howe, *Generations;* Arthur M. Schlesinger, Jr., *The Cycles of American History*. Boston: Mariner Books, 1999.

10. J.C. Fisher and R.H. Pry, "A Simple Substitution Model of Technology Change," *Technology Forecasting and Social Change, 3* (1971), pp. 75–88.

11. Millett and Honton, *A Manager's Guide to Technology Forecasting and Strategy Analysis Methods,* pp. 43–61, 90.

12. Stephen M. Millett, "The Future of Scenarios: Challenges and Opportunities," *Strategy & Leadership, 31,* no. 2 (2003), pp. 16–24. Also see Liam Fahey and Robert M. Randall, eds., *Learning from the Future: Competitive Foresight Scenarios*. New York: John Wiley & Sons, Inc., 1998.

13. See www.dr-futuring.com for more information about the Battelle approach to scenario generation. Also see Willaim R. Huss and Edward J. Honton, "Scenario Planning—What Style Should You Use?" *Long Range Planning, 20,* no. 4 (1987), pp. 21–29; Stephen M. Millett, "Futuring and Visioning: Complementary Approaches to Strategic Decision Making," *Strategy & Leadership, 34,* no. 3 (2006), pp. 43–50.

14. Much of this case history is based on Battelle lore passed down by word of mouth. For Battelle's version of the Xerox story, see Clyde E. Williams, *Bridging the Gap: My Contributions to the Growth of Industrial Research*. Cincinnati: Best Impression Corp., 1976, pp. 95–104; George A. Boehm and Alex Groner, *Science in the Service of Mankind: The Battelle Story*. Columbus, OH: Battelle Press, 1981, pp. 35–48.

CHAPTER 5

DEVELOPING PRODUCTS FOR SENIORS

Anthony A. Sterns and Harvey L. Sterns

More people will live longer than in any previous generation that has ever existed. What this will mean is that there is going to be a shift in economic and political power toward the increasing number of older people. To prepare for this important aging trend, the business and marketing professional must change his or her current mind-set away from the youth-oriented culture and refocus attention on the mature culture of tomorrow. Mature consumers have a different orientation about the world, different interests, and exhibit different behaviors—including consumer behaviors such as shopping and purchasing. Understanding these differences will be an important challenge for the business and marketing professional of tomorrow.

The world's population, especially the developing world, is growing older. By 2050 those over 65 years of age will represent 15 percent of the global population, up from around 7 percent at the beginning of the millennium. Most aging professionals are focused with growing concern on preparing for the medical and social resources this group will require as they enter advanced age. But for business and aging professionals this trend represents a growing market with a myriad of business opportunities for those well educated in life-span developmental psychology, gerontology, gerontechnology, and geriatrics. The future bodes well for those who have an entrepreneurial spirit as well as a penchant for improving the quality of life for older adults.

New life-science technologies are emerging that will extend, transform, and enhance our health. These new "bio-tools" represent growing markets on their own, but also will transform and disrupt existing markets.

We can see in recent mainstream periodicals an increased focus on topics that relate to living longer, staying healthy, maintaining mental acuity and memory, and looking healthy and fit. Some key trends include products and diets related to supernutrition and science-based consumer products like cosmeceuticals that work at the cellular level. Future markets would include wearable computing (think Bluetooth wireless headsets and Nike+ shoes) and personal digital assistants that do everything (think iPod with computer and cell phone functionalities) and customized drugs that eliminate side effects and gene therapies that can correct chronic diseases like diabetes.

MARKET DEFINITION

The future market of tomorrow will be dominated by the mature market. The mature market, sometimes called the gray market, is made up of the products and services purchased for individuals over 50 years of age. The terms may also be used to describe those individuals directly.[1] Those business entities focused on these markets are also referred to as silver industries.[2]

The market is by no means uniform. It is as diverse as the individual countries that make up the global market and as unique and varied as the individuals within those countries: rich and poor, healthy and unhealthy, socially engaged or socially isolated.

The countries aging most rapidly are in the developing world with Japan and Italy leading the way. The consumer-oriented cultures and economies in these societies drive these older and aging individuals to have an interest in products and services that are identifiably different from younger, more conventional target markets.

In many developed countries, this market segment also represents a concentration of wealth as individuals have had an opportunity to build equity and net worth over a half century. In the United States, for example, there are 27 million Americans over the age of 50 with a total income of over $2 trillion. Mature Americans control a disproportionate share of the net worth of all households and have yet to be fully appreciated in the marketplace.

As such the kinds of products and services that can be offered are potentially more lucrative for businesses. On the one hand, the market can support higher margins on mass-produced items. Conversely, unique or customized items produced in limited quality for niche interests can be produced and purchased at prices younger consumers would not be able or willing to pay.

For both corporate and entrepreneurial business professionals this segment represents an opportunity to bring new products and services to the market. The kinds of products and services that will be successful will be well-grounded in the accumulated knowledge gathered by aging professionals. Thus, products and services developed, researched, marketed, and sold to the mature market require business professionals to have an understanding of adult development and aging as well good business acumen.

THE AVAILABILITY OF AGING EXPERTISE IN BUSINESS

There is a relationship between the awareness of society regarding issues of aging and the ability of the business community to be knowledgeable about and responsive to the needs of mature consumers. Consumerism has been transformed, and will continue to be transformed, as the number of older people increases and mature consumers' interests and needs have a greater influence on the market. This level of awareness will determine how quickly the transformation will take place. The effectiveness of the transformation will depend on the availability of information and the existing infrastructure of aging knowledge and the sciences of aging to feed the needs of responsive and capable native industries and entrepreneurs. We propose here a set of developmental stages that provide a gauge of this relationship and provide a framework on which business communities can evaluate their maturity.[3]

Stage One—No Mention or Specific Attention to Business and Aging

In stage one there is no information base or specific interest in aging and business. Historically this would describe the developing world where hard physical labor and minimal access to medicine would make consumerism in general and mature market issues in particular a nonissue. Today, this issue is much more likely to be driven by instability. Regions of the world that have no focus on aging are consumed by regional conflicts and ethnic struggles.

Stage Two—Individual Attention for Specific Market Interests Such as Older Adult Services

Most of the developing world is now aware of the aging of the population and that developing countries are the ones most profoundly impacted by aging and longevity. Specific health care institutions would be utilizing knowledge of biological aging to provide basic universal medical services and living situations to support older adults. There would still be a need for more organized services. Gerontology as an area of study and education, and enterprises that serve this market, will be very underdeveloped and many gaps will exist. These gaps should be viewed as opportunities for local entrepreneurs and organizations from more developed countries to expand their global outreach.

Stage Three—Informal Integration between Business Interests and Aging Consumer Research

At this stage there is an established aging academic community, but the connections between that community and the business community will be somewhat informal for most business endeavors. Applications are likely to be focused on care and housing of the chronically ill, but with increasing attention to issues such as transportation, financial services, leisure, and entertainment. There may be some fledgling efforts to provide support services to attract mature tourists by providing easily accessible transportation to attractive destinations.

Stage Four—Formal Integration and Attention to the Mature Market as a Distinct Consumer Class

At this stage the mature market will be formally recognized and included in market research. A full range of products and services, from automobiles to insurance products to retirement communities, will be available and actively marketed to older consumers. The disciplines of business, marketing, and aging will be integrated in the business community, but will not be formally integrated in the education system. Very progressive businesses will have a few aging specialists to advise and consult.

Stage Five—Formal Positions of Responsibility for Mature Market Products and Marketing

In the final stage business, marketing, and aging are formally linked in both academia and the business community. The mature market is recognized as an important market that requires specially trained personnel to be successful and competitive. There are positions at companies that require degrees in both business and aging or combined degrees, and such training is available at leading academic institutions in the country.

MARKET SEGMENTATION

Marketing to mature consumers is challenging as they display greater diversity than younger consumers. The mature market is split into four categories that mirror Bernice Neugarten's categories of young-old and old-old and are based on life cycle events as well as age.[4]

Those who are 55–64 years of age, generally active, and in good health are referred to as the young-old. Still working, most of these individuals are actively preparing for retirement. In most developed countries this group has the most discretionary income. The young-old are beginning to experience more effects of aging and in combination with disposable income are primary targets for exercise equipment, health programs, and antiaging products of all kinds. In addition, a whole level of luxury and high-quality products is aimed at these consumers:

luxury cars, sophisticated media equipment (for example, large flat-screen televisions, media centers, and so forth), and leisure items such as golf equipment.

We believe these trends will continue as electronic items converge into a hand-held computer that will serve as a communication center, information repository, and memory support. The communication center would include text and voice communication. As a repository, devices would include all personal information from contact information and pictures of the family to favorite music and portable books and media. Memory aides would include calendaring, reminders for appointments and medications, as well as navigation aides. These high-end hybrid devices (at a high but, for this group, affordable cost) are ideal devices for a younger mature market segment that is more comfortable with technology.

The second segment is made up of 65- to 74-year-old mature consumers, called middle-old consumers. This group currently contains a significant number of retirees. In the future an increasing percentage of this segment will remain at work longer. Typical estimates indicate that 30 to 50 percent of individuals will desire to work at least part-time as a member of this age group. These middle-old consumers are interested in nutrition products and services, services for leisure activities like dining and travel, and low-maintenance housing like condominiums and communities that cater to active older consumers. In the future, this group's health is expected to equal the young-old. Because many in each segment will still be working, it is likely that these groups will converge.

The old-old market segment consists of those individuals who are 75–84 years of age. As the individuals increase in age across this segment, they can experience increasing frailty with increased likelihood for chronic conditions and limitations to physical activities. This group is most likely to benefit from home modifications and supportive technologies that provide and help maintain independence. These technologies can be simple consumer products that make transporting groceries and laundry easier or sophisticated medication-reminding robots that prepare and remind individuals to take their medications. For the broader market, products that are developed with universal design principles and are useful and easy to use by everyone will likely be the most widely adopted products. Universal design is particularly important for the housing design market. Tremendous advances have been made possible through smart home technology and intelligent supportive devices.

The oldest consumer group segment consists of those individuals who are 85 and older, referred to as the oldest-old. In the United States, Japan, and Europe this group is exploding. As a group, they are less independent, less mobile, and consume the most services to accomplish the tasks of daily living. This segment commands a large share of medical services and hospital care. They are good targets for home health care products and services, in-home chore services, and assisted living communities.

GENERATIONAL DIFFERENCES

R. Zemke, C. Raines, and B. Filipczak[5] have developed categories to describe different cohorts and describe generational characteristics. These help to understand how to approach and appeal to the different cohort. Zemke et al. refer to these groups as Veterans, Baby Boomers, Generation Xer's, and Nexter's.

Veterans

This group was born between 1922 and 1943 and consists of over 52 million people in the United States. They are characterized as being dedicated, hardworking, and having respect for law and order. They understand sacrifice, believe in conformity, and respect authority. They are willing to delay gratification, adhere to rules, and are patriotic and family oriented.

Veterans have been shaped by several key historical events. These include the Great Depression, World War II, New Deal politics, and the Korean War. Key cultural influences include the golden age of radio, the silver screen, and the rise of organized labor.

Importantly, Veterans do not see themselves as old. According to an American Association of Retired Persons (AARP) report on American Perceptions of Aging in the 21st Century, nearly half consider themselves to be young or middle-aged. One-third of those 75 years of age and older reported being young or middle-aged. Only 15 percent of those people aged 75+ considered themselves "very old." In an interesting twist AARP attempted to create a version of its magazine, *Modern Maturity,* for young-old members and middle-old and older members. However, when given a choice as to which to receive, almost all the members requested the young-old version even though they were not as interested in the content. Today, the magazine is called *AARP The Magazine,* and AARP still has two versions, but they are based on whether or not the individual is still working full-time.

Baby Boomers

Baby Boomers are the largest cohort and consist of those individuals born between World War II and 1964. These individuals are now entering middle age. Because they are such a large group they are changing the demographics of the entire United States. Defining events for the Baby Boomers include the Civil Rights Movement, the Cold War, the Space Race, the Vietnam War, and the Women's Liberation Movement. Baby Boomers have a connection to the golden age of network television, popular and rock music, and life in suburbia.

Baby Boomers, more than any other group, are focused on hanging on to their youth. As the "Me Generation," they fuel an entire industry of antiaging products with over $30 billion in discretionary income. These products include a cornucopia of consumer goods and services that include fitness equipment, organic foods, Botox injections, hair transplants, and antiaging cosmetics for both men and women. This interest in maintaining youth by the wealthiest generation in history is driving investment in pharmaceuticals, biotechnology, the food industry, and the cosmetic industry.

Generation Xer's

This group was born between 1965 and 1980. Generation Xer's consist of 70 million Americans. The interest of this group centers on technology. They are concerned and think about issues globally. They are more tolerant and more comfortable with diversity. This group is more cynical about politics, having grown up in the wake of the Watergate and Iran-Contra scandals. Other defining events include the Challenger accident and the AIDS epidemic. They have seen the world grow flatter with the collapse of the Soviet Union and the falling of the Berlin Wall. Generation Xer's were part of the MTV (Music Television) and personal computer revolutions. Generation Xer's were more likely to be raised by two working parents, so they are both wealthier but have less interaction with their parents.

This is the group that is most likely to be interested in technology-driven products and services for the aging market. At present, marketers want to target this group to purchase products designed to increase the independence of parents and grandparents. The Xer's will purchase and install the goods or arrange for the services, then teach their use. These would include medication-reminding equipment, communication technology such as e-mail or videoconferencing, or online shopping. Services that reduce the demand on the caregiver are most likely to appeal to this group.

Nexter's

Nexter's are about the same size segment as the X'ers, just under 70 million. They are characterized by multiculturalism. Defining cultural events include school violence and the Oklahoma City Bombing. This is the connected generation that grew up with video games, cell phones, and digital media.

This generation is not often in the caregiver role, but their future attitudes about aging are likely to be shaped by the experiences of their Baby Boomer parents who are caring for older members of the Veteran generation. This generation is the most likely to be interested in more radical antiaging technology. This would include implanted supporting devices, wearable computer equipment, and bionics. Breakthrough technologies that are on the cutting edge of science will be available for this generation in midlife and beyond.

FACTS ABOUT THE MATURE MARKET

There are nearly 76 million Americans over age 50, representing about 27 percent of all adults in the United States. The 50+ age group has a total annual income of more than $2 trillion. Mature Americans control 70 percent of the total net worth of all U.S. households—more than $7 trillion of wealth.[6]

Mature market consumers are the most affluent group in the United States, and those aged 50 to 64 are the most affluent of all. Americans aged 50 hold over 77 percent of the nation's financial assets and 50 percent of all discretionary income. Per capita spending is about 2.5 times that of the population.

The "Age Wave" marketing concept is referred to as the life choice model. It views the mature consumer as a multidimensional individual. There are six key components in the model. The first is the age cohort. This is similar to Zemke's generational model. Life stage is the second component, referring to career stage and family. Typical patterns of older Baby Boomers are to have married and had children in their early twenties and retire at or around 65 years of age or even earlier. But for younger Baby Boomers who remarried (50 percent are divorced) in later life and had children in their 40s, it is possible that they are not able to retire early because of the need to build additional assets to make up for losses from the divorce, pay for children's college, and perhaps to keep working because a younger spouse is also working. Thus, affluence is a third component of this model.

Health is a fourth component of the model. Clearly, those with chronic medical conditions, obesity, or disabilities will have different impacts on their life-styles compared to those in excellent health and in good physical fitness. Gender and ethnicity are the fourth and fifth components of the model. Gender is the single best predictor of longevity. Eventually we can expect that the concentration of wealth among Baby Boomers will, for a time, be squarely in the hands of these senior women. This alone has dramatic implications for how luxury items and charitable institutions will be marketed in the latter half of this century.

The final component of the model is called psychographic profiles. These combine activities, interests, and opinions in the kind of analysis that identifies Soccer Mom's and NASCAR Dad's. It ties lifestyle characteristics to segment and target customers with similar identifiable characteristics.

DESIGNING PRODUCTS FOR OLDER ADULTS

We now have some background understanding of the growing mature market and how that market is composed of a diverse but definable group of individuals. Armed with that knowledge, one can anticipate new market opportunities. We next present our method for identifying market opportunities, determining the potential needs and desires that fill the opportunities, and how we refine and test those ideas. We begin by defining demand potential and covering the process of literature and existing product searches, focus group and survey research, and finally laboratory and field prototype market research.

Determine Demand Potential

Market research can play an important role in identifying a need for a product and providing important information about defining a product. As our society changes, there are opportunities created for new and better products. Changes in society can reflect the impact of changes in fashion, in technology, in the economy, or in attitude. These changes create market opportunities and the potential for a product or service to succeed. Combining the level of interest and the number of people who will be interested in a product or service yields what we call demand potential.

In the case of the mature market, the opportunity is to design products and services that can anticipate the needs of those mature consumers by understanding and anticipating changes in the population. What we know is that there will be a very large group of mature consumers that will move from being young-older adults to old-older adults in the next 15 years. That transformation will create demand potential due to changes in physical and mental health, attitudes and interests, and potential changes in life-style as they transition from the early to later stages of aging.

To determine demand potential we utilize the following steps:

- A literature review of professional and academic journals,
- Competitive product evaluation,
- Focus groups to determine the language and concept categories and qualitative assessment of how things are done now and how they might be done with the prospective product or service,
- Targeted survey research to understand the needs and interest level of potential consumers,
- Laboratory studies to explore product features, and
- Testing to verify product features and evaluate potential demand.

Using this process, we can take an identified need, create a set of desired features to fill that need, and assess the prospect of our potential product's success. At each stage of the process we can refine the demand potential and determine the utility of investing in the next stage of product development. At the end of use testing, a clear idea of demand potential will be achieved. To best understand what is already known we begin to assess demand potential by conducting a literature search.

Literature Search

A targeted review of recommendations by aging professionals is often the source of new product and service ideas to help improve the quality of life for older adults. We use the example of some of our previous work on the development of an ergonomic cart, a consumer product with considerable potential market to illustrate the development process.

As aging professionals we concluded there exists a need for a product that minimizes or assists in difficult movements while doing the laundry and that such a product would improve functioning and independence for many older adults. Throughout the human factors and aging literature several conclusions about older adults' performance of everyday activities appeared over the past 15 years, which led to this conclusion (see Figure 5.1). Major findings included the following:

1. Physical and psychological impairments are more likely to occur with increasing age.[7] Over 80 percent of people aged 65 or more have at least one chronic condition. Older women are more likely than older men to have a chronic illness that causes physical limitations.

2. About 46 percent of community-dwelling women aged 65 years and over report difficulty lifting the equivalent of two full bags of groceries with 27 percent over the age of 75 reporting having difficulty in lifting a ten-pound load.[8] Women report having difficulty in lifting about twice as often as do men. A study of activities of daily living (ADL) task analyses showed 53 percent of adults aged 53 to 90 experience difficulty with grocery shopping.[9] Twelve percent experience difficulty with doing the laundry.[10]

Figure 5.1
Subjects Self-Reported Difficulties with Performing Various Tasks

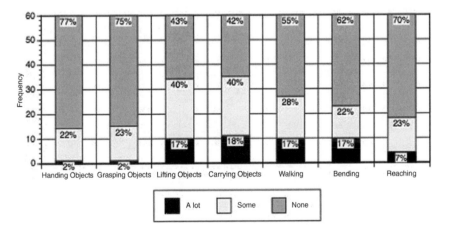

3. Accidents such as falling may be related to changing capabilities and health-related disabilities. Other work has pointed to high-risk activities and products leading to accidents. The Consumer Safety Product Commission singled out the laundry basket as a product needing design improvements for accident prevention among the elderly.[11] Occupational therapists have determined that transferring objects around the home is difficult and hazardous for many older adults.

4. Transport tasks have been identified as a major problem for older adults. Because doing the laundry involves transport, this task is problematic.[12]

This is not the kind of information you just run into in daily readings. These are findings reported in professional academic journals focusing on gerontology. As a marketing professional, that means to work in the market you need to increase your understanding of aging by immersing yourself in the field or working with a team of professionals that includes individuals with a deep understanding of aging issues.

There are also a number of key product design and human factors issues to consider when thinking about mature market products and services. The difficulty older adults experience in performing household activities, for example, is often considered to be a problem with person/environment fit. Human factors research has demonstrated that a more accommodating environment or assistive, easy-to-use products make completing tasks easier and yield fewer accidents.[13] M.P. Lawton focused on the self-maintenance needs of older adults and was one of the first to relate levels of capability to supportive environmental approaches.[14] Past reports such as *Technology and Aging in America* established the need for more household products.[15] D.B. Smith discussed the use of human factors to meet the needs for subpopulations of older people with physical limitations.[16] The performance of home tasks has received considerable attention, including specific instrumental activities of daily living (IADLs) such as doing the laundry and other transport tasks.[17] For example, Clark and her colleagues state that reaching is a frequently reported problem in ADLs and IADL task performance among the general population of community-dwelling older adults. Task demand profile analyses of task observation including a high or extra-high reach revealed that 66 percent of such reaches occur while doing the laundry and grocery shopping; 91 percent of these reaches are performed while repositioning or retrieving an object.[18]

As with basic approaches such as person/environment fit, the application of good industrial design principles can enhance independent living and reduce the risk of accidents. Task analyses for prototypes for continued product development applied good industrial design principles to directly address problems associated with the transport of laundry, grocery bags, and other household items.[19]

The literature contains other useful information about laundry in particular. Problems with doing the laundry stem from age-related characteristics[20] including the following:

- A general decline in strength, which makes it harder to hold objects or containers in an "awkward forward position";
- Limitations in movement, which increase risk of injury while lifting or carrying;
- Bending or stooping may lead to dizziness;
- Grasping the container's handles may be difficult, particularly for those with arthritis;
- Balance may be more difficult to maintain while lifting, due to the forward shift in the center of gravity while carrying the load; and
- Declines in fingering and grasping are also related to declines in strength.[21]

In general the literature provided both a source of ideas for products and helped to define a set of consumer needs that would likely increase as age begins to make a growing number of individuals increasingly challenged. The focus is on challenges brought about by lifting and carrying, in general, and in doing household tasks like grocery shopping and doing the laundry in particular. The next step is then to evaluate how existing products are likely to fill this demand potential.

Competitive Product Evaluation

Our project team reviewed the availability of commonly used household products as well as products for people with physical limitations or disabilities. We completed a search of the literature and examined products available through stores, durable medical equipment suppliers, old and new retail catalogs (Fred Sammons, Inc. Professional Health Care Catalog, 1991; 1994; 1995; Sammons Complete Source for Rehabilitation and ADL Products, 1991; 1995; Comfortably Yours, 1991; Enrichments, 1991; 1995; the now-defunct Ways and Means, 1986; 1987; Sears Health Care Catalog, 1991; 1994; Adaptability, 1991; and others), and electronic databases including AgeLine and ABLEDATA.

A project team evaluation of the strengths and weaknesses of products that proprietary research has shown to be used most often by the general population, including older adults, for transport and application to doing the laundry is summarized below:

- A large or medium-sized plastic laundry basket,
- A laundry chute,
- Shopping cart, and
- Laundry bag or sheet.

While the products listed above are those used frequently by the general population, products currently available for people with physical limitations or disabilities display another set of problems. Products for the disabled are generally perceived by older adults and professionals as difficult to obtain, too utilitarian or institutional in appearance, and too costly. They have a stigma attached; that is, they draw attention to the disability and define the user as belonging to "deviant segments of society"—handicapped, infirm, and so forth.[22] For example, proprietary research on a laundry basket with legs suggests this product is perceived by older women as too cumbersome to use. Also, there is a lack of low-technology products to improve or enhance accomplishing daily tasks.[23]

Smith states that older adults are more likely to accept and use products that are also perceived as useful for and by the general population.[24] Products with acceptance and usefulness for all age groups and ranges of ability have the characteristics of "universal product design." While empowering older adults or people with disabilities, "universal design strives to make every place and product work better for everybody."[25]

With a good understanding of the physical requirements of older adults and the potential number of them who are likely to have problems lifting and carrying, and an understanding of the existing products' ability to satisfy some portion of that group, we can now begin to form a set of focused questions about what the ideal product can and needs to do. Those questions can first be explored in focus groups. From the focus group we can learn the specific language and can understand the basic concepts and categories that exist in consumers' mental frameworks. Once this language and framework are known, we can then develop survey questions and gather more generalizable information from a sufficient sample of potential mature consumers utilizing survey-based research.

Survey Research

In the review of transport task products, results of analyses of competitive products, and a set of focus groups, our development team identified products and product features that displayed potential solutions to the problems in task completion and the weaknesses in transport products cited above (for example, the folding shopping cart with casters and liner). Most elderly recognize changing capabilities and develop compensations to overcome limitations. These elderly want products that help them continue to function, doing activities they have always done. For elderly who fail to compensate on their own or with product assistance, risk of accident or injury increases.[26] Our research intended to bring into existence a product that would be attractive and be perceived as beneficial with or without hands-on experience with the product.

To confirm these findings and determine the potential demand for a product that filled these needs we conducted a market survey of 255 older women. The survey concluded that laundry and moving groceries were the most difficult tasks for older women and products that made the tasks easier would be of interest.

Several questions in the survey focused on doing the laundry and the problems older adult women had in performing its many steps. Nearly all claimed to do their own laundry (98 percent). As shown in Figure 5.2, most of the women

Figure 5.2
Subjects Self-Reported Frequency of Doing the Laundry

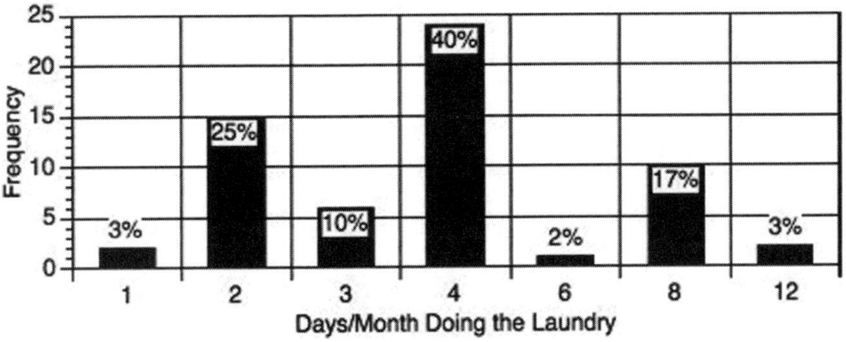

reported that they do their laundry either weekly (43 percent) or several times per week (32 percent). Many indicated that they did their laundry now less often than they used to, citing among their main reasons that they lived alone (35 percent) or had fewer individuals living in the household (34 percent).

Nearly all of those living in a single-family dwelling did their laundry at home. Nearly all of those living in an apartment or condominium (duplex or high-rise) did their laundry in facilities located in their buildings. Very few of the women (3 percent) went to a Laundromat.

In order to reach their washers and dryers, most (69 percent) of the women have to walk downstairs to the basement. Some (22 percent) have their laundry facilities located on the same level as their living area. A few (15 percent) walk upstairs, and a few take an elevator to reach their washers and dryers. Those few respondents who left their homes or apartments in order to access their laundry facilities either walk (61 percent) or drive themselves (36 percent).

We concluded that the frequency with which older adult women do their laundry is related to the location of their laundry facilities. Most of those doing their laundry in facilities located in their single-family homes do so weekly or more often (83 percent). Of those using laundry facilities located in their apartment buildings (single story or high-rise) most (81 percent) do the laundry weekly or less often. Of those (3 percent of total respondents) using a Laundromat, most (62 percent) do the laundry every other week.

When asked if they have any problems doing the laundry, nearly all of the women said no (96 percent). However, when asked about the degree of difficulty associated with specific laundry-related tasks, some problem areas were indicated. Those tasks most difficult for the respondents tended to involve difficult movements associated with the use of a laundry basket: lifting, carrying, and grasping. A majority (55 percent) of the women use a basket to transport their laundry, usually medium-sized or large. Nearly all (93 percent) of their baskets are plastic.

With the results of the survey we now have a clear understanding of how the current population is using existing products and perceptions of their need for existing products. We can also use currently older adults to predict how younger adults are likely to change as they age. Using the research results we can construct a set of features that might be part of the product. These features can be evaluated in a focus group and those most promising features tested using a prototype. In the case of the cart we proceeded to testing to look at combinations of features and settle on the relative importance of each.

Laboratory Prototype Research

We divided the prototype testing into two stages and incorporated what would have been the focus group questions into an interview of the subject at the end of the testing. In the laboratory stage subjects were asked to do a test load of laundry, in a step-by-step procedure controlled by the researcher. The subjects did the laundry using a prototype that was configured to present a number of features, separately or in combination. This allowed a powerful test of only the basket features. In the first stage, the prototype was modified to incorporate the most favored feature combination with the ability to raise and lower the basket. In the second stage, the frame variables were then tested. This resulted in more focused testing, improved statistical power, reduced prototype costs, and a slightly smaller number of subjects. The protocol used is described below.

The testing regimen was similar for both the laboratory setting and the field setting described later. It began by interviewing older women who reported on their difficulty in accomplishing daily tasks including handling objects, lifting, carrying, walking, bending, and reaching above the head. Demographic information was obtained including each woman's age, income, marital status, and if she had arthritis. Various body measurements were taken including height, weight, waist height, and other measures that are important in designing products for older adults (for example, average height the bottom of a basket can be without bending). The women were then asked to do several loads of laundry using a traditional basket and using the prototype. In the laboratory there was a prototype that simulated four configurations of a cart on wheels with (1) a solid attached basket, (2) a solid detachable basket, (3) a front-opening basket, and (4) a detachable, front-opening basket. In the field the prototype with a detachable, front-opening basket was refined to raise and lower the basket. The women were videotaped as well as being observed on each trial. After each trial the women were asked about each task involved in doing the laundry with respect to its difficulty. After completing all trials, the women were asked about which

Figure 5.3
Evolution of the Prototype

The photos above show the progress from the conceptual wooden models to the finished metal prototype. The left prototypes also illustrate the use of the top crank. The white prototype with the basket could be configured with either a side or top crank. The rightmost prototype introduces the easily seen hook on which to hang the basket—another design improvement. The metal prototype moved from intermeshing gears to a belt-driven system.

method they preferred and some questions about their impressions of the prototype.

This design incorporates a human factors motion analysis approach into a traditional market testing approach. This project obtained a database of bodily measurements to allow better matching of product dimensions to older women. The prototypes are shown in Figure 5.3.

Sample

We wanted to study mature consumers who were most likely to be interested in the product, so we focused on women and chose a wide age range. Thirty women between the ages of 57 and 80 were recruited to be subjects for the first phase of human factors testing. The women were divided into three categories, having no difficulty, some difficulty, and having lots of difficulty with daily household activities. Each subject was informed about the testing, signed a consent form, and answered demographic questions. Measurements were taken for various anthropometric measurements, and the women were asked to do a laundry simulation five times.

The five trials consisted of using a prototype with (1) a nondetachable basket on wheels, (2) a detachable basket, (3) a side-opening basket, (4) both a detachable basket and a side-opening basket, and (5) a traditional laundry basket. After each trial the subjects were asked questions about their experiences with the prototypes. After completing all of the trials, subjects were asked for their preferences among the prototype features and the traditional laundry basket.

Laboratory Results

After completing all the data gathering we analyzed the information we had gathered. We found more subjects preferred the prototype with both the detachable basket and the side-opening basket (33 percent). Of the ten individuals who preferred that basket, seven (70 percent) said they would purchase it. A majority of the women felt that the detachability of the basket (77 percent) was valuable. A slightly smaller number indicated that the side-opening feature was valuable (60 percent). Most women (87 percent) indicated that having the ability to adjust the height of the basket was a desirable feature.

Most women (60 percent) found the height of the basket to be "about right." The rest (40 percent) indicated the basket was too low. The size of the basket was found to be adequate according to almost all of the women (93 percent). The height of the handles was equally acceptable (93 percent) and found to be "about right."

A majority of the women said they would use the basket (67 percent) for doing the laundry. The women indicated other uses including transporting groceries, moving things from room to room, and using the cart outside for hanging laundry or doing gardening. Most said they would be interested in purchasing such a device (60 percent). The average price suggested by the participants was $107.88 with the median being $45.

We also asked the women what material they would prefer for the basket handle. The soft handle received the most favorable response (58 percent), followed by the neoprene handle (35 percent), and the hard handle (8 percent).

Based on these results it was decided that the next phase of human factors testing would measure the feasibility of a device that raises and lowers the load. This feature would be tested along with the detachable, side-opening basket with soft handles.

Video Motion Analysis

Video motion analysis was conducted by recording ten parameters of each major motion of subjects while transporting and doing the laundry. Twelve individuals were randomly selected (four from each difficulty category) for coding. The videos were viewed in slow motion and stopped at the end of each major motion (for example, removing a handful of laundry from the prototype, placing a handful of laundry into the dryer). The activities, body postures, actions, object, location, grip, and difficulty of each major motion of subjects while transporting and doing the laundry were recorded. This resulted in 7,059 coded motions for a total of 70,590 observed data points.

Once the coding was completed, data were assembled into component maps. Component mapping is a technique for summarizing a task's activities and identifying the frequency of task actions. Maps are divided into person and environment components. Person components are the postures, actions, and hand positions that an individual performs during the task. Environment components are the objects handled, locations visited, and difficulty encountered during the activities. Once all of the activities and component elements are identified, they are reported as a percentage of their respective component. In this way, it is possible to identify what activities, postures, or actions are carried out most often and on what objects and at what location. Once the component maps are generated for each task, the differences between task conditions can be examined by computing the percentage change in component elements. A negative number indicates a decrease in the component element. Comparisons of doing the laundry with each prototype configuration were made with the traditional laundry basket. An example of the comparisons is provided in Table 5.1.

The motion analysis demonstrated the prototype's success in reducing bending, lifting, and carrying. This reduction was found in the comparison component maps of all four prototype configurations. Reduced lifting, lowering, and carrying of the basket were replaced by pushing and pulling the lightweight cart. Use of the floor (requiring stooping, lifting, and bending) was also reduced. Decrease in the dryer as a location is an indication of the scooping action used by some of the women to move the laundry from the front opening basket into the dryer.

The video motion analysis technique used to study the task of doing the laundry provided a useful method for demonstrating how a product can affect and improve an older adult's or mobility-impaired individual's ability to accomplish daily tasks that involve lifting and carrying.

FIELD AND USE TESTING

With the completion of laboratory testing we now have a product with defined features that we know does what it claims to do—reduces the amount of lifting, carrying, and bending. We also have a well-supported estimate of the potential market size for this product. The size is bounded by those individuals who actually have difficulty doing laundry at the upper bound and those who recognize they have difficulty, want help, and are willing to purchase on the lower. We also have a good idea what people are willing to spend, and that determines the target manufacturing costs for this product. But these estimates are based on only a brief exposure to the product. Now we want to put the product in the mature consumers environment and demonstrate that they will want to keep it and that they will use it as designed. This is particularly important for mature consumers who are more frail and may continue to use the device with some physical or cognitive impairment.

Table 5.1

Percent Difference in the Component Maps of the Prototype with Detachable Basket and Front-Opening Side and the Traditional Basket*

	Person Components		
Activities	**Body Posture**	**Action**	**Hand**
Put in Container 0.38%	Being Helped −13.07%	Lift/Lower −1.83%	**Left**
Transport −3.70%	Standard 7.44%	Carry −2.15%	Finger Grip 2.56%
Take out of Container 2.16%	Slight Bend 12.28%	Place in −0.94%	Full Grip 0.61%
Place in Washer −0.18%	Moderate Bend −1.98%	Place on −0.90%	**Right**
Take out of Washer −0.35%	Deep Bend −6.30%	Remove 0.74%	Finger Grip −3.20%
Place in Dryer 0.28%	Knee Bend −1.52%	Push 3.02%	Full Grip −4.17%
Take out of Dryer −1.44%	Reach −0.82%	Pull 1.89%	**Both**
Place on Table 2.04%	High Reach 2.67%	Open 0.17%	Finger Grip 4.06%
Take off of Table 0.80%	Lean Reach −1.01%	Close 0.09%	Full Grip 1.26%
	Twist 2.28%	Hold 0.64%	
	Bend & Twist 0.40%		Action w/o Grip 0.27%
	Reach/Twist −0.22%		Other/Help −1.39%
	Environment Components		
	Object	**Location**	**Difficulty**
	Laundry 3.63%	Floor −1.45%	None 2.86%
	Basket −6.48%	Table 4.50%	Some/A Lot −0.85%
	Washer 0.08%	Washer −0.92%	
	Dryer 0.02%	Dryer −3.27%	
		Laundry Room 0.38%	
		Basement −0.10%	
		Chair 1.01%	

*Prototype = Traditional Basket; N = 2,571 Observations.

Field Sample

To determine the answer to the use question we recruited 60 older women [mean age = 72.46 (s.d. = 6.06)] between the ages of 56 and 84 for a field test. The group was racially mixed and consisted of 85 percent Caucasian women and 15 percent African-American woman. Approximately half of the sample lived independently in a single-family home (55 percent), and the remainder lived in an multistory apartment setting (45 percent). A majority (72 percent) of the subjects lived alone, while the remainder lived with a spouse (25 percent). Of the remaining individuals one lived with a roommate, and the other lived with her sister.

Subjects were asked if they had been diagnosed with arthritis and about the degree of difficulty they have performing tasks related to mobility. Each subject was asked to indicate whether she experienced none, some, or a lot of difficulty completing a list of tasks. A "1" indicated no difficulty and a "3" indicated a lot of difficulty. The list included handling objects, lifting, carrying, walking, bending, and reaching above the head. The tasks that subjects reported having the most difficulty with were lifting (mean = 2.27) and carrying (mean = 2.23).

Self-Reported Laundry Behaviors

Of the 60 subjects, all but one indicated that they did their own laundry. One woman indicated that her husband usually did the laundry. Most of the subjects did not receive any help in doing laundry (83.3 percent). For those who did receive help (16.7 percent), it usually involved transporting the laundry to the machines. The women who lived in an apartment building (n = 27) used the building facilities, and the women who lived in a single-family house (n = 33) used a home machine. The subjects spend an average of 4.26 (s.d. 2.51) days per month doing the laundry.

Analysis of Observed Data

Video motion analysis was conducted by recording ten parameters of each major motion of subjects while transporting and doing the laundry. Twenty-four individuals were randomly selected (four from each difficulty category) from each field setting (apartment and home settings) to be coded. This resulted in 2,687 coded motions for a total of 20,687 observed data points.

Videotape of the participants was digitized as described above. The activities, body postures, actions, object, location, grip, and difficulty of each major motion of subjects while transporting and doing the laundry were recorded.

The data were assembled into component maps in the same manner as described in the laboratory setting above. Once the component maps were generated for each task the differences between task conditions could be examined for each setting. Comparisons of doing the laundry with the prototype were made with the individuals' own method for doing the laundry.

The motion analysis again demonstrated the prototype's success in reducing deep bends. This reduction was found in both the home and the apartment setting. Reduced lifting, lowering, and carrying of the basket were replaced by pushing and pulling the lightweight cart. Use of the floor (requiring stooping, lifting, and bending) was also reduced.

Table 5.2 presents the change in the percentage an activity represented between doing the laundry with the prototype and doing the laundry by the residents' own methods in an apartment setting. Many of the women in this setting used some

Table 5.2
Comparison of Component Maps between the Prototype and the Individual's Own Method in an Apartment Setting*

Activities	Person Components		
	Body Posture	**Action**	**Hand**
Put in Container 1.36%	Standard 1.64%	Lift/Lower −0.47%	**Left**
Transport 1.53%	Slight Bend 2.39%	Carry −3.93%	Finger Grip 2.32%
Take out of Container 0.19%	Moderate Bend 3.36%	Place in 1.32%	Full Grip 1.68%
Place in Washer −4.02%	Deep Bend −4.00%	Place on −0.74%	**Right**
Take out of Washer −3.38%	Knee Bend −0.62%	Remove 0.14%	Finger Grip 3.98%
Place in Dryer 0.60%	Reach −1.02%	Push 3.94%	Full Grip −2.76%
Take out of Dryer 2.92%	High Reach −1.53%	Pull 1.06%	**Both**
	Lean Reach −0.30%	Open 1.40%	Finger Grip −9.10%
	Twist 1.58%	Close 0.00%	Full Grip 4.66%
	Bend & Twist −0.30%	Hold −3.76%	Action w/o Grip −0.79%
	Environment Components		
	Object	**Location**	**Difficulty**
	Laundry −4.34%	Floor −0.40%	None 5.61%
	Basket 9.25%	Table −0.81%	Some/A Lot −4.85%
	Washer −2.57%	Washer −3.29%	
	Dryer 0.04%	Dryer −1.38%	
		Hallway 0.85%	
		Laundry Room −0.62%	
		Basement 3.15%	
		Prototype −0.57%	

*Apartment Differences (Prototype—Own Method).

kind of device, often a shopping cart, for carrying the laundry the long distance to the laundry room. Again, a negative number represents a decrease in the activity when using the prototype. A decrease in the body posture components of deep bends and knee bends is demonstrated. The decrease is less dramatic than in other comparisons, as many of the women already have a carrying device. However, many of these carts have their bottom near the floor, requiring a deep bend. Also of concern is that many women place a laundry basket in a two-wheel grocery cart that is top-heavy compared to the stability of the prototype.

Looking at the environment components, several other trends can be seen in the component map. In the object of focus component, a decrease in the percentage of the laundry and the dryer and an increase in the percentage of the basket is a reflection of the increased use of the prototype to move the laundry around. Most of the transporting activities were done with the prototype when it was available. Decreases in the use of floor, table, and washer and increases in the prototype as the location component are also a reflection of this behavior. A decrease in difficulty is also shown, which is a reflection of the decrease in deep bends as a result of reaching into the low bottom of two-wheeled grocery carts.

Specify Product Features and Functions: Refine Prototype and Field Test Again

Above we have covered an iteration of the market research cycle in detail. With the prototyping complete and the design refined, a short run of the products was then initiated. Participants were recruited to use the device in their apartments for 90 days. The participants were interviewed monthly and at the end asked if they wanted to keep the device. Over half of the participants kept the cart. The remainder returned the cart because it took up too much room in their apartments. They preferred the cart to their previous carts and if the cart folded up they would have kept it. This prompted further development, and another cycle identical to the development above was conducted with a folder version of the cart as shown in Figure 5.4.

The most challenging aspect of the folding cart was to develop a folding mechanism in which the wheels would not leave the ground. Just as the target market had trouble carrying groceries, lifting and opening a large object like a cart would prove challenging. Opening up the cart needed to be nearly effortless and never place the individual off balance.

The final model uses a handle to push open a set of wheels that scissor together with the aid of a spring to reduce the force required. Although the model is top heavy, a kick stand that is deployed when the wheels are brought together allows the folded cart to be freestanding. The basket also folds and can be hung back on the basket hook for easy storage. The cart can be shipped in a box less than 8 inches wide. The final model was made of aluminum to bring the weight down

Figure 5.4
HomePal Conceptual Drawings

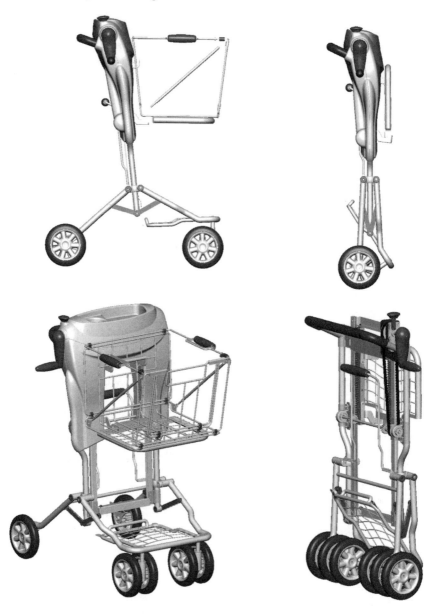

The final conceptual model showing the folding legs. This prototype folds without bending, the wheels never leave the ground, and with the addition of a kick stand (not shown) can stand on its own.

to 22 pounds. With further refinements and a plastic rack, the weight can be reduced to around 15 pounds.

CONCLUSIONS

As the mature market grows and expands, it is creating new demands for products and services. To develop a great product for this diverse group of consumers takes an in-depth knowledge of many aspects of aging, including physical, cognitive, and attitudinal components. While the current oldest-old may be tolerant of medical-looking walkers, the next cohort of active, independent, and affluent consumers is looking for style as well as functionality. Therefore, to create products for this market requires a multidisciplinary team of designers, engineers, researchers, and marketers working in conjunction with aging specialists. This team must understand not only attractive design and engineering costs to be successful, it must understand the experience of aging physically as well as understand the aging experience of the cohort and how the latter influences the former.

NOTES

1. Sterns, R.S., and Sterns, H.L. (1995). The mature market: Older consumer issues. In G.L. Maddox (ed.), *The Encyclopedia of Aging*. New York: Springer Publishing Company.

2. Cutler, N. (2005). Silver industries: Introduction. *Generations, 28*, 6–7.

3. Cowgill, G., and S. Orgren (1979). The international development of academic gerontology. In Sterns, A., Ansello, C., Sprouse, P., and Layfield-faux, J. (Eds.), Gerontology in Higher Education: Developing Institutional and Community Strength. Belmont, CA: Wadsworth Publishing Company.

4. Sterns, H., Sterns, A., and Hanson, R. (2005, February 24). Business and Work: Managing Transitions in an Aging Society. An invited pre-conference intensive presented at the 31st Annual Meeting of the Association of Gerontology in Higher Education. Oklahoma City, OK.

5. Zemke, R., Raines, C., and Filipczak, B. (2000). Generations at work: Managing the clash of veterans, boomers, Xers, and Nexters in your workplace. New York: American Management Association Publications.

6. Dykwald, K. (1999). *Age Power: How the 21st Century Will Be Ruled by the New Old*. New York: Tarcher/Putnam.

7. National Center for Health Statistics (1987). Havlik, R.J., Lier, B.M., Kovar, M. G., et al. Health statistics on older persons, United States, 1986. Advance data from vital and health statistics, Series 3, No. 25 (DHHS Pub. No. [PHS.] 87-1407). Public Health Service: Hyattsville, Maryland.

8. Ibid.

9. Clark, M.C., Czaja, S.J., and Weber, R.A. (1990). Older adults and daily living task profiles. *Human Factors, 32*, 537–549.

10. Lawton, M.P. (1984). The older person in the residential environment. In Robinson, P.K., Livingston, J., and Lawton, M.P. (eds.), Aging and performance of home tasks. *Human Factors, 32,* 527–536.

11. Canon-Bowers, J., Lerner, N.D., Sterns, H.L., and Koncelik, J.A. (1987). Development of a booklet on "Safety products for older consumers." Prepared for the U.S. Consumer Product Safety Commission, Contract CPSC-C-87-1157. Comsis Corporation: Maryland.

12. Sterns, H.L., Barrett, G.V., and Alexander, R.A. (1985). Accidents and the aging individual. In J.E. Birren and K.W. Schaie (Eds.), *Handbook of the psychology of aging* (2nd ed.). 703–724. New York: Van Nostrand Reinhold Company.

13. Sterns, R.S., Nelson, C.A., Sterns, H.L., Fleming, J.C., Brigati, P., McLary, J., and Stahl, A. (1997). *Public Transportation in An Aging Society: The Potential Role of Service Routes.* Washington, DC: The American Association of Retired Persons.

14. Lawton, The older person in the residential environment.

15. *Technology and aging in America* (1985). U.S. Congress Office of Technology Assessment. OTA-BA-264. Washington, DC.

16. Smith, D.B. (1990). Human factors and aging: An overview of research needs and application opportunities. *Human Factors, 32,* 509–526.

17. Faletti, M.V., and Clark, M.C. (1984) In Robinson, P.K., Livingston, J., and Birren, J.E. (eds.), *Aging and technological advances.* NATO Conference Series III: Human Factors. 313–324. New York: Plenum Press.

18. Clark, Czaja, and Weber. Older adults and daily living task profiles.

19. Koncelik, J.A. (1982). *Aging and the product environment.* Stroudsburg, PA: Hutchinson Ross Publishing Company.

20. Canon-Bowers, Lerner, Sterns, and Koncelik. Development of a booklet on "Safety products for older consumers."

21. Clark, Czaja, and Weber. Older adults and daily living task profiles.

22. Enders, A., and Hall, M. (Eds.). *Assistive technology source book.* RESNA Press. Washington, DC.

23. *Technology and aging in America.*

24. Smith. Human factors and aging.

25. On the eve of universal design. October, 1988 in *Home, 34,* 95–104.

26. Lonero, L.P., Clinton, K.M., Wilde, G.J.S., Holden, R.R., McKnight, A.J., McKnight, S., and Young, M. (1994). *Awareness of risk and self-restricted driving in older drivers.* Ontario, Canada: Ministry of Transportation, Safety and Regulation Division.

CHAPTER 6

PATH-FORWARD THINKING: CORE COMPETENCE AND THE VALUE PROPOSITION

Ken Dickey

With all that has been written about the subject of core competence, why is it that the present-day strategic planning process has proven so frustratingly difficult and yielded continued poor operating results for so many companies? One wonders if the process of strategic thought, which must take place before action, can provide serious benefits. If so, can companies learn to utilize this powerful tool?

If core competency is the anchor of the strategic thought process, why do companies struggle?

It seems that the concept of core competence is too abstract and theoretical for real-world consideration and use. Apparently, this is a topic for the classroom that corporations never apply to their strategic thought processes. If this concept of strategic thought anchored by the core competency process is to deliver on the promise of the future, why do so many companies continue to struggle to implement it?

As a practical matter, many business leaders view the core competence subject in isolation, as though conversational mastery of this topic will prove to be the "secret ingredient" missing from their recipe for success. Often discussed as the latest and greatest one-minute business solution, "core competence" is interwoven with those classic phrases "back to basics" or "returning to our roots;" it is never really understood and therefore is superficially applied.

In reality, most strategic plans contain little genuine forward thought and are no more than an exercise in spreadsheet arithmetic. Companies take the year's numbers, add x percent, build a series of action steps that are good enough to get through the presentation meeting, and next year blame poor results on the economy, competition, weather, and so forth. The strategic planning process in use by companies that take the time to generate a long-term plan is similar. An abundance of numbers, data, charts, graphs, comparisons, analysis, plans, and action steps are all built through a backward-looking prospective; not a single eye looks to the horizon or what might lie beyond.

A quest for understanding is embedded in the core competence process. The real power of this understanding is in the intellectual work and thought process, which involves dynamic discussions, tough introspective questions, and brutal intellectual honesty. The product of these efforts is a clear direction for the future of the enterprise, which will continue to produce increasingly superior results. "Superior results" means growth rates two to five times the industry norm and financial results (measured by return on capital employed) of the same magnitude when compared to competition. The delight of customers who place serious value on their strategic relationship with the firm is the true testimony of the firm's success.

Addressing the real barriers requires intellectual honesty—something that not everyone finds easy. The intellectually honest discussion process that will soon be addressed is not for the timid, casual, or unwilling, as it will expose difficult, perhaps painful, and unpopular topics requiring attention. A commitment to producing superior results demands intellectually honest and open discussion on all subjects. Remember, if superior results were easy, everyone would produce them.

Readers may find it amazing that so many companies continue to struggle year after year simply because they fail to address the most basic issues. Hopefully the case examples given will be beneficial in making the connection from theory to practice.

CASE EXAMPLE 1: CONFLICTING FUNDAMENTALS

The owner of an enterprise makes all the politically correct statements about growth, long-term career opportunities, future plans, and so forth, but in fact is unwilling to fund growth projects. The owner's level of satisfaction for risk and complexity of the enterprise has been achieved, and additional capital investment or risk is not necessary for him to further benefit. The owner's desire to preserve the status quo remains unspoken, but the intellectual honesty required for the core competence process will quickly uncover this watershed issue. The enterprise cannot deliver on the promise of growth if its basic fundamentals are in conflict. The conflict between the personal life of the business owner and the needs, expectations, and aspirations of employees, customers, and vendors is ever present. There is no easy answer or quick fix, and the frustration of those team members trying to execute a long-term growth strategy will continue to grate against the true agenda of the owner until the problem is solved.

For any plan to deliver on the promise of the future, the importance of every stakeholder must be acknowledged. The reality of expectations (business and personal) requires that a company consider the aspirations, desires, and needs of all stakeholders, not just the owners. The stakeholders' responses to future plans must also be considered; it is important to remember that all stakeholders have an opinion, positive or negative, about the future of the firm. Stakeholders are raised to the forefront of corporate attention depending on the issue, hence the need to recognize their importance.

Understanding and using core competence does not require investment, but the success and growth of customers will dictate future investment pace as the firm gains a greater share of an expanding market-based opportunity. Investment decisions should be centered on serving the needs of customers.

Building a great business, not just an average business, is a matter of conscious choices. The size of the company is no guarantee for success. In the example of the business owner who was satisfied with merely the status quo, the choice had been made, though probably never discussed, to accept the concept that "okay is good enough." Usually these owner-focused companies slowly settle and fade over time. Bright new employees are not attracted, vendors share their new ideas with companies on the move, customers look elsewhere for value innovation, and lending institutions view the lack of growth as a sign of management weakness and stagnation.

The greater the need for superior performance, the more critical the task of comprehensive strategic thought becomes. An understanding of core competence is at the heart of this process. (See Figure 6.1.)

The strategic thought process utilizing core competence as a driver is difficult, painful, and awkward. It requires one to think on multiple levels (vertical, horizontal, and concentric), deal with an unknown number of variables (including business and personal), and recognize the simultaneous occurrence of those variables. In this example, the business owner has made a personal choice, factoring in comfort level, risk tolerance, family status, and so forth. This basic unspoken decision will drive the future of the enterprise, for better or worse. This example used a small business as a case model; however, larger firms are subject to their own series of barriers and blinders. Size or product diversity is no guarantee for success.

The process to harness the power of core competence is not a stand-alone, one-time event; the discussions usually span months and are conducted best by a neutral moderator. Furthermore, the process includes the key people running the business. These busy people are stressed already with the events of the day. Most managers are short-term tacticians; they look for immediate resolution of "today" issues. Unfortunately, many of their tactics prove toxic to the long-term success. Many times the flood of everyday activity and their training or instincts prevent

Figure 6.1
Multi-Level Simultaneous Thought Process for Today's Businesses

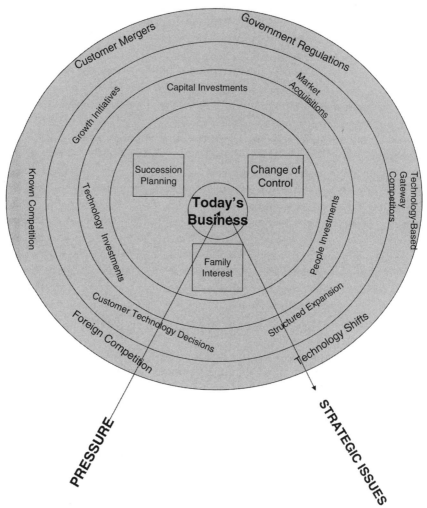

them from seeing the world from a position of opportunity driven by understanding, a position that comes from the core competence process.

Some team members may have difficulty grasping or accepting the concept of core competency, while others may fear change and take on obstructionist roles. In many companies that I have had the opportunity to assist, we have found that time to understand and digest this new lens to the world is a great ally in gaining an opportunistic perspective.

An open discussion process often reveals strong differing opinions about what the company actually does and what it needs to do. As employees have an opportunity to speak openly about their feelings regarding what they believe is really happening in the company, these latent feelings and issues will surface. The example's small business owner might be surprised at his employees' reactions to his speech about growth. Their reactions would show him the reality of the consequences that flow from his unspoken agenda. His agenda may have greater influence on the business than any other single issue.

Keeping all stakeholders in mind, a company must decide what it wants to do and does not want to do, how it wants to do it, what needs to happen and when, and how it shall deal with the variables.

CASE EXAMPLE 2: THE BOEING COMPANY

Not long ago, The Boeing Company referred to its firm as being in the "transportation business." This comprehensive, all-inclusive corporate direction led to multiple paths. Transportation includes everything from planes, boats, cars, bikes, elevators, trains, to walking, and some of these ideas may have been good for Boeing. In reality, however, the heart of Boeing was airplanes. So after years of less than satisfactory operating results, Boeing was forced into serious reconsideration, and attention was again focused on the core competence of Boeing: airplane design and manufacturing. As an affirmation of its newfound focus, Boeing even began calling itself The Boeing Airplane Company. Today, Boeing is the world leader in commercial aircraft and the envy of global competitors.

Imagine the vigorous discussion at Boeing during this period of self-examination, particularly between the corporate managers defending the transportation theme and the operating people opposing it. In the end, they achieved success by hearing the voice and needs of the customer, initiating the core competence process, and forging the value proposition.

In an article in *BusinessWeek,* Stanley Holmes writes, "Another success driver [is] Boeing's newfound discipline on the factory floor. It has come a long way from the troubles it faced in 1997, when production problems shut down two assembly lines and cost the company $2.5 billion."[1] Boeing's core competence and discipline to the design and manufacturing of commercial and military aircraft is at the heart of its success.

Core competence is a way of thinking about the total enterprise and how the people within it view the world served by their customers. Cultivating and developing a thought process centered on core competency does not require outspending competitors on research and development. The core competency process has nothing to do with vertical integration. Outsourcing is a tool, while a thorough understanding of the company is the true value.

Consider the issue of the stakeholders in a business and which of the stakeholders has the most significant stake. These stakeholders are united in their desire for a successful business, each for their own reasons.

The listing of stakeholders includes but is not limited to employees, customers, vendors, the financial community, shareholders, union leaders, joint development partners, distributors, representatives, dealers, integrators, users, original equipment manufacturers, and so forth. All of the stakeholders are important, but only one can reside at the top of this list: customers.

To emphasize this point, a company could ask each member of the strategic planning team to create his or her own list of the stakeholders in order of priority. This listing will provide insight into how the employees see the company and whom the company should serve. Without customers, the remaining names on the list of stakeholders simply disappear. Serving customers better must be the first priority of all strategic thought processes.

Sufficient time must be allowed for this early step since it will create the unity of purpose upon which the enterprise will rest. Team members will come to this strategic thought process with a narrow focus and must be given time to internalize the most fundamental reason why their enterprise is in business. Once customers favor them with orders, then all the stakeholders can share in the celebration. A simple review of how the enterprise responds to a business downturn validates this point; in a downturn, the company will launch a new marketing and sales theme focused on customers, which is quickly abandoned once the bookings crisis appears over. The company then moves on to the next hot topic, unaware that its path is circular.

Core competence discussion requires decisions concerning what the company is about and what it is not. Having had the opportunity to participate in this core competence process with many firms, I have found that many companies stall at this very first step. They simply cannot agree on what the business is about and what it is not. Management has allowed the direction of the business to be self-defined—that is, defined by the desires of individual self-serving units—to the point of paralysis. Nothing more can be accomplished until senior management clarifies this basic question, ironically a question that it has caused in the first place.

CASE EXAMPLE 3: SWISS WATCHES

One of the more widely discussed case studies used by universities is the example of the mechanical watch business located in Switzerland. For years watches produced in Switzerland were the world hallmarks of fine watches. This precision mechanical manufacturing business, however, failed to notice the threat coming from the emerging market of electronic components in Japan. The Japanese competitors planned to compete through a complete change of technology. Electronic component watches were cheaper, feature rich, more reliable, and easily mass-produced. In a period of a few years, more than 90 percent of the Swiss mechanical watch business was gone, replaced by the new electronic watches from Japan. Thousands of employees who produced these fine parts were out of work, and the economy of Switzerland that depended on these craftsmen suffered.

In the aftermath of this market crash, the core competence process revealed to the Swiss leaders that their real competence was their ability to produce small precision mechanical parts. Watches just happened to be one of the uses for these precision parts, so any product that had a requirement for this level of precision could be considered to recover business losses.

While the list of potential consumer and industrial products was lengthy, one of the most promising possibilities was the upscale single-lens reflex camera product line. (See Figure 6.2.) With the realization that Swiss precision parts competence could be applied to many products in multiple industries with customers worldwide, the Swiss turned their failure into success.

Although the Swiss were absolutely certain they were in the mechanical watch business, when viewed through the lens of the core competence process they saw their business as a series of capabilities that extended far beyond watches.

Figure 6.2
Swiss Watch Industry

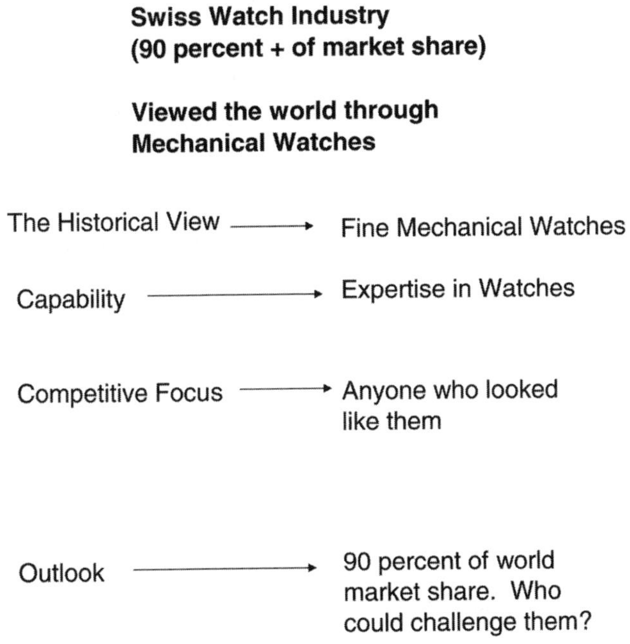

Swiss Watch Industry
(90 percent + of market share)

Viewed the world through
Mechanical Watches

The Historical View ⟶ Fine Mechanical Watches

Capability ⟶ Expertise in Watches

Competitive Focus ⟶ Anyone who looked like them

Outlook ⟶ 90 percent of world market share. Who could challenge them?

The power of core competence is not visible unless a company looks for it in a deliberate manner, which is why it took such a long time for the Swiss to view themselves as having a series of competencies rather than just as producers of mechanical watches. The Swiss found that a useful core competence must be difficult for others to imitate, and it must make a significant contribution to the end product or service.

In consideration of the case of the Swiss watch industry, it is important to remember that the use of the core competency thought process is no guarantee or protection from competitors. Nothing the Swiss could have done would have prevented the Japanese from entering the watch business with new technology and creating a major market shift from mechanical to electronic watches. The metrics were in favor of the electronic components; it was the Swiss watchmakers' narrow perspective that caused the true damage.

It is important to realize that new and powerful competitors will enter the market from distant arenas using technology as their gateway. The Swiss business leaders did not realize this, and so they failed to see the threat from the Japanese electronics industry. A comprehensive understanding of their core competencies would have facilitated a far quicker response to the threat; it would have allowed them to expand into other products and markets that utilized their ability to produce fine mechanical components and parts (see Figure 6.3).

CASE EXAMPLE 4: HONDA MOTOR CO.

If the Swiss watch industry is a negative example, Honda Motor Co. provides a positive example of core competency thought process. In my class studies, I ask the students to define Honda's core competency. Their responses are typically quality, value, choice, manufacturing, culture, engineering, or price. The correct answer surprises many.

At the heart of Honda's success resides a competence fired by passion to be the world's best designers and manufacturers of gasoline engines. Therefore, any product or application that uses a gasoline engine as its prime fuel is fair game for the Honda product teams.

Just as the Swiss did not see the Japanese electronic threat coming from that distant arena, the U.S. lawn care industry did not see Honda coming into its industry. Until that point, Honda produced only cars and motorcycles, and these upscale transportation products were a long way from the business of consumer lawn care products. The Honda lawn care product, however, entered the market with a 30-percent+ price premium and captured a significant share of market. When consumers are willing to pay a price premium for a product with demonstrated superior value and features, a competitive action based on lower price is not an effective response. The premium price serves as the point of validation for superior content.

Figure 6.3
Swiss Watch Industry

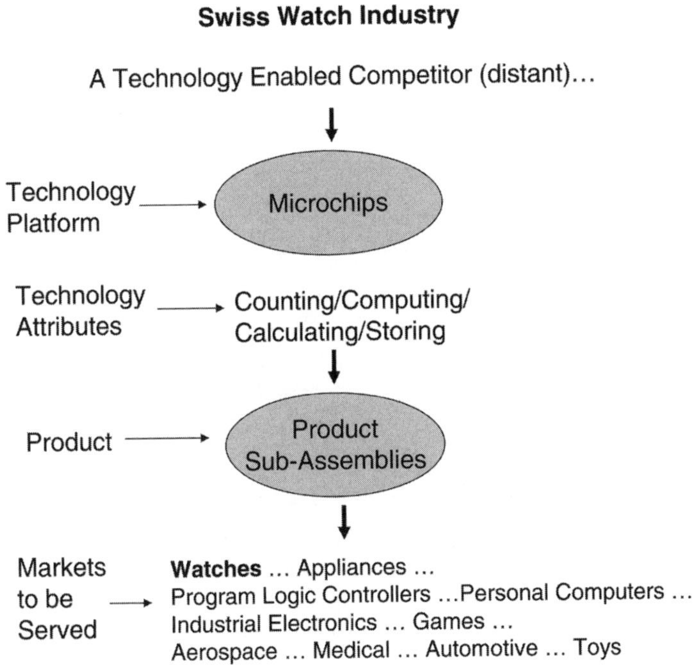

Swiss Watch Industry

A Technology Enabled Competitor (distant)...

↓

Technology ——→ (Microchips)
Platform

Technology ——→ Counting/Computing/
Attributes   Calculating/Storing

↓

Product ——→ (Product
                    Sub-Assemblies)

↓

Markets   **Watches** ... Appliances ...
to be   ——→ Program Logic Controllers ...Personal Computers ...
Served   Industrial Electronics ... Games ...
                    Aerospace ... Medical ... Automotive ... Toys

The Honda business leaders clearly understand the power of core competency and have remained extremely loyal to the principles that differentiate competencies, technologies, and products.

Today, this portfolio of competencies allows Honda to participate in multiple products where the common link is a desire for a high-quality gasoline engine. The list continues to grow and currently includes standby power generators, lawn mowers, outboard marine engines, snowmobiles, automobiles, motorcycles, power sprayers, and its new venture, aircraft engines. If a product utilizes a gasoline engine, consider it fair game for the Honda product teams. While competitors have tried to imitate the Honda business model, none have done it better.

Honda's success shows that core competence will provide access to a wide variety of markets. The Swiss watch industry was late to understand the value of its competency, while the leaders of Honda were early adapters and enjoyed a profitable growth curve for more than 50 years.

Honda's success also proves that it is important to differentiate competence, technologies, and products. Technology alone is not a core competence, but the organizational capacity to integrate human expertise across various levels of the organization is. Individual technology streams are not the issue, but the ability to harmonize the hard and soft issues across an enterprise is at the center of making competency an effective tool. In the case of Honda, it took the experience and knowledge gained from the racetrack and delivered that knowledge to various product design teams worldwide.

The knowledge gained from technology investments must have the capacity to move through the organization. It does little good to spend resources on technology development and then not have a competency to move that knowledge through the organization to people who can convert this knowledge into benefit for customers.

A company collectively learns and improves by developing a culture centered on learning, working together, and moving knowledge to those who need to know. Those responsible for stewardship of technology absolutely must have a shared understanding of customer needs and technical possibilities.

CASE EXAMPLE 5: LAWN TRACTORS

Recently, a local lawn implement dealer sent a very angry letter of resignation to the factory headquarters when his flagship supplier signed a national arrangement to source lawn and garden tractors to a national big box store organization. Until this time all lawn and garden tractor sales had gone through the exclusive dealer organizations, which enjoyed protected territories. The dealer could not understand how the loyal dealers could be expected to compete for new equipment sales against such a large volume organization.

What the dealer did not realize was that his core competency was not new equipment sales, but it was supplying parts and service for the lawn care tractors. New product sales, as well as the employees, facility capability, revenue, and customer perception were all based upon aftermarket parts and service. The competency to provide technical service and support to customers was a capability that few could imitate or duplicate. Thus, his supplier's shift to a big box store that does not provide parts or service could only help his business.

CASE EXAMPLE 6: A FOOD PRODUCTS COMPANY

Lately a large producer of processed foods decided to make a significant acquisition of a firm that used many of the same raw ingredients. The difference in the two firms was that one company used the national grocers wholesale distributors organization while the other company used the association of frozen food distributors. It seemed straightforward enough, as both frozen foods and dry goods foods used many of the same raw ingredients.

Unfortunately, because the original food products company had no competence in the frozen food industry and proved its ineptitude with its actions, the penalty administered by the frozen food distribution organization was a loss of revenue of more than 75 percent in the first 12 months. The frozen food acquis-ition was sold in less than 18 months and the food products company took a write-down on the acquisition of more than $80 million. It was an expensive les-son for such a basic principle.

Acquisitions made in the name of vertical integration, sourcing, raw materials, and so forth are often the very worst performers because they are viewed from an incremental operations perspective and not from a core competency perspec-tive. No one takes the time to examine the two companies in terms of a series of competencies. This example of the food products company is not extreme, but it is a real example in which the core competencies of the companies were not known or understood until well after the fact.

These six case studies illustrate the power of the core competency process to deliver on the promise of the future. Competency, or a portfolio of capabilities, is essential to a path-forward strategic thought process.

In Figure 6.4, a flow chart illustrates the entire strategic thought process. Once this chart is completed for an individual business, the entire strategic thought

Figure 6.4
Graphic Map of Strategic Thought Process

Graphic Map of Strategic Thought Process

Vision	Strategic Vision for Enterprise
Core Competencies	#1 #2 #3 #4
Core Technologies	Enabling Technologies Requiring Investment
Core Products	The Platforms Flowing from Technologies
Product Families	Like Kind Products Flowing from Core Products
Business Units	Centers for Customer Interaction
Channels to Market	Distributors, OEM's, Resellers, Packagers, Etc.

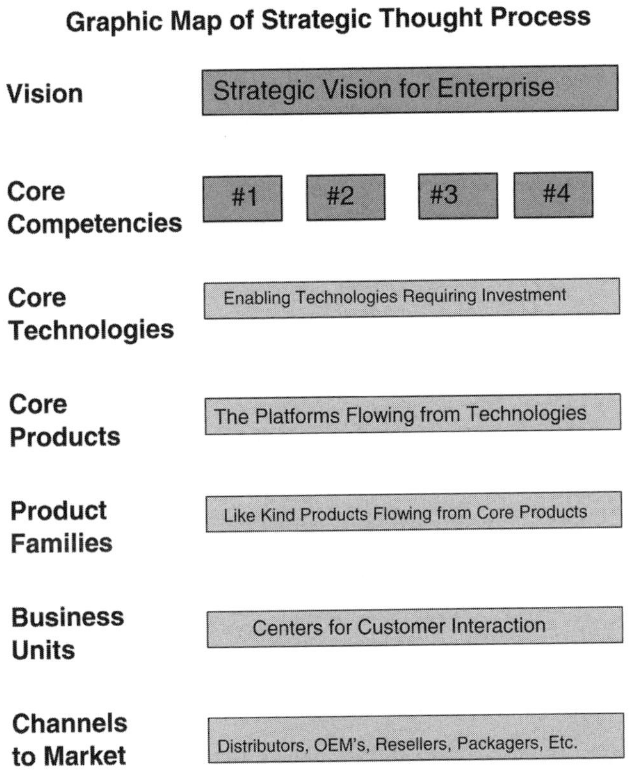

process is there on one large chart. Consider the power of being able to discuss your entire strategic thought process from a single chart. Any stakeholders will have a genuine interest in hearing and understanding what and how you think about the business both in short- and long-term periods. The core competency process will unite stakeholders in a common understanding, and nothing is more powerful for company growth.

NOTE

1. Holmes, Stanley. "Boeing Straightens Up And Flies Right." *BusinessWeek*. May 8, 2006, 69.

Part II

PROMOTION

CHAPTER 7

How to Clean Up with a Start-Up: Tricks and Tips from Entrepreneurs

Robert Black

You have come up with a smashing new labor-saving product for the home. You want homemakers everywhere to run out and buy it; what do you do? Clean Shower was introduced one bottle at a time. Samples were given to northern Florida employees of Winn-Dixie supermarkets and their family members to try in their own homes. Company officials were lobbied until finally the store's buyer relented and agreed to allow the product on the shelves of the Jacksonville division. The inventor-entrepreneur-manufacturer-salesman then visited most of the 120 stores personally to ensure the product was available as agreed.

Then the creativity began. Beauty parlors near the Winn-Dixie locations were targeted. Those beauty parlors were likely to contain local women who were careful about their appearance and their homes' appearance. In the beauty parlor, they also had time to talk while waiting or even while sitting in the chair. The product was explained, some features demonstrated, and then they received a free sample to try at home. "If you like it, buy it at Winn-Dixie. If they're out, be sure to ask for more."

The captive audiences were captivated. Clean Shower took off. The rest, as they say, is history.

DEVELOPING PRODUCTS

Delivering new benefits or substantially improved benefits to the consumer is a must with a start-up company. To break through the noise and clutter, the offering must be outstanding in its own right. Me-too products will not work to kickstart a company. It is important to have a proprietary position. This can be as complex as securing patents or copyrights, registering trade names, or developing secret formulas or processes. It can be as simple as staking out a location on a busy street corner.

The most important proprietary position is the one in the mind of your customer. You, and you alone, occupy that place, nurture it, and defend it. Volvo has established itself with a classic positioning on safety. Similarly, Rolls-Royce has laid claim to ultimate luxury. Clorox has defended itself as "bleach" at the risk of becoming generic and being forced to share its position. As entrepreneurs, the first vital task is to set a goal for the positioning you want to establish for your new product. The rest of the introduction revolves around winning this spot and finding ways to defend it against intrusions from others.

How do you know you can achieve this unique positioning? There are many sources of statistics describing product launches, successes, and failures. It is claimed that only one out of five new products succeeds and that half of new products in the planning cycle are expected to generate less than $10 million in annual sales.[1] ACNielsen's consumer goods research operation, BASES, reported that in the year 2000, 30,000 new consumer brands were met with a 93-percent failure rate in the United States. The cost of these failures was put at a conservative $20 billion estimate.[2] Other sources cite somewhat different numbers, but the conclusion is inescapable: launching a successful product is very difficult.

One necessary but not sufficient requirement for success is that the innovation fulfills a need in the market. Ambi Pur Liquifresh 2 in 1 Air Freshener and Bowl Cleaner is a toilet cleaning product sold by Sara Lee Corporation. In its first year, sales grew astronomically. This said less about the product than about the market. Many new toilet cleaning products enjoy excellent initial sales, then drop off. Customers continue to have a need for a better product in this market and are willing to try newcomers. None has been established as the dominant toilet cleaner.

In a classic product introduction, Crisco, the leading—almost sole—shortening available to homemakers was challenged by Spry. The introduction came with the marketing muscle of Lever Brothers. Although the challenge seemed insurmountable, the introduction succeeded. This was due in part to the fact that the market for shortening expanded as the fierce competition between Lever and Procter & Gamble reminded consumers of their needs in this category.[3]

The needs do not have to be significant or radical. Addressing small but lingering needs can lead to success as well. Take, for example, the fragrance of products that are not designed to provide or enhance fragrance. This characteristic is easily overlooked, but can greatly influence purchase, use, reuse, and other desirable responses. Observing behavior at the retail shelf, shoppers will select those products that stand out, read some of the label, and then smell the product. Even some products in sealed metal cans are subjected to the smell test. Why? Consumers may be searching for an indication of good products or merely trying to avoid bad (spoiled) ones. Once the product is in a consumer's hands, she is looking for confirmation that she has made the right decision or to discover a reason to put the product down and select another.

This rejection may not be the fault of the product at all, but due to some aspect of the package, merchandising, and the like. Staying with our olfactory example, a sealed and precooked canned ham may be rejected by a customer if the label's smell is reminiscent of a dead animal. (Some glues used to seal labels to containers still are made from rendered animal flesh.) Inside the can the product is perfect, but the marketing has been stymied by a label defect. This creates a secondary need for label printing that does not harm the ability to sell the labeled product and might perhaps enhance the experience. A fragrance of cloves or other spice associated with ham will reinforce the decision to buy. One might ask, "Who cares what the label smells like?" The answer is, the consumer cares. The fragrance should be consistent with or even enhance expectations of product performance. A hammer's handle should smell like wood rather than like the fish oil preservative that has been used to treat the wood.

Delivering the right fragrance at the right time to communicate the right message may well be serving unmet needs. More attention is being paid now to the concept of headspace in products. Headspace is the volume of gas in the container or in the product that allows gases to accumulate. The so-called new car smell is the most recognizable and most often noted headspace example. Similarly purses, makeup, chocolates, and other products have very familiar headspace aromas. Often the headspace is not representative of the product, but rather is a byproduct of production, packaging, or shipping. It takes time for the fragrance to develop, and it may be marred by outside events. Even "good" fragrance experiences may mask harmful chemicals (automobile headspace includes chemicals from colorings and adhesives).

A start-up would do well by attending to the fragrances of the business. Seeing that the aromas present an appealing mix with the product may move the customer to purchase. A purse that smells richly of leather is more apt to be purchased than one lacking this cue. Some leather preservatives, for example, contain formaldehyde, which would not offer customers as pleasant an experience. Research in psychology is only now beginning to document the strong relative influence of smell on memory and attitude. Entrepreneurs should keep this in mind in designing products, packaging, or even in selecting conducive retail outlets.

RESEARCHING THE NEEDS

How do we discover the needs? Traditional marketing research methods like focus groups, surveys, and in-depth interviews are obvious answers. The fragrance example above shows the power of programmed observation. Watching the consumption process from the first signs of need recognition through and past disposition may give insight into the choices, use patterns, and satisfaction with products.

One useful observation tactic takes disposition directly into account. Garbology, as the name suggests, is the study of garbage. There are many applications of this approach, including the archaeological examination of ancient or modern trash dumps. In a consumer setting, examining the garbage can tell us what has been consumed or not consumed and in what condition. US Airways' president had the airline's trash analyzed to better understand the customer preferences and satisfaction with meal selection and preparation. He knew intuitively that too much waste suggested poor choices by the dietary staff and used that to change menus and preparation methods. This was before garbology had taken hold as a respected scientific endeavor.[4]

Items do not have to end up in the trash to tell a story. Products left on the shelf or, worse, purchased and never opened or used also indicate problems detected by consumers. Apple Inc.'s iPod may have run its product life cycle already or at least the growth stages. The market has slowed and people are using the technology less or not at all. As the mainstream entered the market, the innovators and early adopters (the earliest groups to adopt an innovation) appear to be turned off now that the product has become mainstream and boring. The effort required to locate, save, and program music is no longer rewarded with uniqueness and coolness. An effort to revitalize the market with video downloads of movies may not be sufficient to rejuvenate the brand. It depends on how many holiday gifted iPods are returned or unopened because the market has moved on to the next technology.[5]

Frank Perdue saw that consumers could not find cues to quality in uncooked poultry, so he created a market by creating new cues. Rejecting convenience for taste, Perdue emphasized that his birds were fresh, not frozen. Still requiring a cue by which consumers could judge the quality of uncooked poultry, he settled on the use of marigold leaves in the feed. Among the useful side effects of this nutrition decision was the fact that marigold leaves contained a substance that would change the skin color of the chickens to various shades of gold. This, then, becomes the immediate discriminatory variable in chicken selection. Watching customers in the store now, they can be seen to select chicken based on richness of color—as a surrogate for richness of taste or even nutritional quality.[6]

Others observe customers as well. The Perdue chickens do enjoy a better diet and better conditions, so the color marketing is not considered deceptive or dangerous. Marketers who create false attributes or overstate the usefulness of features may be in for trouble. Government interpretation of what is fair and appropriate can vary. In its early days, The Coca-Cola Company suffered from intervention by the courts and the United States. The product never contained cocaine, but adding caffeine prompted oversight and examination of consumers to see if they were being harmed by this substance. Eventually, the product was given the green light, and no further attempts were made in the United States to intervene.[7]

A more recent beverage creation and introduction, Snapple, did not receive this kind of government scrutiny. The producers introduced natural bottled drinks using at the time unorthodox communication methods. The product was targeted to specific niches of customers identified through observing who was dissatisfied with what was available in the market.

Clean Shower was also designed for niche markets. The product and the approach were modified as feedback was gained by interviews and observation of the early trial markets. This research was tricky though. Many early triers were friends and family who may not have given the most realistic feedback versus offering "support from the family."

The Clean Shower customers being targeted were women more than 25 years old with a household income above $40,000 and below $200,000. Working women were a high priority. With many consumer goods, younger women are the more logical target. Observation of usage and discussion with customers convinced Clean Shower that a different group was needed. Women under 25 were not focused on cleaning techniques. Older women usually select their brand loyalties and are often not targeted, but this category was new and loyalties had not yet formed. So the age range was skewed upward. The narrow band of income may look odd, but there are reasons for this, too. Below $40,000 the cost of the product seemed high and perhaps prohibitive. Those in the $200,000+ income groups often had maids to handle the cleaning duties and were unaware of the benefits offered by the product. Although men requested clean showers, they were seldom the ones doing the work, so they were seldom targets for the company. Finally, it was found through observation that potential customers spent considerable time in the car commuting. This opened the door to some of the novel advertising techniques discussed below.

START-UPS AND NEW PRODUCT INTRODUCTIONS

A start-up has different characteristics than a more mature company. By definition, a start-up enters the world as naked as a baby—no products, no money, and no customers. The trick is to find a way to generate positive cash flow with initial successes. Once that has been accomplished, it is necessary to analyze what went right to develop a model that can then be replicated.

McDonald's Corporation started from just one location. Ray Kroc was selling milkshake mixers when he stumbled on a customer who wanted enough to make 48 milkshakes simultaneously. The smell of success was unmistakable, so Kroc went personally to investigate the techniques and processes being used. After a relatively short time Kroc bought out the McDonald brothers and created a franchise system that ensured adequate cash flows and controls over quality and service.

McDonald's continues today in part by continuing to innovate. A successful product line and operating plan from the 1960s cannot survive in the twenty-first century, but a successful philosophy and value system can. McDonald's has maintained close contact with its customers and made changes along the way. Not everything works. Doing things that look dumb in retrospect are inevitable. The important thing is to do inexpensive dumb things (and learn from them). When something does work, understand how it works and replicate it.

NEW PRODUCT MANAGEMENT

One of the great success stories of product development happened almost by accident, but has been replicated many times over. Coca-Cola began as a syrup for headaches and indigestion and was only incidentally mixed with carbonated water to become a beverage. The plans for bottling and distribution certainly were no accident, however.

Also not an accident was the selection of the name of the product. Coca-Cola was selected to be descriptive of the product and to be attractive in advertisements. The look of the name and the type style have been duplicated worldwide. Competitors and copycats still abound, much as other products with similar names were offered in the early 1900s: Candy Cola, Hoca-Nola, Kel Kola, and Kaw-Kala.[8]

Product naming itself is part science, part art, mixed with a bit of luck and a dash of magic. The name of the product and the name of the company should say what you do and why consumers should buy. The following are examples of product names that give a mental image and will attract the target customer:

- Tony's Deep Dish Pizza
- Biker Pub and Grub
- Family Friendly Video
- Dermal Science Anti Aging Face Cream
- Nickermans Menswear
- Best Way Trucking

These names do part of the selling. Everyone has their own preconceived mental images associated with words and phrases. The start-up needs to take advantage of these images and use its name to send a message. Even if the founder's name is Edward Smith, a pizza shop needs an Italian name. People who ride motorcycles are shunned in some places and may think of themselves as part of a clique. A name like Biker Pub and Grub would attract bikers and probably repel many in search of a family friendly or quiet dining establishment. The name itself helps to define the focus of the business and identify the niche market targeted.

Nickermans Menswear is the actual name of a tailor shop in Bangkok, Thailand. The owner is an East Indian. When asked where the name originated, the owner said that he thought a Jewish name would be more likely to attract European and American customers who had had good experiences with Jewish tailors in Europe and America. A nearby tailor shop that is also owned by an East Indian is called Raja's. We leave it to the reader to decide which shop is more likely to attract walk-in business from European and American men.

The concept works in the business-to-business sector as well. When placing purchase orders, purchasers sometimes specify the shipping company desired. Usually, the purchase order form has a place in which to indicate the transportation company. It was usual practice to select "best way" on the form when it was left to the supplier's discretion to pick the shipping company. By naming a trucking company Best Way, the founders took advantage of this custom. Stories abound that similar strategies were used in the days when telephone directory assistance was the primary method for long distance shopping. Operators asked for the number for a local florist would find themselves giving the number for A Local Florist. Clever and innovative naming can reduce some of the need for media advertising.

A name is also a promise. It gives the consumer expectations. What is delivered must be congruent with what is expected. Miss Evelyn's Tea Shoppe needs china, crystal, and white lace tablecloths. Biker Pub and Grub needs Formica tabletops and Harley-Davidson décor. Potential customers would do an about-face at the front door of Miss Evelyn's if they saw Harley-Davidson décor in the seating area.

A name can also be limiting. Wile E. Coyote (the Road Runner's foe in so many cartoons) had found that the Acme Company could supply him with many different products. Conversely, he is unlikely to try Beautyrest for explosives. Once a company name becomes associated with a product or line of products, it can create a negative attribution for incongruous products. Beautyrest has become linked with mattresses. Beautyrest ice cream will not work. Similarly, Sealtest mattresses might be a bad choice.

Some companies are, however, able to use brand names for their products that unlink the corporate name from the brand or product line. Sara Lee is a company that markets shoe polish along with its apple pies. The shoe polish is sold under the Kiwi brand, and the pies are sold proudly sporting the corporate name.

Names that are hard to pronounce or are spelled incorrectly to be clever can cause dissonance and may create consumer avoidance. Consumers do not want to be made to feel inadequate at not being able to pronounce or spell a name, and it makes it more difficult to establish a place in customers' memories. Some examples of difficult names might include Kwick Schop, Abdjinger, and La Pountinifique. As firms go global they increasingly seek to identify names that will be memorable, pronounceable, nonoffensive, and perhaps not restrictive in whatever language they are doing business. The lists of candidate names tend to run short as more firms seek names they can use.

McDonald's may be viewed as a nondescriptive name. The brothers who ran the original hamburger stand that grabbed Ray Kroc's attention were named McDonald and the name seemed adequate for their needs. Perhaps some of the expansion came about because the franchises opened with signs that read McDonalds 10¢ Hamburgers in a time when 25¢ hamburgers might have been considered the norm. Apparently the neutral name did not hurt the franchise system. Some businesses with good names have failed; others with names that do not convey value succeed. A good name choice does not guarantee success, but it may be considered to be of particular advantage for a start-up.

Start-up companies require innovative approaches to marketing. Large, mature companies like Procter & Gamble will spend years and millions of dollars developing a new product and researching the market. They will then launch a product with a media budget of $20 million plus while simultaneously sending out representatives to retail stores to ensure shelf space. The stores feel the market's pull pressure from consumers coming in to ask for the product in response to the advertisement. As a contrast, Clean Shower was launched with a $70,000 budget that included manufacturing, marketing, and overhead. Marketing was personal, the inventor selling one-on-one to prospects in informal surroundings. Store employees pulled the product into the stores, and consumers drew reorders.

Naturally, the different types of organizations have different expectations of the results they will achieve with these programs. In either case, results should be measured against objectives. One formula for setting objectives is the SMART model, which sets the dimensions of effective goals. Objectives need to be Specific, Measurable, Attainable, Relevant, and Time bound. This enables even the least organized entrepreneurs to establish a test of success or failure versus the standard that was set prior to launch.[9]

Traditional advertising is becoming less and less effective. The public is saturated with advertisements and turns them off mentally. New technology enables television viewers to skip the commercials or fast forward through them. In an effort to grab attention, producers of advertising add comedy, sex, and special effects. Often these are the only parts of the commercial that are remembered. In the case of some of the most talked about and memorable Super Bowl or World Cup commercials, viewers often fail to accurately recall the brand advertised. One of the reasons is that the attention is on the comedy, sex, and special effects rather than on the product.

Another reason for the limited effectiveness of Super Bowl advertising is that one exposure has little impact on purchase. The objective is to create sufficient motivation within the consumer to drive purchase. Big companies use this in scheduling media. The classic metric used to choose and measure media campaigns is the reach (number of prospects seeing the ad) versus frequency (average number of times the ad is seen during a purchase cycle) tradeoff. One exposure of an ad to 100,000 people will not drive as many purchases as will ten exposures of that same ad to 10,000 audience members. In an introductory ad campaign, you have to reach beyond a minimal level of exposures and ensure that the target audience views the ad at least enough times to increase the probability of purchase. It is also possible to have too many advertisements. The trick is to select a frequency high enough to have the desired effect, but not so high that the final exposures are wasted.

There are many ways to determine how much frequency is enough. Some large companies use the "rule of nine" as a guideline for new product introductions. If you are in their target audience, you can expect to hear the message more than nine times. The audience is selected based on the media they see and hear and how often the media overlap (the same people hear the same message in multiple places). The rule of nine is based on an average product, an average media presentation, and an average susceptible consumer. Therefore, this is a rule that a start-up must break. For a start-up, the product must be better at delivering benefits, the media must be better at motivating the consumer to purchase, and the message must reach the most susceptible audience.

One way to excel at reach is through creative use of media. Radio is an oldie but a goodie. Consumers turn off advertisements on radio. They do this by pushing the next button on the car radio or simply by mentally turning them off. Ratings produced by independent companies measure the number of radios tuned to a particular station. Listening is another story. To be effective, the potential consumer must be tuned to the station and listening actively. This author changes the station at the first shout of a car advertisement.

To overcome this radio problem, only personality-driven programs are effective. Talk radio is good because the audience is tuning in to listen actively. Personality music can be good if the patter between songs keeps the audience listening actively. As soon as the consumer realizes the program has shifted to an advertisement, it is turned off physically or mentally. Early Clean Shower radio commercials were simply the radio personalities relating their true experiences with the product. The personality was given the product, allowed to use it, and asked to tell his or her story about the experience. These had sufficient impact that in many cases one exposure was sufficient to obtain purchase by susceptible consumers.

These outside-the-box campaigns are hard to manage. An advertising agency on a 15-percent commission could not do this and remain profitable. One of the most economical radio purchases at Clean Shower was a Scandinavian music program in the Pacific Northwest. The audience actively listened to the host and when he said, "Buy Clean Shower," the Scandinavians purchased Clean Shower.

Another good example of successful radio is Snapple. Traveling salespeople use convenience stores to get snacks, use the comfort facilities, and get something to drink. Snapple was introduced with a wide mouth so that it was possible to drink out of the bottle while driving and reclosed between stops. Canned carbonated beverages were not reclosable and had small openings. Recognizing that music listening looses its appeal after hours in the car, Snapple ran commercials on Rush Limbaugh's program. Salespeople in his audience listened, asked for Snapple, and looked for a variety of Snapple products. This Limbaugh audience, salespeople in cars, sought out the wide-mouth container with the reclosable top in the noncarbonated product niche and made Snapple a success.

When a radio campaign is done properly, the results can be spectacular. On the other hand, giving radio personalities the freedom to tell their own story can lead them to make promises that the start-up company cannot fulfill. Undoing the problems can consume large amounts of time and money that are not readily available to start-ups.

WORD OF MOUTH

Radio personalities speaking on behalf of a product are spokespersons. Your neighbor telling you about a great new product is engaging in word-of-mouth communication. Word of mouth can be particularly helpful to the start-up. The product must be revolutionary and not only an incremental improvement. Word of mouth is best with a product in a niche market. For example, an improvement in racing sail development would spread quickly through the sailboat racing community. If it is shiny, functional, and fits on a Harley Davidson, word of mouth will work in that community.

In the youth market, Homestar Runner is an entrepreneur with a series of comic figures. The company sells T-shirts, hats, posters, CDs, and other branded items through its Web site (http://www.homestarrunner.com). The consumers are 9-, 10-, and 11-year-old children. The only marketing is the Web site itself and word of mouth among children. The target audience returns frequently to the Web site, and events on the site become a topic of conversation within that age group. The markup on the products is substantial, and the media budget is zero.

Giving Clean Shower away in beauty parlors in Winn-Dixie shopping centers was completely outside of any conventional marketing approach, yet generated considerable discussion about the labor-saving product. The idea started by thinking about people who would care about appearances, shower regularly, have sufficient disposable income, and a wish for more free time. The company found this group in beauty parlors and they told their friends and family. It was successful, but beauty parlors no longer allow access to their customers, so this word-of-mouth experiment cannot be repeated.

Steve Marks and Harvey Nelsen founded Main Street Gourmet, a producer of muffins and muffin and cookie batter. Harvey wanted a broader distribution and to get the muffins into McDonald's restaurants. He arranged to play in a charity golf outing with the owner of a major franchise group and then got him to agree to a one month trial of his muffins. To get business started, Harvey encouraged all of his friends to purchase the muffins—even handing out money for them to do so. This got people to try the muffins, share them with their friends, and talk about the experience. People liked the muffins and, as a result, he was able to generate sales that impressed the franchise owners enough that they expanded the product line.

Barry Easterling is another creator/entrepreneur. He designed a better surgical table that was attractive to surgeons. Prototypes were produced and physician friends were recruited to try the product and get it placed in hospitals. Once placed and tried, the surgeons discussed the improvement among themselves and pulled more tables through distribution channels through their word-of-mouth advertising.

Jerry R. Wilson wrote the book *Word-of-Mouth Marketing,* literally.[10] He describes a word-of-mouth marketing blitz as a way to orchestrate discussions in launching a product or start-up company. The essential element is *to keep it simple and systematic,* streamline everything, and orient everything to action. Wilson describes the steps to creating communication through word-of-mouth networks by creating teams to work through planned tactics to achieve specific quantified objectives. The book itself was marketed successfully through these channels.

Word of mouth works both ways. One bad customer experience can be spread to large groups that will not patronize a product. Clean Shower found that negative word of mouth could be reversed. Customers who did not use the product correctly reported problems to friends and neighbors. When these customers called to accuse the company of fraud and threaten to complain to the Better Business Bureau, opportunities arose. The person who initially answered the phone was able to identify the problems and reinstruct in the use of the product. This turned the complainers into loyal customers, and they began to spread the word on how well it worked. The telephone specialist began training the customer-service staff that was added to the company and she later became the Vice-President of Operations.

OTHER PROMOTION

The word-of-mouth and sampling strategy of Clean Shower as a start-up somewhat mirrors that used by Lever Brothers to introduce Spry shortening. To introduce the product, one-pound sample cans, recipe books, and coupons were sent to one-third of U.S. households. This was supplemented with a mobile cooking school, model kitchen, and eventually a cooking program on the radio. With over

4 million mid 1930s dollars spent on the campaign, the product became very popular and put a significant dent in Crisco's market. Of course, Spry is gone now and Crisco remains.[11]

True start-ups have it a little more difficult. A rule of thumb in the grocery business is that 60 percent of buying decisions are made at the shelf. An easy-to-read label that describes the benefits will go a long way. A recent example is Cleanest Dishwasher. The package has the product name in bold type and adds, "Cleans the machine that cleans the dishes." The need fulfillment is clear, so who could resist the special value 2-Pack?

Color is important as well. If it is a consumer product, it should stand out on the shelf. If all of the competitors are dark blue, your label should be red and white. It is hard to go wrong with light and bright. Different and appealing are an absolute must. In the case of Cleanest Dishwasher, the aisle where it is likely to be located (dish and laundry detergents) has product labels that are dark with greens and blues. As a contrast, the product's package is white with a bright yellow label.

Labels and signs tend to collect text. The name, the logo, multiple messages, consumer suggestions, company name, admonitions, address, telephone number, and the like are all included. Remember—less is more. The rule of thumb is that a highway billboard should contain no more than seven words, two of which should be "This Exit." The front label on a start-up product is a billboard. It has to work as quickly as the highway sign. Cleanest Dishwasher has 14 items including the logo. Even this is pushing the envelope. The back label can contain the details. This too should be concise enough to be read quickly. Details like the company name and address can be in smaller print. The best billboard this author has seen is a McDonald's "M" followed by "Playland Next Exit." One letter and three words delivered a complete message. Consumers who do not like McDonald's are not going to patronize in any case. Consumers who like McDonald's and have children are very likely to stop. Children in the car may even lobby their parents to stop (to put it mildly!).

Beyond the label, the rest of the package has to appeal to the customer as well. A start-up needs to have a good "feel" to it to make the long trek from the shelf to the cart. Fine wines are now being introduced with screw caps in place of the traditional, but awkward and messy, corks—much to the delight of this author. Purchasing the product in its package should be pleasant. In the late 1960s and early 1970s Hanes Corporation created a hosiery product that was meant to break into a new distribution channel. The product itself, panty hose, was improved so that there was better fit with fewer individual sizes. The channel selected was supermarket distribution. The unique packaging, a large plastic egg, contributed to the visibility and memorability of the brand. It was easy for retailers to manage (and Hanes did much of the work). The package also felt good.[12]

Making products easy for the retailer is one way to break in. Start-up companies are tempted to try to push their products through the supply chain. Pushing is marketing to agents and distributors who are given an incentive to push the products through to retail outlets. These in turn are given an incentive to push the product to the customer. In each case, the next layer has other interests and usually has more pressing present business. This has been described as pushing a chain and is about as effective as pushing an anchor chain. The alternative is the pull strategy described earlier in which, for example, Clean Shower prospects were encouraged to ask Winn-Dixie retailers to stock the product. The best alternative is to design a product and package that are good for the retailer and then get the consumers to pull it into the store.

Hanes not only made the package attractive, it took the handling duties away from the retailer. The rack and product were delivered directly to each store, so the retailers' storage and delivery costs were zero. Afterward, restocking and other maintenance were performed by Hanes' "route girls." These women, in distinctive uniforms, oversaw the displays and gathered intelligence daily in the field. A start-up may offer to do this sort of consignment placement on much smaller scales to get a product established.

Establishing a product sometimes comes down to timing. If the three most important things in real estate are location, location, location, the three most important things in business start-ups are timing, timing, timing. The Spry shortening product mentioned previously was developed and was ready five years before it was introduced. The launch of the product was held up while the economy recovered enough that a new item might be better received. Start-ups seldom have the luxury of waiting that long, but some entrepreneurs may choose not to make the shift until the timing is right.

CASE HISTORY

How did Clean Shower come to market anyway?

Fair is fair, so in return for help in the manufacturing company the author was helping around the house. One chore was cleaning the shower. After one cleaning, it was time for a trip to the store in search of a better product. Finding nothing, the author returned to the workbench and developed Clean Shower.

After trying it and discovering how well the product worked, friends, neighbors, and employees were encouraged to test it as well. One use cycle later the people who were trying it came back and demanded more, "I can't go back to cleaning the shower—you have to make me some more." So, we applied for a patent, developed a label, bottle, sprayer, boxes, and a manufacturer to put it all together. The first 4,000 units were produced and stored before getting placement in a local convenience store.

A local marketing company had a public relations person who was able to get the story on the local news. The news show drove customers into the convenience stores. Samples were then given to employees at the local stores in the Winn-Dixie supermarket chain. This created more local buzz. As mentioned above, it was at this point that sampling occurred in the beauty parlors that were often in the same plazas as the Winn-Dixie stores.

Within four weeks, Clean Shower became the number one seller in the household cleaner aisle. Additional television appearances and newspaper articles caused additional growth. With the initial success, investors were interested and funding became available. Then a Boston media buyer suggested talk radio as an advertising vehicle. The initial radio was a morning talk show featuring a liberal and a conservative. The commercials were simply the two personalities discussing their experiences with the product.

In less than four weeks, Clean Shower became the number one selling shower cleaner in the Boston area. The system of having a radio personality use the product and describing his life-changing experience was then replicated throughout the country. As the product rolled out and became available in new areas, new media vehicles were phased in. Clean Shower grew 20.6 percent per month for 34 months with a peak of over $10,000,000 per month. (Author's note: This brief history does not include the stumbles, hiccups, and just plain dumb things that also happened along the way. Those come with the territory, too!)

CONCLUSION

A start-up is a difficult, frustrating, time-intensive, labor-intensive, and fun enterprise. It also requires marketing techniques different from those used by established firms. Some of the ones that have been mentioned include the following:

- Me-too products do not launch start-up companies;
- Create a name that is easy to understand, pronounce, spell, and describes the company;
- Color should add to the message and not reduce legibility;
- Fragrance, sound, and feel of the package count;
- Word of mouth and public relations are low cost and high impact; and
- You have to know your consumer and what makes your target market susceptible to your offering.

NOTES

1. Pollack, Judann, "New Products, Same Old Mistakes," *Advertising Age,* 67, Issue 41 (October 7, 1996).

2. Dominiak, Mark, "Avoid New Product Release Pitfalls," *Television Week,* 24, Issue 6 (February 7, 2005).

3. Hartley, Robert F. *Marketing Successes* Second Edition, New York: John Wiley & Sons (1990).

4. Wilson, Jerry R., *Word-of-Mouth Marketing,* New York: John Wiley & Sons (1994).

5. Smith, David, "Why the iPod Is Losing Its Cool," *The Observer,* September 10, 2006.

6. Hartley, *Marketing Successes.*

7. Ibid.

8. Ibid.

9. Wilson, *Word-of-Mouth Marketing.*

10. Ibid.

11. Hartley, *Marketing Successes.*

12. Ibid.

CHAPTER 8

MARKETING'S BIGGEST CHALLENGE: MARKETING BEHAVIOR CHANGE

Cheryl Agranovich and Mark Bednar

Marketing products and services is not easy. Marketing behavior changes is tougher still. Marketers develop products and services to reach diverse groups of individuals with unique wants, needs, and desires. In addition marketers develop specific messages to meet the motivations for purchase of each group. One group of Baby Boomers may purchase baby oil to soften aging skin, while Generation Y consumers may purchase baby oil to remove makeup, and Generation X consumers may purchase it to keep their infant's skin soft and moist. This form of match between target group's desires, or end goal, and the product as means for achieving the goal is central to the concept of marketing. Marketing is, in essence, meeting the wants and needs of consumers.

Marketing is often about asking people to change their behavior: buy "Fluff" laundry detergent rather than "Puff," buy brand "X" beer rather than brand "Y." This is not easy, as marketing professionals recognize. Even more challenging than getting consumers to change the brand of detergent or beer they purchase is getting individuals to change their behaviors. This chapter addresses the marketing of behavior change, a unique and challenging aspect of marketing, with application across a number of domains. As we consider how to obtain consumer buy-in to address health, education, and lifestyle issues, this chapter presents insights and issues that have application across many services, ranging from financial services to health and beauty services as well.

MARKETING BEHAVIOR CHANGE: MEANS TO AN END?

The End Goal

The skyrocketing cost of health care today is hardly news. Hence, employers increasingly are offering health management programs to their employees in the hope that employees ultimately will improve their health and, in turn, save the company money by lowering health care claims costs and through increased attendance. Data show that when employees are healthier they miss less work and are meeting and/or exceeding the requirements of their jobs (thereby increasing employee productivity) versus employees in poor health who are not performing at desirable levels.

Effective health management must contain an array of programs in order to reach a diverse population. For that reason, programming often is referred to as population health management. When looking at a typical population, three states of health generally are represented—three different market segments if you will. These segments are shown in Figure 8.1.

Segmentation of Markets

As evidenced in Figure 8.1, employees in the high-risk state already have an illness or disease they manage; those in the moderate-risk state have risk factors for diseases or illnesses (obesity, high blood pressure, and tobacco usage), but do not yet have a disease or illness; and those in the low-risk state are, for the most part, healthy. The smallest population in an organization represents the largest health

Figure 8.1
Fifteen Percent of Employees Are at High Risk for or Already Have a Chronic Condition

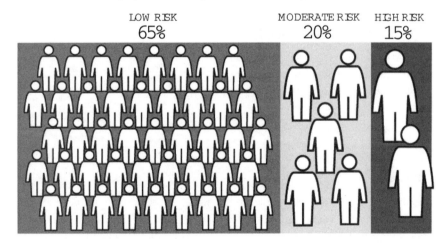

care costs, while those in the low-risk state make up the largest number of employees. The goal is to help those in the low-risk state remain in the low-risk state, move those in the moderate-risk state back to the low-risk state before they move into the high-risk state, and manage the diseases and illnesses of those in the high-risk state in order to control costs and maintain the level of health of employees in this state.

To address the needs of each group, a range of marketing strategies is used. A typical mix of programs to address a diverse population would start with disease management, which may include marketing tactics such as one-on-one telephonic counseling to help an individual manage a disease or illness; lifestyle management, with one-on-one telephonic coaching to help an individual reduce his or her risk factors and potentially avoid developing diseases or illnesses; a nurse line, which includes a 24/7 telephone line for employees to call when they have a health question or incident. In addition, more traditional marketing materials such as educational components, consisting of newsletters and health education Web sites, and other more traditional point of purchase materials would be available and would be targeted at specific health-related issues. In addition, more creative and innovative approaches are used, including a health risk appraisal (HRA), or self-reported questionnaire, for employees to complete that ideally is populated with their personal, individual biometrics data, such as cholesterol level, heart rate, blood pressure, weight, body mass index, and other dimensions of health.

However, convincing employees to take advantage of health management programming is a daunting task, as many programs require an individual to change a lifestyle behavior. Unlike marketing a product (such as a laundry soap), lifestyle behavior change (for example, quitting smoking, implementing an exercise program, and changing the way one eats) can affect all aspects of one's life. Marketing such drastic behavior changes is not asking someone to change an aspect of his or her life, but rather to change who he or she is, and his or her entire life focus, in some cases.

The challenge in marketing lifestyle change programs hinges on four areas:

1. Educating employees about their new benefit and how it can work for them;
2. Incentivizing employees to take advantage of the programs;
3. Showing consumers their personal return on investment; and
4. Changing the sociocultural environment, for example, the groups of people that surround the individual in the workplace, home, or group setting.

Ethical Issues

Confidentiality also plays a role in marketing behavior change since personal health information is an important part of the equation. This especially becomes important when dealing with the workplace, as employees need to understand that their personal health information is protected by law from their employer. The confidentiality issue often cannot completely be resolved, though a certain percentage of individuals will, based on good communications and marketing, feel more at ease with the issue and, consequently, take advantage of the programming. The first two challenges can be resolved only by effective communications and marketing.

MARKETING BEHAVIOR CHANGE

Marketing behavior change is not the same as marketing a soda or marketing a line of clothing; instead, marketing behavior change needs to be applicable to persons of both genders, all socioeconomic backgrounds, all age ranges, and all levels of education—and still be interesting enough to engage the wildly diverse audience. While target marketing to a particular client certainly will be more effective (even within seemingly narrow client types, such as a law firm), several groups of employees are represented—e.g., lawyers, administrative assistants, communications specialists, human resources (HR) generalists, information technology personnel, and paralegal assistants. These groups each respond to marketing materials in their own manner.

Additionally, behavior-change marketing simply is not as sexy as soda marketing or tennis shoe marketing. Because health is a serious topic, many typical marketing approaches cannot be utilized. Health often is a topic that does not excite individuals—and it is a topic about which they do not often want to think. They view health as a private, confidential topic and, unfortunately, many people have the viewpoint that health is not something they can change.

But it is this thinking that behavior-change marketing aims to combat. Because health management is a relatively new field, the marketing of health management also is a new field. As a result, the behavior-change marketing model is still being developed. When one places the behavior-change model in the larger context of the health management model, one can see how this particular model is one part of a larger model that employees need to experience to reach optimal health.

What has become apparent is that marketing behavior change rests on a foundation of traditional marketing versus a model based on the health benefits of positive change. Historically, getting people to make a positive change in their health was driven primarily by doctors. But as the health industry matured and employers recognized the amount of money that could be saved by implementing health management programs, getting individuals to change behaviors became a monetary issue and something that could benefit from traditional marketing techniques, such as the hierarchy of effects model. One of the most often referenced models, within marketing, is the hierarchy of effects group of models, also known as the AIDA model, which suggests that consumers go through a laddering process, of attention, interest, desire, and action, suggests that consumers go through a series of steps as outlined in Figure 8.2.[1] The hierarchy of effects model suggests that advertising, or more generally promotion, leads consumers to move through a series of steps, starting from awareness, knowledge, liking, conviction, and ultimately to action.[2]

Applying behavior change (such as quitting smoking) to the hierarchy of effects model yields the foundation of behavior-change marketing and manifests in the following manner:

Awareness

Orient employees to the benefits of good health by making them aware that choices and behavior are at the heart of good, or bad, health—and that the choice is in their hands. In the smoking example, employees need to recognize that smoking is bad for their health.

Knowledge

The next step is to give employees the knowledge they need to make healthy choices. In the smoking example, employees need to understand that not smoking

Figure 8.2
The Hierarchy of Effects Model[3]

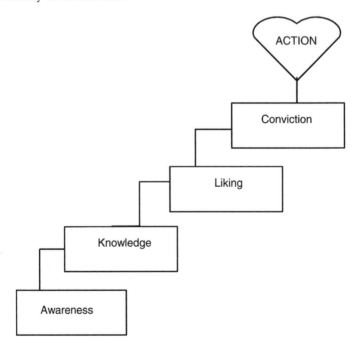

will improve their health by reducing their risk for cancer, heart disease, coronary obstructive pulmonary disease, and diabetes.

Liking

Next, employees need to want to change and be able to recognize the benefits of behavior change. In the smoking example, the employee needs to want to quit smoking—though at this stage, he or she may not know how to quit smoking. At this stage, the perfect opportunity exists to introduce many health management tools (for example, mail-based or telephonic lifestyle management programs). Employees at this point are ready to heed the message that resources are present to assist with their goals.

Conviction

Employees need to commit to behavior change and make a plan to change—but this can be done only once the employee understands the tools that are available. In the smoking example, the employee will pick a date to quit smoking and commit to the change. He or she also will have access to all the tools necessary to be successful.

Action

Finally, the employee actually makes the behavior change. In the smoking example, he or she reaches the quit date and does not smoke on that date.

However, as one can foresee, if the behavior-change marketing model would end there, success would not be attained since the real work begins AFTER the purchase stage. The stage after the purchase stage is a very perilous one unless the employee successfully can make the change permanent. If the change is only temporary, the employee will revert to the liking stage, and no cost savings is gained, no quality of life improved.

This is why the traditional hierarchy of effects model, when viewed through the lens of a behavior-change approach, has morphed into a somewhat different model in the health management arena. This model, the marketing behavior-change model, combines both the psychological effects found in a traditional health theory.

Awareness

Using the hierarchy of effects model, the employee first needs to be aware of his or her choices and understand how they affect his or her health.

Education

The individual needs to be educated about how to attain good health and about the benefits of good health. Because education is a key aspect of health management, this stage is referred to as the education stage in the industry as opposed to the knowledge stage.

Recognition

This is where the behavior-change marketing model deviates from the hierarchy of effects model. In the recognition stage, the individual recognizes the negative behavior choices in his or life and understands how he or she can benefit from the change. This often, from a health perspective, is termed the "imagining" or "projection" stage, in which the individual imagines himself or herself as having made the change (for example, picture what your life will be like when you are not smoking or you are at a healthy weight—how will you feel or what will you be able to do?).

Conviction

The individual can teeter back and forth between the recognition and conviction stage for some time, as the conviction stage is where he or she decides whether to make a change. Many individuals already are aware and educated as to why a particular behavior is negative for health reasons and recognize that a change needs to occur. Individuals often also enter the conviction stage (for example, "I'll go on a diet after the holidays," or "I'll quit smoking after my job gets a little less stressful."), but this stage often does not move employees to the all-important action stage. Instead, the individuals move back to the recognition stage.

Action

The action stage involves some positive action from the individual—quit smoking, start a diet, begin an exercise routine, and so forth. In the action stage, the individual must implement a change in his or her life. He or she must get involved in this stage beyond thinking and assimilating information and actually make the behavior change.

Proof

In this stage, the individual has to experience the proof of the benefits of behavior change. This proof either can be revealed independent of outside measures (for example, the individual can breathe easier after quitting smoking or loses weight and goes down a size in clothing) or can be shown by tangible numbers (for example, cholesterol level improves or blood pressure improves). However, for the employer purchasing the health management program, the proof needs to be tangible and must translate into dollars saved based on employees' improved health. It is the return-on-investment data that frequently, if not consistently, motivates an organization to make an investment in health management for employees.

Maintenance

This stage can be viewed as the most important stage in the model, as the individual must recognize how being in a state of good health is ideal and desirable. The health management program, theoretically, will provide tools to allow the individual to maintain good health once it is achieved. Otherwise, the individual reverts back to the first stage. In other words, health is not a one-time-only purchase, whereas a lot of other marketing (clothing, electronics, and furniture) focuses on a one-time or infrequent purchase.

While the education and the incentive/reward aspects have distinct stages, the thread of community support is woven throughout the model. For example, the awareness and education stages cannot occur in the workplace if the individual's organization does not support the message; the conviction and action stages cannot be successful unless support of the individual is provided, either at home or at the work site; and finally, the maintenance stage becomes more successful when the individual is in a supportive environment—having both supportive programming and supportive individuals who also are reaching for the same goals or have achieved the same goals.

As in the marketing hierarchy of effects model, the individual must travel through all stages, and the stages can occupy various time periods. But individuals cannot skip stages in the marketing behavior-change model.

Also, what must be taken into consideration are the diverse effects of health on an individual's complex body. This also differs from the traditional marketing model. In other words, while the results of using a certain bleach can be universal (all who use it will have whiter clothes), the results of a lifestyle behavior-change program can be wildly divergent. For example, one who starts a walking program may lose ten pounds over two months, yet another may lose only two pounds, based on other controllable risk factors (that is, eating habits, tobacco use, and so forth) and noncontrollable risk factors (that is, genetics). Therefore, if one experiences a less-than-desirable result, he or she may incorrectly conclude that the behavior change itself is ineffective. This greatly affects the proof stage and may force the individual to revert to the education stage.

Behavior change also is not something with which people often are confronted, unlike many other products, making the marketing of behavior change more challenging. Behavior change is not as universally essential to one's life as food, air, or clothing. It also is not associated, at least in the beginning stage, with any sort of entertainment, such as music, films, and books. Making a behavior change is not perceived as an "enjoyable" task, but rather as work on behalf of the individual making the change.

In order to best understand the ideal method to market behavior change, one must first understand behavior change from the perspective of a health change model. This model provides the mind-set from which an individual can make a behavior change.

ECOLOGICAL HEALTH CHANGE MODEL

In order to best understand the ideal method to market behavior change, one must be well served, by understanding the behavior change from the perspective of the ecological health change model, as this focuses on the interaction of people and their surroundings—physically and socioculturally.[4]

Relatively new in the health management world, the ecological model was developed to provide guidance to researchers and practitioners during the assessment and intervention phases of behavior change; it identifies five levels:

- interpersonal factors,
- primary groups,
- institutional factors,
- community factors, and
- public policy.

The multidimensionality of this model, as compared to the somewhat narrowed focus of other health models, establishes this as—while time-consuming to implement—a comprehensive solution for behavior change. As such, this model is utilized more frequently in the public sector, as is evidenced with the current approach to the smoking issue.

Utilizing other health models, the approach to the smoking issue historically has been to educate the smoker about the health hazards behind the habit—focusing on just the interpersonal factors. But in the recent past, the most prudent method to combat smoking has incorporated a more ecological model of health to drive behavior change, employing tactics such as the following:

- prohibiting smoking in any public buildings or workplaces,
- raising health insurance premiums for smokers, and
- increasing taxes on cigarettes.

By approaching the issue from multiple perspectives, the habit of smoking becomes more difficult to maintain. Research also supports this model, as workplace smoking bans have been found to reduce smoking prevalence by about

10 percent and reduce overall cigarette smoking by 29 percent. Restrictions on smoking in public places also produce environments in which smoking is marginalized.[5] Household smoking also can greatly affect the behavior, as illustrated in Table 8.1.

BRANDING BEHAVIOR CHANGE

Behavior change happens over time. This is another way in which the model differs from the traditional hierarchy of effects marketing model. In theory, one could experience marketing for a soda, for instance, at point of purchase; go through all stages of the hierarchy of effects model almost instantaneously; and make the purchase. Rarely does that happen with behavior change. Because making a lifestyle change can be seismic to an individual's life, this cannot be entered into lightly.

Table 8.1
Smoking Patterns among Adolescents and Young Adults: Smoking History Categorized by Home Smoking Rules[a]

| | Home Smoking Rules | | |
Smoking History	No One Is Allowed to Smoke Anywhere, Percent (95 Percent CI[b])	Smoking Is Allowed in Some Places or at Some Times, Percent (95 Percent CI[b])	Smoking is Permitted Anywhere, Percent (95 Percent CI[b])
Ever smoked 100 or more cigarettes (yes)	12.0 (11.2–12.9)	24.0 (22.0–26.0)	30.3 (28.1–32.4)
Smoking status			
Current	8.5 (7.8–9.3)	19.2 (17.2–21.2)	26.5 (24.5–28.5)
Former	3.5 (2.9–4.0)	4.8 (3.8–5.7)	3.8 (2.9–4.7)
Never	88.0 (87.1–88.8)	76.0 (74.0–78.0)	69.7 (67.6–71.9)
Smoking intensity (no. cigarettes/day)			
≤5	40.1 (35.7–44.4)	31.9 (27.0–36.9)	20.6 (16.3–24.8)
6–10	27.8 (23.9–31.7)	29.4 (24.6–34.1)	29.7 (25.2–34.2)
>0	32.2 (27.6–36.7)	38.7 (33.5–43.9)	49.7 (45.0–54.5)
Quit ratio[c]	28.9 (25.2–32.6)	19.9 (16.1–23.8)	12.5 (9.9–15.2)

[a]Based on data from the 1998–1999 Tobacco Use Supplement to the Current Population Survey. Includes self-reporting respondents aged 15–24 years.

[b]CI indicates confidence interval.

[c]The proportion of ever smokers who reported that they were former smokers at the time of the interview.

Source: Clark, Pamela I., Michael W. Schooley, Bennett Pierce, Jane Schulman, Anne M. Hartman, Carol L. Schmitt. "Impact of Home Smoking Rules on Smoking Patterns Among Adolescents and Young Adults." Centers for Disease Control, April 5, 2006, 15, http://www.cdc.gov/pcd/issues/2006/apr/05_0028.htm.

Also taking into consideration the socioeconomic model, one can see why the marketing for behavior change needs to take this gradual shift into consideration. A culture shift at the organization ideally needs to occur for change first to happen and second to be successful and lasting. The socioeconomic model also outlines the need for community involvement.

For individuals to take advantage of health management programming, and in order for them to move from the education stage through recognition and conviction to action, the individual must have a strong level of trust in the programming being offered. The individual must trust not only that his or her personal information will be kept confidential, but also that the resources available to assist with the lifestyle behavior change are expert and valid. This is especially true because the individual is dealing with behavior change that has the potential to cause poor health, if implemented incorrectly.

This level of trust becomes a more difficult hurdle when one makes a behavior change in the workplace. Many employees are skeptical of any ulterior motives behind health management programs.

Building a level of trust becomes the first step in establishing programming that is designed for maximum utilization. After crafting a program that will target the company's needs, one of the first actions is to brand the program as an expert, reliable, resourceful, and trustworthy initiative. To maximize the chances of success, this branding should be as exhaustive and comprehensive as the branding for a product or company. As such, the theory and principles behind a name and logo can be established, and common goals can be sought.

The branding also serves to separate the program provider and its staff from the company offering the health management program. This will begin to combat the fears surrounding confidentiality and help to build trust. If employees think that people from within their own company are running the program (which would violate the Health Insurance Portability and Accountability Act), chances for trust building are severely reduced.

As branding is established, employees begin to recognize the tools available and how those tools can help them achieve or maintain good health. The program name and logo also relay the importance of the program to the employees.

Once the branding of the program is established, it is important to market any behavior-change program under this umbrella and within the scope of this program. This conveys the desirable third-party feel of the program and links together resources that can support the individual as the behavior change is being made.

The branding should be representative of the employees and of their culture, and the name and logo should be unique to the company, creating the targeted effect that evidences a program's usefulness in an employee's life.

Brand building often can take a significant amount of time, and companies implementing health management programs often do not have the luxury of waiting for brand building to occur before implementing programs; thus, programming is introduced under the umbrella of the brand almost instantly, and, as the brand building occurs, the early adopters of the health management program serve as the driving force behind culture change at the company. It is this group of early adopters that function as the community for those who make behavior changes in the second wave.

TOOLS FOR SUCCESS

Capitalizing on the early adopters' success is key to motivating more behavior change in a company. There are several ways to capitalize on this success, including

- testimonials,
- word of mouth, and
- reporting of success.

Testimonials become very useful for marketing behavior change. These testimonials can be solicited from those who have had success since this group often is pleased with the results and is willing to share. Ideally, the permission to utilize a testimonial should be gained at the onset of the program.

The testimonial, once gained, can be used in various venues, including all-employee meetings, company literature at the work site, and printed information sent to employees.

Word of mouth is an uncontrollable yet highly effective means to capitalize on success. Word of mouth can be encouraged by those assisting with the implementation of the behavior-change program (that is, the nurse working with the individual enrolled in a disease management program can encourage the individual to speak to co-workers about the program), but is most successful when organically developed.

Reporting of success is an important tool in marketing behavior change that often is overlooked. This reporting is important to both the decision makers who have opted to implement health management at the workplace and the individuals.

In the former case, the reporting of employees' success spurs the "decision makers" (often made up of human resources professionals and upper management team members) to recognize the value in the programming, thus prompting them to become better ambassadors of health management and spurring them to reach for more success by allocating funding for additional programming. In the latter case, reporting back to the individual enrolled in a program drives the first two tools in this section—word of mouth and testimonials. While both of these tools are possible without reporting of results, the reporting validates what the individual may be feeling and serves as the "proof" stage to allow the behavior change to be successful and permanent, allowing the individual to progress to the maintenance stage.

CHALLENGE 1: EDUCATION/ACCESSIBILITY OF TOOLS/ COMMUNICATIONS

The first challenge in marketing behavior change comes during the awareness and education stages in the marketing behavior-change model. The level of difficulty of the challenge varies based on the following:

- education level in regards to health information of the employee population,
- readiness to change of the individual,
- company culture,
- company budget for communications,
- company budget for programming (including educational tools, such as Web sites and newsletters), and
- perception of confidentiality.

The awareness stage of the marketing behavior-change model is best conquered through multiple mediums and diverse information, taking in a wide segment of the population. Ideally, the awareness stage includes on-site, online, and mail-based marketing and communications, including health management awareness campaigns (informational brochures about health), newsletters, and Web sites. This stage also should be met in conjunction with available resources already at the work site in order to begin to capitalize on and meet Challenge 3 (community involvement/support). In other words, a company's on-site nurses or fitness center employees should be involved in the awareness and educational stages, assisting with the communication of the message.

The education stage must be built on the foundation of success from the awareness stage. The education stage presents information about ways individuals can improve their health and provides the answer to the "what's next" question that inevitably follows the awareness stage.

Because of the product diversity necessary to meet the various demands of individuals, the education stage also must offer various media and messages. Preventive care reminders accompanying educational products often are an ideal way to lead the individual to the next stage in the marketing behavior change model (recognition). One example of this is a client with a population of state workers based in the Southwest that receives a newsletter focusing on all benefits. The newsletter includes a preventive care reminder in the form of a Post-it note affixed to the front page. This preventive care reminder, based on the stage of the individual receiving the message, rests either in the education stage or in the recognition stage of the marketing behavior change model.

Targeted information can include preventive care reminder communications sent to groups based on age and gender. For example, a preventive care reminder postcard focused on the fact that a prostate-specific antigen test can assess the risk for prostate cancer—which is sent to men over the age of 50 (the group that requires a yearly test)—becomes more successful than a general postcard about the fact that losing weight will reduce one's risk for various diseases and illnesses.

The education stage also includes education about certain programming and how it functions. Convincing an individual that a lifestyle management program is beneficial is part of the communications effort and is what drives many in the lifestyle management industry to employ individuals in the call center who specialize in program enrollment. It is this individual's immediate task to educate employees about the program and convince them to enroll.

The next stages, recognition, conviction, and action, are largely self-driven, meaning if proper information is presented through the awareness and education stages, the individual must come to recognition, conviction, and action on his or her own. These stages are greatly influenced by factors such as community support, confidentiality, and incentives; but, ultimately, these three stages prove more difficult than others to affect a mass population level.

CHALLENGE 2: FINDING INCENTIVE/PROOF

When marketing behavior change, as mentioned previously, the stage of proof is vital. This stage can take several forms, and all can hold varying value to the employee, necessitating, ideally, a multidimensional approach.

One of the more public (and, consequently, necessary) proof methods is that of participation and the tie-in of an incentive. The incentive is chosen based on the program, the level of involvement necessary from the individual, and, obviously, the company's budget. For example, for a disease management or lifestyle management program—a program that involves considerable life-altering behavior change and commitment—an incentive of greater value is necessary. This value often is implemented in the form of a cash incentive or a percentage off a benefit such as health care. Yet for a behavior change program, such as a fitness incentive program (usually a three- to five-month program focusing strictly on the individual implementing a fitness program in his or her life), an incentive such as a $20 gift certificate often serves as enough motivation for the employee to join.

When looking at an HRA—which serves the recognition stage of the marketing behavior change model very well—incentive is an important factor to consider. The incentive, again, greatly drives participation, as evidenced in Table 8.2.

In Table 8.2, the company remains the same, and the time an HRA is offered also is consistent; the incentive is significantly increased, support is increased, and marketing dollars slightly are increased. Because of the consistencies, the driver behind the increase in participation must be attributed to the incentive

Table 8.2
Incentive versus Participation

Incentive Product	Incentive Amount	Participation
$15/month reduction health benefit contribution	$180	85%
$25/month reduction health benefit contribution	$300	85%
Fitness towel with company logo	$5	15%
First-aid kit	$2	2%
T-shirts	$5	7%

and the increased support of the program. Another factor to consider, however, is the perceived value by the employee, which contributes to the need for incentives other than monetary ones in order to meet the diverse tastes of employees.

In addition to participation, the other proof is the less visible yet solid one that, truly, positively impacts health. This proof varies by individual, but can come in the quantifiable form of improved biometrics information or in the difficult-to-quantify form of a general feeling of improved health in the individual.

The next stage, maintenance, is the all-important change that allows good health to permeate the individual's life. The maintenance stage, like the recognition, conviction, and action stages, is again largely self-driven by the employee and is difficult to affect the population on a grand scale. Often, the one factor that most influences this stage is the proof stage—the more proof presented, the more likely an individual is to succeed in the maintenance stage.

CHALLENGE 3: SENIOR-LEVEL SUPPORT AND/OR COMMUNITY/FAMILY SUPPORT

The marketing of behavior change is impossible to accomplish without support —both at the workplace and in an individual's personal life. The support at the work site comes in several forms:

- by giving employees time to participate in programming,
- by offering support materials offered to assist with the behavior change and to educate employees, and
- by supporting programming at all levels of the organization (CEO, HR, upper management, and so forth).

The first two usually are based on budget and/or company regulations. Companies that can offer employees time to participate in programming often see better participation rates than companies that require employees to participate outside of normal working hours.

The last form of support is an area that is less quantifiable because it often is based on both unaffectable qualities (such as an individual's thoughts on health) and affectable but difficult-to-track qualities (such as relationships between health management implementers and the individual).

Additionally, the larger the organization implementing the health management program, the more difficult it is to reach all upper management and human resources representatives responsible for supporting the program.

Because of this complex issue, this form of support is best approached by first formulating relationships with the contacts at the organization. These initial contacts often create the program's original ambassadors. Concurrently the health management provider should be utilizing all available and attainable methods to keep this key group aware of upcoming programming, especially in regards to programming that positively affects lifestyle behavior change. Methods to keep this audience abreast of programming include conference calls, mailings, promotional timelines, and materials with commonly asked questions from employees. Of course, any sort of incentive sent to members of this group that encourages them to support programming is advisable.

Support in personal life comes in several forms as well:

- through resources available in the community to assist with the behavior change (for example, fitness facilities),
- from family members, and
- through consistent messaging offered in media.

Support in one's personal life is difficult to track and control. With more than 60 percent of Americans being obese, more meals being eaten away from the home, and an increasingly sedentary population, forces often work against the individual making the change.

Fortunately, American society is at the cusp of change, as sales of healthy items, such as bottled water and organic food, are at an all-time high. This paradigm shift, while in its infancy, certainly assists the individual in making a lifestyle behavior change.

One method for success with lifestyle behavior change is to extend the program to spouses, as this can instantly provide family support, should both the employee and his or her spouse enroll in a lifestyle behavior change program.

Support at both the work site and in one's personal life becomes necessary as this encourages the individual and assists with movement from the proof stage to the maintenance stage. Once an individual reaches the maintenance stage, it becomes less likely that he or she will regress to the education stage, though he or she can slip back to the recognition/conviction stage. The important aspect is that the individual now has been through these two stages and hopefully can see their importance.

CONCLUSION

Marketing behavior change is a relatively new concept, as behavior-change programs in general are in their infancy. Yet the ability to market these programs rests at least partially on more conventional marketing methods. The twist is that in order to successfully market the programs, the best approach is to marry traditional marketing techniques with health models to allow for the life-altering change that, in theory, occurs with lifestyle behavior-change programs. The research and knowledge that comes from better understanding the strategies that most directly impact behavior change can then be transferred to other domains of marketing, leading to better insights and ultimately greater impact on behaviors of individuals, whether health related, or related to the purchase of products or services.

NOTES

1. Vakratsas, Demetrios, and Tim Ambler, "How Advertising Works: What Do We Really Know?" Journal of Marketing, Vol. 63, Issue 1, January 1999, pp. 26–43.

2. Lavidge, Robert J., and Gary A. Steiner, "A Model for Predictive Measurements of Advertising Effectiveness," Journal of Marketing, October 1961, Vol. 25, Issue 6, pp. 59–63.

3. Ibid.

4. Sallis, James F., and Neville, Owen, *Health Behavior and Health Education.* San Francisco, CA: Jossey-Bass, 2002, p. 462.

5. Clark, Pamela I., Michael W. Schooley, Bennett Pierce, Jane Schulman, Anne M. Hartman, and Carol L. Schmitt, "Impact of Home Smoking Rules on Smoking Patterns Among Adolescents and Young Adults." *Centers for Disease Control,* April 5, 2006, http://www.cdc.gov/pcd/issues/2006/apr/05_0028.htm, pp. 6, 12, 13.

CHAPTER 9

SALES PROMOTIONS: BOOM OR BUST FOR BRAND LOYALTY?

Michael Hardman

"Half the money I spend on advertising is wasted. The problem is, I don't know which half." Among the people to whom this aphorism is attributed is department store magnate John Wanamaker.

What would Wanamaker say about sales promotions in the 21st century? How much of this money is wasted? How much of it is well spent? How can we know the difference?

Varying definitions of sales promotion and the difficulty of tracking expenditures make estimation of annual spending difficult. The Promotion Marketing Association (PMA) has tracked the industry into the 21st century and has endeavored to maintain comparability over time. The PMA estimated overall spending on promotion in 2004 to be $429 billion, including both consumer targets and trade targets. This compares to an estimate of advertising spending that reached only $156 billion using similar procedures.

Promotion spending had dipped in 2001 along with world economic markets. Since that time, spending has rebounded, in some areas more strongly than others. Investment in consumer promotions has continued to increase, up 7 percent from 2003 to 2004, although trade promotion has not gained as much and was down from 2003 to 2004 by 3 percent.[1]

Spending levels vary by sector as do the strategies and goals of the spending. Procter & Gamble alone, for example, spends in excess of $2 billion annually on trade promotion alone. Best estimates are that more than a quarter of such trade spending ends up as profit or margin contribution for the retailers rather than being shared with the end consumers. Procter & Gamble is undertaking a program to increase the effectiveness of its promotions by tying retailer payoff to consumer benefit. "Whenever you can get the retailer to actually apply 80 to 90 percent of those funds to actual in-store merchandising, temporary price reductions, end-aisle displays, what have you, it's very good for P&G," according to a quote in a trade publication.[2]

Total spending on sales promotions as well as spending relative to advertising is likely to continue to increase according to many in the industry. These increases are attributable to a fragmentation of traditional advertising media and the evolution of customer targeting techniques. The increasing use of micromarketing encourages the use of specific tools to encourage immediate responses. Some clients are seeking very specialized tactics including sales promotion, while others are seeking more holistic approaches, incorporating all marketing disciplines.[3]

A word of caution is in order. One industry publication, *Marketing Week,* has likened sales promotion to the "reality television of the marketing world."[4] It argues that in its early days, sales promotion was innovative and vibrant. Consumers benefited from promotions because they perceived and received an actual value in excess of investment. Now, promotions dominate the landscape and consumers have become blasé or hostile toward the techniques. The comparison with reality programming is apropos and well-timed. Some of the most excessive promotions are introduced on the backs of the reality programs themselves.

TECHNIQUES OF SALES PROMOTION

Traditional methods of consumer sales promotion such as deals (for example, buy one, get one free or BOGOF programs), sampling, coupons, refunds, rebates, premiums, and sweepstakes have been joined by event marketing, product placement, and online promotions. Given the choice, many consumers would prefer a cash incentive over one involving additional product or premium gifts. "The best promotion is to get something for nothing. Buy one get one free (BOGOF) is so much more compelling than a promotion inside the wrapper of a Kit Kat [candy].[5]

Customer loyalty programs continue to gain popularity among consumers and marketers. Television networks have experimented with a new form of sampling new programs. CDs containing new shows are tipped into magazines or sometimes newspapers (in the United Kingdom). Product sampling to large audiences takes place at sporting and entertainment venues. Another new activity has been occurring in the direct marketing sector. *Promo* magazine is now including direct mail in its inventory of sales promotion techniques. Various forms of e-commerce promotions, including reminders, viral marketing, incentives, video games, contests, and sweepstakes have helped to fuel the growth of online customer relations. Many commercial sites offer instant win sweepstakes or facilitate sweepstakes entry in some form. Those sites that allow repeated entries on a daily basis encourage return visitors. Most sites have some restriction, requiring UPC or other product codes. Many also collect data useful in creating a customer database.[6] Regulations vary from state to state and globally as to what can be required and what information can be gathered to qualify as a legal sweepstakes.

Promotion to individuals to prompt word of mouth and opinion leadership has grown as techniques to identify and contact those who are most likely to be effective communicators have improved. The Haygarth marketing agency has developed a proprietary approach to this called SMART TARGETING. This technique locates, identifies, and profiles those consumers who are most likely to be innovators and market leaders and determines how best to interact with them. Sophie Daranyi, Haygarth's managing director, offered as example Nokia Corporation's participation at the Newquay Rip Curl Boardmasters sports festival targeting the active lifestyle market. By the end of the festival, attendees had increased their association among Nokia, youth, and sport.[7] In a similar fashion, Procter & Gamble (P&G) is using a teen buzz-marketing program, Tremor, to generate awareness and hype for its products. For example, P&G contacted the males in its 250,000 teen database with a communication designed to use coupons for Schick Quattro razors to inoculate the market against the introduction of the Gillette Fusion razor. "Each Tremor panelist is getting 11 of the booklets with free-razor coupons—10 are intended for distribution to friends—totaling more than a million. That adds up to nearly $100 worth of free razors per panelist."[8] This continues what has become the cornerstone strategy in the razor market—giving free or greatly discounted razor handles to encourage purchases and/ or block a rival's introduction of a new blade.

Another way to muster strength against a rival's introductory campaign is through partnerships. Partnerships are regaining attention in the promotion field. In the United Kingdom, for example Walkers Snack Foods successfully teamed its crisps (that is potato chips in the United States) with the News International Books for Schools campaigns. Using an access via entertainment durables, Britvic soft drinks company partnered with PlayStation 2 for an instant-win on-pack promotion with an investment of $4 million. Partnerships that come together by convenience and are not seen to provide a relevant relationship or message to consumers may be doomed to failure. Many partnership promotions have failed in recent years due to lack of synergy. Giving another brand as a gift or premium may not help either brand if the products are not used together, or at least appear to address the same lifestyle audience or similar usage situations.[9]

Event sponsorships continue to grow. National Automotive Parts Association (NAPA), an automotive parts retailer, has participated in support of motorsports for years. Customers do not expect to buy the same parts, but brand exposure is the key factor in utilizing this form of promotion. A regional approach is taken to reach segments of consumers/fans. NAPA credits the effective use of this tool to drive sales to users who find awareness and credibility from the promotion. In a similar fashion, the National Institute for Automotive Service Excellence

(ASE) sponsors the NASCAR (National Association for Stock Car Auto Racing) Craftsman Truck Series. The organization began its involvement with the Craftsman Truck Series in order to recognize auto technicians. Emphasis was placed on certified technicians, convenient for the only industry-wide certification program for automotive professionals. In this case, the promotion is expected to reach both a consumer, do-it-yourselfer audience as well as the trade audience of technicians whether presently ASE certified or not.[10]

Trade promotions continue to be important to the management of distribution channels. Slotting allowances, performance allowances, case allowances, dealer rebates, trade shows, and the like continue to be popular for use by business-to-business (B2B) firms. More recently, we have seen the emergence of account specific promotions, e-commerce, and business loyalty programs in that sector. Not all of this has been in the fast-moving consumer goods (FMCG) arena. Matthew Hooper, chairman of the Marketing Communications Consultants Association, is quoted as observing, "The money is simply not there in FMCG any more, so agencies are having to find new routes to market."[11]

It is difficult to settle on one authoritative measure of the scope and impact of sales promotion. Global marketing estimates are difficult to locate, but one source claims that worldwide, suppliers spend at least twice as much on promotion as on advertising.[12] See Table 9.1.

Tracking of effects is better for promotion than for advertising, but is still primitive. Nevertheless, sales promotions continue to serve their traditional purpose of achieving timed sales increases. These increases come about through the specific call for action that is inherent in a sales promotion. The actions typically fall into one of two categories: creating trial or encouraging larger purchase volumes.

Up to now, these objectives have been viewed as running counter to a longer-term goal of encouraging the development of loyalty. However, more recent discussions find a role for sales promotion in loyalty-based strategies.[13] The Promotion Management Association tracks spending on promotion-related customer relationship management programs (loyalty cards, reward points, and similar tactics) and estimated this would exceed $16 billion in 2006.[14] The question arises, though, whether customers want or need such loyalty programs. The perception may change depending on the type of firm involved. With higher-risk products, consumers may feel more secure in a long-term relationship. Conversely, they may not want a relationship for lower involvement products.[15]

The cellular telephone industry encouraged consumers to reconsider the meaning of loyalty in the face of sales promotion. Customers are expected, even required, to commit to seemingly long-term relationships. Recent U.S. legislation that enables the "portability of telephone numbers is intended to provide more flexibility, but the impact has been modest.[16] Perhaps it is a form of inertia that keeps consumers with the same company even in the face of promotions from

Table 9.1
Select Promotion Spending 2004 (with increases from 2003, some categories omitted)

Category	2004 $Billion	Percent Change from 2003
Direct Mail	$56.8	+8
B2B Promotion	45.68	+5
Premiums	31.56	+5
Trade Shows	24.88	+6
Point of Purchase	18.0	+6
Ad Specialties	17.75	+5
Sponsorships	11.03	+8
Couponing	9.98	+8
Licensing	6.16	+1
Fulfillment	4.70	+15
Interactive	3.50	+25
Sweepstakes	1.84	0
Sampling	1.80	+18
In-Store	0.89	−2
Total Consumer	*293.07*	*+7*
Total Trade	*136.41*	*−1*
All Promotion	*429.48*	*+4*

Advertising Spending 2004 (PMA)	
Category	2004 $Billion
All TV	$67.79
Radio	19.14
Magazines	12.25
Newspapers	46.64
Outdoor	5.77
Business Public	4.07
Grand Total	*155.66*

Source: Promotion Marketing Association.

competitors. A more insidious effect, perhaps, may be the resentment felt by loyal customers at the "perks" offered to the "newbies" joining the fold.

Do these customers remain loyal because of inertia? Or is there an impact from promotions that do target loyal customers' additions of services or enlistment in new programs or extended time periods? Can promotions act to positively affect brand loyalty?

This requires a consensus view of loyalty, which may be difficult to achieve. Many measures and concepts have been used to evaluate loyalty in academic and practitioner studies. These have included (a) the percentage of consumers buying a brand, (b) the number of purchases per buyer, (c) the percentage who continue to buy the brand (repeat buyers), (d) the percentage who are 100 percent loyal, and (e) the percentage who also buy other specific brands (duplicate buyers). It may be that a better descriptor of behavior in the marketplace is "polygamous loyalty" in which customers are "loyal" to a set of brands. Examples include having a set of preferred restaurants or hotels, membership in multiple reward programs within the same product class, and even having service with multiple providers although one could satisfy multiple needs (for example, land-line telephone, wireless phone, broadband Internet, and television programming can come from one or separate providers to one household).[17]

A brand-loyal user of a product would likely respond differently to a sales promotion than a customer who typically purchases a competing brand. This changes the strategy of sales promotion. One goal may be directed to brand switchers, those not yet strongly loyal to one given brand. These customers may be newer to the product category and not yet have the experience on which to base loyalty. They may switch as a response to market efforts by various brands or as a way to collect information from experience. Indeed, within most product categories it is rare to find consumers who exclusively purchase one brand, and thus a brand-loyal consumer may be considered one who (usually) purchases a given brand.[18] A potential additional goal of sales promotion is to create an impact on brand equity and thus loyalty to the brand. One study, described below, evaluated whether sales promotions consisting of bonus merchandise with each order would reinvigorate purchases by "lapsed" customers.

SALES PROMOTION AND BRAND LOYALTY

In the long term, brand loyalty is perceived to be the key to sustainable competitive advantage.[19] Brand loyalty can be defined as the consumer's desire to buy the same brand on a regular basis. Just as people are more likely now than ever to change jobs, homes, even spouses, brand choice is also in question. New products, more media communicating choices, wider variety of distribution channels, and greater choice in financing lead to difficulty in maintaining loyalty. Shari Caldron attributes this decline in brand loyalty to rising consumer price sensitivity, a decrease in advertising effectiveness, and an increase in new brands.[20] As a result of these changes, marketers have become interested in the potential effect of price promotions on brand trial, repurchase intentions, and long-term brand loyalty.

As noted previously, just as there are many ways to understand loyalty, there are also many ways to influence and improve loyalty. The three M model proposes a strategy of measuring, modeling, and managing. Companies that measure customers beyond mere financial performance levels can be shown to have stronger performance than non-measurement-driven companies in multiple key indicators according to one source. A comparison of measurement-managed versus non-measurement-managed organizations showed that (a) 83 percent of the measurement-managed group were rated in the top third of their respective industries as compared to 52 percent for others, (b) 74 percent are recognized as industry leaders versus only 44 percent for nonmeasurement organizations, (c) 80 percent realized a three-year positive return on investments as compared to 45 percent for non-measurement-managed organizations, and (d) a whopping 97 percent of measurement-managed organizations experienced success in their last major change effort compared to a 55-percent success rate for others.[21]

In order for measurement to be useful, the measures have to have some grounds in a realistic definition and theory. The best definition is one that is consistent with how other related concepts are present in an overall theory or model. Statisticians have developed a way to evaluate whether cause-and-effect relationships really hold through chains of variables. These causal modeling techniques allow marketing managers to put their concepts of the marketplace, including influences and effects of brand loyalty, to the test.

It has been said that knowledge becomes power only when it is put to use. That simple perspective summarizes the essence of any marketing management theory, but was offered as the reasoning behind the third M of the strategy, managing customer loyalty. For the process to work, the loyalty measures have to become part of assessment of brand management, internal relationships within the organization, part of the objectives for quality improvement, and a way to track and direct other customer research. This can be accomplished through strategic planning around loyalty management, senior-level adherence to the models, communication of loyalty trends and goals throughout the organization, and the building of an overall culture that recognizes the importance of loyalty.[22]

Often it is the brand-loyal consumers who benefit most from a pricing promotion versus more novice consumers. This is attributed to the fact that brand-loyal consumers have greater exposure and greater knowledge of actual market conditions of their brand.[23] In an analysis of price-related promotions across 13 different product categories, Andrew S. C. Ehrenberg, Kathy Hammond, and G. J. Goodhardt found price promotions often reward the brand's existing customers.[24] Consumers rarely respond to a price promotion if the brand has not previously been tried. When these one-off purchases do occur, it is the result of a "selective consumer reaction" not likely to result in additional brand-loyal customers, according to the researchers. At best, these are temporary brand switchers.

Brand loyalty may seem strong, yet still be short-lived, leaving brands vulnerable. In research of brand loyalty across 27 brands, Allan Baldinger and Joel Rubinson noted that after a year only 53 percent of "high loyalty" users remained highly loyal to the brand.[25] These authors identified three distinct loyalty groups: (1) high loyals, who have a 50-percent probability of purchasing the brand, (2) moderate loyals, those having a 10- to 50-percent probability of purchasing the brand, and (3) low loyals and nonbuyers, having a 0- to 9-percent probability of purchasing the brand. The brand loyalty of moderate loyals, who may or may not buy the brand on any given occasion, can be enhanced through promotional programs. Price promotions such as rebates, cash discounts, and other promotional offers can serve as a mechanism to say "thank you" and recognize and reward long-term loyal customers. Therefore, making the promotion a reward rather than an enticement at least for the long term can serve as a positive reinforcement for loyal purchasers of the brand.

Price promotion strategies have been linked directly to customer brand loyalty. One study found that if all brands in a product market have high brand loyalty, price promotions will not be useful to any of the brands. In more competitive markets, where both stronger and weaker brands compete, the picture is more complicated. When a stronger brand competes with a weaker one, the stronger should use promotion less often. Brand loyalty was found to have the potential to explain the use of price promotion as well as the frequency and depth of discounts in various markets. "The data are consistent with the finding that there is a positive correlation between the number of competitors and a brand's likelihood of using price promotions in a product market, and that stronger brands promote less often than weaker brands."[26]

Another potential goal for sales promotion is to address the "moderate loyals" or "system beaters" who are not yet loyal users of the brand, but have the greatest potential for becoming long-term brand-loyal consumers. Sales promotions reinforce the brand for this group, and some people may even convert into highly loyal product purchasers.

Simply put, "a loyalty program must enhance the overall value-proposition of the product or service. This in turn will help to motivate buyers to make the next purchase of a product and therefore support other aspects of the firm's offensive and defensive marketing strategy."[27]

AN EXAMPLE WITH LAPSED BUSINESS BUYERS

A Midwest medical products company (MedProd) wanted to find a way to increase response rates from its current direct mail marketing campaign. MedProd sought to increase sales from its database of physicians and physician suppliers. Checking the files, a three-year sales history showed that sales levels had stagnated at just over $3 million. Relatively few new customers were placing orders, just over 600 per quarter.

With these numbers leading into the study period, MedProd was anxious to find a way to reinvigorate its direct marketing. The company felt that previously loyal customers could be brought back, with the right incentives. Prior studies have shown that, in business-to-business situations suppliers who formed close working relationships with customers tended to experience more loyalty and to receive a greater proportion of the orders. Further, the customers found that they enjoyed "better" suppliers when the relationships were stronger.[28] So it makes sense to strengthen ties with prior customers who may have grown to feel neglected or unappreciated.

The company found that it had a significant number of these customers lapsing over time. By one measure, customers were falling off at a rate of 726 each month in the "lapsed from 4 to 12 months" category. These lapsed customers were to be the target audience for the sales promotion program. To ensure a more valid study, the company focused its efforts on two subsegments of customers in only one sector of the business. Although the company deals in both equipment and nonequipment merchandise, the study would examine only the more frequently purchased nonequipment goods.

How important are the lapsed customers? Too often, marketing departments obsess over acquisition of new customers and retention of current customers without sufficient attention to profitability or cost-effectiveness. Beyond a certain point the cost of acquisition or retention may exceed the revenues generated. Many methods are available to assess the value of customers and compare that value to the cost of service. One such model in a consumer domain is ARPRO (Allocating Resources for Profits), a regression analysis that combines behavioral and psychographic descriptions of a company's customer base with the buying behavior and cost of serving those customers.[29]

At the time of the promotion test, customers who had lapsed between 4 and 12 months numbered 5,809 with an average (nonequipment) prior order of $83.82. Data on longer lapsed customers, those without an order in the prior 13 to 33 months (longest consecutive data available) counted 5,120 in this group, with prior average orders of $83.35.

Each group contributed a sample of 2,500 names for a test of a direct mail program designed to reactivate their business. The program consisted of a self-mailing over the course of 90 days.

The products promoted in the mailings were selected to be appropriate for lapsed customers, popular, and of general usability. These were chosen from among MedProd's most popular stock keeping units (SKUs) as well as the SKUs that were most popular among the specific target audiences. The same products were featured in each of the mailings. Additionally, three products per mailing were featured in a separate insert as further promotions. This amounted to a total of nine new products being featured in each communication.

The sales promotions that were used to stimulate purchases were FREE offers with a qualifying purchase. The first mailing offered free self-grip tape. For the second incentive, free X-ray envelopes were offered. Finally, one pint of a specific medical product was featured in the third promotion. In each case, a $50 purchase was required in order to qualify for the free gift.

The initial mailing was sent to all of the 5,000 customers who had been selected. The sampling used a replacement approach; that is, as initial customers purchased, they were removed from the mailing list and new customers were added from the appropriate list of lapsed accounts. The second mailing went to 4,735 addresses one month after the first mailing. The third mailing, an additional month later, was sent to 4,494 addresses. There was a total of 6,001 unique addresses in the final database.

Purchases could be tracked to a specific mailer either by customer identification or by citing an assigned code. Despite instructions, 85 percent of those ordering from the mailer did not mention the code specifically. Overall, the multiple coding systems enabled a very good measure of effectiveness.

By the end of the trial period, 987 of the targeted customers had placed orders totaling over $140,000. This level of reactivation was achieved at a cost of $29,000 over the course of three months.

The mail program was successful with the customers, achieving many of the company objectives. Both segments purchased SKUs in the database, whether they cited the offer or not. A total of 987 customers from a total group of 6,001 responded for an average response rate of 16.4 percent. Spending level per customer increased from $83.00 to $145.98 during the study period. The return on marketing investment was estimated at 4.87. This level of return was determined to be acceptable, given the goals of the company. There is a further expectation that returned customers will become once again loyal.

BUSINESS-TO-CONSUMER EXAMPLE

In the business-to-consumer realm, sales promotions and loyalty may interact positively as well. Promotions encourage customer activity—visits and/or purchases—without which loyalty programs cannot benefit the participants. The trick is to avoid the discounting effect that may result from customers attributing their own purchase behavior to the deals. Promotions have to be designed to reinforce relationships to encourage loyalty.[30]

Aradhna Krishna, Imran S. Curim, and Robert W. Shoemaker proposed a model that can be used to understand the response to sales promotion.[31] As shown in Figure 9.1, the model suggests relationships among sales promotions,

Figure 9.1
Model of Promotional Activity

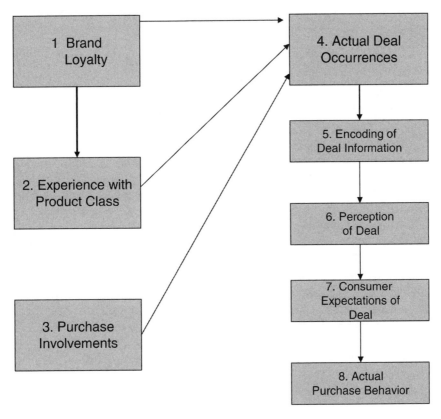

Source: Adapted from Krishna, Aradhn, Imran S. Curim, and Robert W. Shoemaker, "Consumer Perceptions of Promotion Activity," *Journal of Marketing,* 55 (1991): 4–16.

consumer characteristics, product characteristics, and managerial actions. A reduced version of that model has been evaluated in a business-to-consumer context.

This framework proposes that rational consumers respond to promotions through a thoughtful information processing. Brand loyalty, experience with the product class, level of involvement, and consumer characteristics combine to generate customer response. Responses to promotions can be estimated as resulting from individual consumer characteristics including (1) frequency of shopping, (2) brand loyalty, (3) interest in deals, (4) frequency of exposure to actual market conditions, and (5) degree of involvement and ability to encode information.

These elements of the model were evaluated in a study looking at consumer response to promotions for paint.[32] Paint was chosen because consumers have a range of experience levels, and they tend to plan purchases of the product for specific uses. Paint does not store well enough to be stockpiled for long periods, so demand cannot be skewed excessively. However, paint has a relatively high per unit price, so price-related promotions are more valuable and more immediately attractive to customers.

Paint promotion was tested using a nationally branded product sold through large building supply centers, home centers, and independent specialty paint stores. The price promotion consisted of a rebate on the paint product over a six-week period in the southeastern United States. Consumers were offered a $4.00 per unit rebate on a $22.00 product, resulting in an 18-percent price reduction per unit. Purchases of between 2 and 25 units qualified for the rebate.

A dealer promotion supplemented the consumer promotion. Dealers were offered a special purchase incentive of a 5-percent discount off the invoice, a special cooperative advertising program for newspaper advertising, and an upgraded point-of-purchase merchandising display. A total of 4,478 rebates were redeemed by consumers during the eligible promotional period. A mail survey was sent to the first 3,500 rebate redeemers and 385 completed questionnaires were returned.

Low- and high-loyalty groups were compared and differed significantly on two measures of consumer perception of the deal. Consumers who were more brand loyal had higher perceptions of the quality of the promoted product. Likewise, consumers who were more brand loyal had higher perceptions of the attractiveness of the promoted price than those consumers who were less brand loyal.

What happened with actual purchasing? Were there any differences among loyalty groups? The more loyal buyers had higher perceptions of the quality and value of the promotion. These loyalists also purchased significantly more units of the promoted product than did their less loyal counterparts. Purchase volumes also showed a loyalty effect. Although users categorized as "high loyal" were only 26 percent of the sample, they purchased 43 percent of the product sold during the promotion period. Consistent with this finding, the "low loyal" group, 23 percent of the sample, purchased less than 5 percent of the product sold during the deal period.[33]

These results suggest a new perspective on customer response. Traditionally, sales promotions have been viewed solely as a mechanism for producing immediate short-term sales effects. Promotions have been assailed as the very "antithesis" of rewarding loyalty. Manufacturer positioning suffers to benefit the short-term gains of retailers.[34] Now it seems that viewing sales promotions as merely a tool for achieving short-term goals may not be valid. Loyal buyers have a considerably more positive perception of the deal, which translates into higher purchase volumes. This may be due to their added knowledge. Therefore, sales promotions may assist in sustaining long-term product loyalty of present users. This is in addition to their more traditional role of creating trial among new users. For the brand-loyal consumer, a price promotion can serve to encourage repeat usage and neutralize the competition.[35]

There is another potential explanation for the effects on loyalty. Loyal customers may have more realistic (lower) expectations of product performance than those customers attracted for the first time by advertising or other marketing communications. The reduced expectations meet the actual performance, and enhanced satisfaction levels result. The more satisfied customers are then more likely to become loyal customers, requiring less investment to create or maintain brand loyalty.

This study provides further evidence that brand managers must concentrate their focus on the highly loyal consumer who purchases in considerably higher volumes than their less loyal counterparts. In this field study investigation, for example, the highly loyal group purchased an average of 8.92 units compared to 5.58 units for moderately loyal brand users and 4.71 for low loyals. While together the high brand loyals and moderate loyals produced 95.5 percent of the revenues, based on the amount of product sold during the promotional period, these two groups comprised only 77 percent of the firm's customers.

To neutralize the effects of intense competition, marketing managers must begin to view sales promotions as a brand management strategy to improve relationships with the existing customer base, while avoiding the promotion-only buying behavior of some customers.[36] In this field study of a price-based paint promotion, very real differences existed between high, moderate, and low loyalty consumers. Highly loyal consumers have a considerably higher perception of the deal than those who are less loyal to the promoted brand. This relationship was true for both quality perceptions as well as price perceptions.

The research found that highly loyal customers, who bought the brand during the promotional period, had quality perceptions that were nearly 40 percent higher than their low loyal counterparts. Likewise, the perception that the promotion made the price attractive was nearly 70 percent higher for the highly loyal group as compared to the low loyal group. As reflected in the Krishna, Curim, and Shoemaker model, these higher perceptions of the deal led to higher consumer expectations of the deal, and ultimately higher purchase volume for the promoted brand.[37] It seems clear from the results of this study that brand loyalty may be critical in determining the impact of a price-based promotion. This research also found that experience with the product class was not a significant criterion associated with perceptions of the deal or participation in the price-based promotion.

There are other processes that might add to the effectiveness of sales promotion on brand loyalty. Promotions that are repeated over time or require some input from the customer might make the experience "sticky," to use an e-commerce term. That is, the customer's personal investment and involvement may encourage returning to the process if for no other reason than merely to amortize that investment. This may be true, in particular, if the transaction occurred in a service environment. Whatever the case, if customer performance is required to redeem a promotion, the event becomes a "coproduction experience." Customers who become involved in these more elaborate transactions may play their role in one of these ways:

Transactionals. They like to execute everyday business themselves. They use self-checkout at the grocery store, eat at buffets, and book travel online.

Traditionals. They favor do-it-yourself in terms of home improvement, gardening, financial management, auto repairs, and so on. They frequent The Home Depot, Smith & Hawken, Charles Schwab Corporation, and Kragen Auto Parts.

Conventionals. They acquire tangible, self-contained products that enable them to perform tasks independently. For example, a Viking stove facilitates gourmet cooking, and a snow blower clears snow from a driveway.

Intentionals. They engage in coproduction experiences to customize goods and services (for example, at Build-A-Bear Workshop or at the Nike iD.com design center where customers can create their own pair of athletic shoes).

Radicals. They take coproduction experiences to new extremes. They include the man in California who modified his Toyota Prius's batteries to achieve 80 miles per gallon and the Apple iPod aficionados who create podcasts (audio programs featuring comedy, music, and sports).[38]

In order to make the process as simple, yet involving, as possible, it is important to manage the process of promotion redemption. To the extent that customer participation is required to return rebate forms, track usage, register for sweepstakes, or perform any of a myriad of tasks, the promotion manager must take care to create a "designed experience." That is, cross-functional teams integrate company and customer feedback into the process specification.

If the process of claiming a sales promotion incentive creates a delay or is problematic for the customer, the value of that promotion in creating motivation to purchase or to remain loyal is jeopardized. That is why accumulating benefit programs, such as frequent flyer promotions from airlines or points clubs from credit cards or retailers, send regular statements of progress toward the next level of promotion. Often these statements include further reinforcement for the program and the rewards to be gained. This reduces the need for record keeping by the customer and potentially alleviates the stress for those personality types who do not choose to invest in monitoring their own performance in the promotional experience.[39]

GENERAL CONCLUSIONS

The traditional view of sales promotions as being good for short-term effects alone has been shown to be outdated. Loyal customers are more aware of the true value of deals they receive, are often more invested in acquiring those deals, have experienced learning as part of the deal process, and feel more positively about the deal provider. All of this argues for a stronger effect on loyalty of sales promotion than had been understood previously.

Sales promotions do not always create negative attributions of value and quality, nor do they diminish the value of relationships between sellers and buyers (whether trade or consumers). In fact, some promoted products have rated higher in quality after the promotion, when tested. Sales promotions can reward loyalty rather than replace loyalty.

NOTES

1. "A Summary of U.S. Trade Promotion Practices," http://us.acnielsen.com/pubs/2005_q2_ci_tpp.shtml.
2. Neff, Jack, "P&G Trims Fat off Its $2B Trade-Promotion System," *Advertising Age* 77, no. 23 (June 5, 2006): 8, via EBSCOhost.
3. Barrand, Drew, "Sales Promotion Top 45," *Marketing (UK)* (October 6, 2004): 35–41, via EBSCOhost.
4. Lester, Robert, "Time to Take a Break from Sales Promotion?" *Marketing Week* (November 18, 2004): 24–25.
5. Ibid.
6. Seligman, Terri J., "Marketing through Online Promotions," *The Computer & Internet Lawyer* 21, no. 4 (April 2004): 22–26.
7. Barrand, "Sales Promotion Top 45."
8. Neff, Jack, "P&G Slits Own Throat with Razor Promotion," *Advertising Age* 76, no. 40 (October 3, 2005): 6, via EBSCOhost.
9. Lester, "Time to Take a Break from Sales Promotion?"
10. Molla, Tony, "High-Performance Promotion," *Aftermarket Business* (May 2004): 60–63.
11. Barrand, "Sales Promotion Top 45."
12. Vuyk, Chris, "Promotions: Understanding the Impact," *Beverage World,* 23, no. 3 (March 15, 2004): 84.
13. Ehrenberg, Andrew S.C., Kathy Hammond, and G.J. Goodhardt, "The After-Effects of Price Related Consumer Promotions," *Journal of Advertising Research,* 34 (July 1994), 4.
14. Promotion Marketing Association, "7th Annual State-of-the-Promotion Industry—2005 Report,"
15. Dowling, Grahame, and Mark Uncles, "Do Customer Loyalty Programs Really Work?" Research Brief 001 Centre for Corporate Change at the Australian Graduate School of Management.
16. *RCR Wireless News,* "Survey Finds Little Impact from LNP," February 9, 2004.
17. Dowling and Uncles, "Do Customer Loyalty Programs Really Work?"
18. Totten, John C., and Martin Block, *Analyzing Sales Promotions,* 2nd ed. (Chicago: The Dartnell Corporation, 1996).
19. Aaker, David A., *Building Strong Brands* (New York: The Free Press, 1996).

20. Caldron, Shari, "Brand Loyalty: Can It Be Revived?" *Industry Week* (April 1993), 11–12, 14.

21. Crosby, Lawrence A., and Sheree L. Johnson, "The Three Ms of Customer Loyalty," *Marketing Management* (July/August 2004), 12–13.

22. Ibid.

23. Aaker, *Building Strong Brands*.

24. Ehrenberg et al., "The After-Effects of Price Related Consumer Promotions."

25. Baldinger, Allan, and Joel Rubinson, "Brand Loyalty: The Link between Attitude and Behavior," *Journal of Advertising Research*, 36 (November/December 1996), 22–34.

26. Raju, Jagmohan S., V. Srinivasan, and Rajiv Lal, "The Effects of Brand Loyalty on Competitive Price Promotional Strategies," *Management Science* 36 (March 1990), 276–304.

27. Dowling and Uncles, "Do Customer Loyalty Programs Really Work?" p. 1

28. Dowling and Uncles, "Do Customer Loyalty Programs Really Work?"

29. Thomas, Jacquelyn S., Werner Reinartz, and V. Kumar, "Getting the Most out of All Your Customers," *Harvard Business Review* (July–August 2004), 116–123.

30. Ruszala, Jim, "Promotions and Loyalty Can Play Nice," *Direct* (July, 2004): 47.

31. Krishna, Aradhna, Imran S. Curim, and Robert W. Shoemaker, "Consumer Perceptions of Promotion Activity," *Journal of Marketing*, 55 (1991): 4–16.

32. Owens, Deborah L., Michael Hardman, and Bruce Keillor, "The Differential Impact of Price-Related Consumer Promotions on Loyal versus Non-Loyal Users of the Brand: A Field Study Investigation," *Journal of Promotion Management* 6 (January/February 2001): 113–131.

33. Ibid.

34. Bashford, Suzy, "Price Promotion: The Brand Killer," *Marketing (UK)* (June 30, 2004): 42–43.

35. Totten and Block, *Analyzing Sales Promotions*.

36. Dowling and Uncles, "Do Customer Loyalty Programs Really Work?"

37. Krishna et al., "Consumer Perceptions of Promotion Activity."

38. Honebein, Peter C., and Roy F. Cammarano, "Customers at Work," *Marketing Management* (January/February 2006): 26–31.

39. Dowling and Uncles, "Do Customer Loyalty Programs Really Work?"

CHAPTER 10

WHEN PERCEIVED VALUE IS FLEETING: PROMOTION OF EVENTS

Rob Piekarczyk

Something that strikes me as funny is, if you think back to the most recent NFL Super Bowl, can you recall which teams participated? However, you could start a weeklong debate regarding the best commercial on the live television broadcast. For the organizations that pay millions of dollars for the 30-second commercial spots, one can ask, is it worth the money for the exposure? There are hard numbers that can be reviewed regarding the television coverage, overall event attendance figures, and other statistics, but it is difficult to assign a monetary value to return on investment. Looking at those figures, it is easy to ask the question, is an event worth being a part of and, if so, why? In this chapter we are going to look at event marketing from several different angles to better understand why billions of dollars worldwide are spent each year to be a part of something that really may not give any immediate tangible results.

AN EVENT: THOSE INVOLVED

The most notable participants in event marketing are the organizations that give money to the event, otherwise known as sponsors. A sponsor invests in an event for many reasons that can include television exposure, brand association, or insert-your-favorite marketing buzzword here. Ultimately an organization invests in what it hopes will deliver a strong marketing message that will produce measurable results.

Next we need to look at the other obvious participant of an event, the viewer. The viewer can be at the event in person, watching on the television, listening on the radio, and reading print media revolving around the event. Viewers may have several reasons why they are attentive, most of which are positive, and as such, they can be very impressionable. There is always a "feeling" associated with an event, and if an organization can tap into the positive feelings of the viewer, a bond begins to form. This starts the snowball effect that will eventually lead to tangible results, though they might not be immediate.

Finally we need to look at the event promoter. After all, this is a business world, and there needs to be an entity to not only organize the event but also to reap the financial benefits. The promoter is the machine that serves as the hub and the catalyst for all activities that make the event a roaring success or a miserable failure. We need to look at the promoter from the inside to better understand what must take place to ensure that the event is a success.

THE SPONSOR

At face value, most view a sponsor as a company that wants its logo visible on TV or to the local spectator base. To a point this is an accurate assumption, as most sponsors do want to receive the value of logo exposure at an event. However, if a sponsorship is done properly, it should serve as much more than just logo exposure. We need to look at why an organization would want to sponsor a particular event and how a sponsorship can be utilized as a multifaceted function to benefit many business units within an organization.

To better understand how to fully activate a sponsorship gaining the most bang for the marketing buck, we first have to look at why an organization would want to spend valuable marketing dollars to be a part of an event.

A.R.E.: Association, Retention, Expansion

Association

Why would a company want to be associated with an event? Let us use auto racing as an example to further develop the concept of being associated with an event or, in this case, sport.

Auto racing in many parts of the world is considered to be a sport on the cutting edge of technology; it is fast-paced and exciting. Our first example would seem to be an obvious one, that of Red Bull energy drink sponsoring Formula One cars. Red Bull spends millions of dollars—$110 million in 2005—supporting four race cars in Formula One, which is the pinnacle of motorsports technology and automotive development. Formula One is enjoyed by fans who are attracted to the speed, energy, sights, and sounds that make up what is essentially nothing more than humans in cars driving really fast. However, the passion that these spectators have for their beloved Formula One drives them to be associated with an activity that they perceive as sexy and energetic. Red Bull has targeted this demographic and views the association as a way to bridge the gap between the sport and the fan, which ultimately generates revenue for Red Bull.

To find a less obvious example of brand association, we are going to shift our thinking from sports to entertainment. The Hershey Company, the confectionary company, sponsors a country concert that travels to 35 venues throughout the United States. Looking at this at face value, it may not seem to make much sense. However, an understanding of its target demographic will help us to better understand why it sees value in sponsoring a concert tour. Hershey's corporate image is family oriented and wholesome. By sponsoring the "Tim and Faith Soul2Soul II" concert tour, it is strategically aligning itself with a couple (Tim McGraw and Faith Hill) that people view as a wholesome, down-to-earth family. What gives this sponsorship added value is that it travels throughout the country, hitting major markets with the same association of product and wholesome goodness of a highly visible country music family.

Retention

Retention refers to keeping loyalty with current customers. According to Scarborough Research, event fans are 64 percent more likely to have a loyalty to a sponsoring brand than a nonsponsoring brand. For example, Mercedes-Benz has been the title sponsor of the Mercedes-Benz Championship since 2004. Though the association between Mercedes and golf is pretty obvious, as golf has always been considered a sport for the more affluent, the retention factor will take a little more thought. The Mercedes customer who enjoys golf comes to expect that the Mercedes Championship will occur every year and, as such, he or she will remain loyal to the brand. Though it cannot be directly correlated quantitatively, one can make the assumption that if BMW were to entitle the tournament, the loyal Mercedes customers are likely to become slightly annoyed that their favorite brand no longer supports the traditional event. Even though the customer may still have a loyalty to the Mercedes brand, there would be a gap that may allow another brand to sabotage that loyalty.

Expansion

Every company wants to obtain new customers and create a greater brand awareness. On a global scale, this may be the largest contributing factor in the decision-making process in whether or not to sponsor an event. Every four years the Olympics serves as a global marketing platform that, though expensive, gives an excellent opportunity to reach millions of fans and viewers (184 million in the United States alone for the 2006 Winter Olympics). VISA, the "Official Credit Card of the 2006 Winter Olympics," spent millions of dollars for the rights to that sponsorship. Through the association with the Olympic Games, it used this sponsorship globally to expand business into new areas and to convert those who were using a competitive product.

THE AUDIENCE

Event marketing would be difficult to justify from a business standpoint if there was not an audience to receive the message that is trying to be communicated. An audience can consist of event attendees or those who pay attention to any other form of public media. Most of the time, the audience is voluntarily subjecting itself to the event and therefore is more receptive to a marketing message. The challenge that event marketers face is how to keep a consistent and effective message through each form of media to best maximize each dollar that is spent.

First, let us talk about the event attendee. The attendee can best be defined as the individual who attends the event in person. Voluntarily, this person has made the decision to witness firsthand, and this decision makes him or her an obvious target for a marketing message. Being that the person has decided he or she wants to attend the event, we can assume that he or she has a positive association with the event, which creates a tremendous loyalty to brands that have a presence. A perfect example would be the Rite Aid Cleveland Marathon. Rite Aid is a locally based pharmacy and convenience store chain located in the Cleveland, Ohio, area. Knowing that the attending audience is predominantly from its geographic area, Rite Aid is able to create several messages that impact the local attendees effectively. First, the Rite Aid sponsorship of the Cleveland Marathon creates an association with a healthy lifestyle. Second, and possibly more important, is that Rite Aid supports the local community. Many organizations utilize sponsorships on a local level to show support for the local community, which is a terrific way to win over customers within that community. Though a local sponsorship is a smaller dollar amount, there can be effective ways to generate awareness in key targeted areas.

Second, we should look at the viewer, or the person who does not attend the event in person but uses a different form of media to learn of the event. Let us turn our attention back to motorsports by analyzing Budweiser and its involvement in the NASCAR Nextel Cup Series. Budweiser is the primary sponsor for Dale Earnhardt, Jr., who was voted most popular NASCAR driver starting in 2003. Dale's image is young and edgy as well as fashionably trendy. Although the image is somewhat subjective, these intangible qualities make the association for Budweiser key to reaching one of its target demographics. Knowing that Earnhardt Jr. is viewed so highly by NASCAR fans, Budweiser is able to dovetail onto the same loyalty that generates $40 million worth of merchandise revenue per year. Although the attendee marketing for Budweiser is also a success, the television broadcast and print media that cover each NASCAR event are equally effective mediums. For the 2006 season, NASCAR had an estimated 570 million television viewers and countless others that read attentively about the sport. Simply put, if you ask any NASCAR fan who drives the Budweiser car, you can safely assume that he or she will know the correct answer.

Previously in this chapter we discussed the association of a sponsor with the feelings of the audience. This point is key to understanding how successful sponsorships work so effectively. To illustrate this, let us think in slight generality and look at a bridal fair. Typically these fairs are attended by brides-to-be or by someone who is a part of the wedding planning process. Since weddings are typically viewed as a positive emotional experience, those who attend are prime targets for association with a sponsor who is supporting this important event in their personal lives. The power of emotion is very influential in the consumer decision-making process, and the best sponsors realize this potential business opportunity.

THE PROMOTER

Just as the brain controls the human body, the promoter is the nerve center of an event. Given the nature of an event, there are various branches within the promoter that consist of varying responsibilities involving the organization, promotion, and revenue generation of an event, all of which lead to the ultimate goal of profitability. We need to look closely at an event promoter to understand all aspects of event promotion and what needs to happen to run a successful event.

What is an event promoter? Typically, though not always, a promoter is a third-party organization that specializes in event promotion. Within this organization, there are departments that include sales, marketing, operations, government relations, and accounting. Though many of these cross over into each other's domain, we need to look at each business unit separately to understand how it fits into the organization.

SALES

Sales is probably the most easily identifiable and definable group within an event promotion organization. Most simply put, the sales department generates revenue. To help pay for the event staff, location, and operational expenses, there must be a flow of cash to the event; otherwise that event will not be around for very long. The revenue generation can take many forms.

The most common form of revenue is event sponsorship. This is where the highest profit margin lies for the promoter, as depending on how the contract is structured, there is relatively little cost that the promoter incurs. In essence, the sponsor is paying for the "rights" to be associated with the event. Those rights, though they can be assigned a value, are more or less an intangible asset that illustrates the earlier discussion about Association. For example, Tostitos annually sponsors the NCAA College Football "Tostitos Fiesta Bowl." Although the promoter sold the naming rights to the game—and I promise you it was a lucrative deal—the cost to the promoter to do this was minimal though the revenue generated was immense.

Another form of revenue is through the sales of corporate entertainment, otherwise known as hospitality. Although a corporate suite, whatever form it may take (lodge, chalet, and so forth), may seem to be nothing more than a place to eat and drink for free, it does serve as a major point of positive cash flow for an event. Most of the time there is a hard cost associated to the suite that takes away slightly from the revenue, but the profitability still remains fairly high. Different venues will have varying profit margins due to operational costs, but rarely does that number fall below 50 percent. Suites are purchased for varying reasons, but always serve as a terrific venue for business activities such as client entertainment, employee appreciation, and even consumer promotions.

Sales can also involve what we can refer to as "second-tier" revenue generators. The second-tier generators can include advertising in a program, vendor space to sell or promote merchandise at the event, video screen advertisements (if applicable), in addition to other less valuable assets of the event. Though comparatively smaller than a sponsorship, the percentage margins are still relatively high for the second-tier sales and can serve as a substantial revenue generator.

Up until now we have not spoken much about trade, otherwise known as barter, but we certainly need to address it. Usually the sales department takes a look at top line numbers. However, events live and die by the bottom line. As we move further along into our discussion of the promoter, we will discuss operations and the costs associated with that. Where sales crosses into operations oftentimes starts with a barter agreement. For example, an event may need $20,000 worth of telephone service to function effectively. Rather than pay the $20,000 tab, an organization can offer up some of its assets in trade reflecting that amount. Although the number does not hit the sales top line, the $20,000 will never hit the bottom line for telephone service. When used effectively, barter is a way to save costs that would otherwise be incurred by the promoter.

MARKETING

In its purest sense, the main goal of marketing is to gain awareness for an entity or product. Event marketing does not differ greatly from that concept. To that point, we need to look at a few of the activities that make up what we refer to as "marketing an event."

First, let us examine traditional marketing to the spectator. To give value to all entities participating in an event, there needs to be an audience. The scope of the event and the audience outreach will determine the marketing strategy.

Although it is possible to purchase media marketing time, most organizations cannot afford to effectively market in this medium because it is strictly a function of cost. If done wisely, media marketing time can be traded off to effectively benefit both parties without a money exchange. This is an extremely beneficial way to utilize a barter arrangement. Please take note, however, that not all media marketing is necessarily applicable or effective for an event.

When marketing an event, keep in mind that the scope of the intended audience directly dictates how and where advertising should be placed. For example, if a local fair were being advertised that might have only 10,000 local attendees, purchasing a television spot on an international broadcast would be overkill. Similarly, while marketing the Olympic Games, it does not make much sense to advertise in every small town weekly bulletin. It is crucial to assess and understand your market through extensive research, identify the most efficient way to get in front of your target market, and then make a decision on how to best reach it.

Timing is everything. It is commonly thought that to make a lasting impact on an individual, he or she must see or hear a message three times before acting upon it. As such, depending on the purchase cycle, messages must be placed at key times. If the purchase is more of an impulse buy, such as a ticket for an event, a two-week marketing blitz may be the best way to go. Conversely, when soliciting sponsorship, which can take an extended amount of time to convert a sale, the messages should be spread out over a longer time period.

Another fantastic way to reach part of a target audience is through public appearances. Depending on the size of the event and the marketing budget, this can reach a fair amount of individuals. Let us look at how to utilize this for a larger event first. For the 2005 Indianapolis 500, the Indy Racing League staged a public photo with each participating race car driver on Times Square. Although only the New York City public saw the appearance in person, the images taken of that public appearance were seen in magazines and newspapers throughout the world. This is a great example of a very effective public appearance on a large-scale audience. In contrast, a local radio station may be out promoting one of its summertime concerts by having a personality or DJ roaming the streets asking silly questions. Again, this individual is in the public, and though only those in the area can see this person, the promotion is heard over the radio waves and perceived as if the listener were taking part in the conversation as well. This is a very effective public appearance on a small scale, as it still reaches a vast majority of the target audience without much cost involved.

Now let us look at public relations (PR), which if done correctly, not only serves as damage control but also as a tremendous way to make an impact on a local community. For example, many events donate a portion of their profits to local charities. Not only is this an ethical thing to do, but it also reaches into the heart of the audience, showing that the event is a responsible part of a community no matter the scope of the community. An effective PR group can create such a positive image for an event; it is an essential part that may not often be thought of, but can be sorely missed if not present.

OPERATIONS

Serving as the backstage crew, the operations group within an event plays an integral part in the overall marketing success of an event. As the old saying goes, the greatest ideas are nothing without a well thought-out plan. The operations group implements the ideas that top-level management determines need to take place. But the question can be asked, how does operations fit into the overall marketing of an event?

Operational planning, if done properly, will be able to maximize assets that an event has and develop a method to achieve the set goal. For example, let us look at the Grand Prix of Cleveland, a Champ Car World Series auto race that is held on airport runways. One of the most obvious aspects of this event is the fact that it is held on what serve as airport runways for 362 days out of the year. For three days, this venue is morphed into a temporary racetrack. Assets that are difficult to take advantage of, but obvious to see, are the actual runways themselves. While marketing the event to potential sponsors, the airport venue offers a unique opportunity for an organization to utilize a facility outside of the norm. In 2002, FedEx Corporation wanted to place an airplane on the runway while the race was going on, and it offered a large sum of money for the rights to display the airplane during the race. It was the operations group, headed by Vice President of Operations Graham Hearns, that logistically made it possible to land an airplane on the runway and have it safely staged for the racing activities.

It is crucial to remember that, although the operations group may not have a high-profile role in an event, it is a tremendous resource for event marketers. If approached properly, a sound operational plan can assist in maximizing a venue and all of the resources available for sponsors and attendees.

GOVERNMENT REGULATIONS

With any event, there needs to be a cognizant effort to ensure all activities are legally permissible. Not only are there local permit issues that need to be addressed, but from a marketing standpoint, event promoters have to make sure that advertising regulations are met as well.

International events are often some of the stickiest when it comes to advertising regulations, especially when it comes to sponsors. One of those sponsor categories that serves as a fantastic example of this is the tobacco industry. Many countries will not allow a tobacco company to sponsor an event or a sport, while others, like the United States, will allow only a certain number of sponsorships for a tobacco company. Let us look at a specific company that partakes in international marketing of events and how it is affected by local regulations.

Philip Morris USA, best known for its cigarettes, is a company that sells its tobacco products worldwide. Here in the United States, there was a law passed in 1997 by the Food and Drug Administration that states that a tobacco company may advertise in only one Auto Racing series. Marlboro, with its worldwide branding strategy, has sponsorships in many racing series, most notably in the United States within the Indy Racing League and also Formula One. It is up to Marlboro to decide which series it will support from an exposure perspective. Due to the sheer number of events, it has decided to place its logo on the U.S.-based Indy Racing League and Marlboro Team Penske.

So what about when Formula One races in the United States? Although there are not any regulations against supporting the Formula One efforts financially, Marlboro is not allowed to place a logo on the Scuderia Ferarri cars that it sponsors for the event held in the United States.

In sum, when marketing an event or events internationally, a considerable amount of homework must be done to make sure that there are not regulation infringements that could ultimately put a halt on all efforts.

MARKETING TO SPECTATORS: GET THEM TO ATTEND

To most people, time and money are valued commodities that are not spent without much thought. With this in mind, potential attendees must be approached with a message and product that appeals to them as a worthwhile venue to spend their valuable time and money. The question to ask is, how can we reach potential attendees cost-effectively with enough attraction for them to decide to attend the event?

First and foremost, an organization must conduct research to best understand what and who its target market is and what appeals to them. For example, let us assume we work for a promoter who is organizing a professional tennis tournament that hosts the top men and women players in the world. To a tennis fan, the event looks like an attractive way to spend a weekend. For the attendees who we know will purchase tickets, we need not worry too much about them because the content—tennis matches—is enough to bring them through the gates. The challenge is how to reach those who may or may not want to attend, and this is where research comes in. By setting geographic parameters and deciding how large the sample size should be, we can start to evaluate the best way to appeal to these folks. The key is not to ask what about tennis appeals to them, but instead focus on what other things attract them to spending money and time. Quite possibly we may find that our target market appreciates the very best of anything. To market to these folks, our message can focus on the fact that the best players are in this tournament and it offers a unique opportunity to see them all at one location. Another trend we may see is that our target market likes to attend social events for the opportunity to be around a crowd. If this is the case, focus on the fact that it is such a large event, and many networking opportunities possibly exist. The key point that must be understood is that there are other aspects, tangible and intangible, that will attract a nontennis fan to the event, and if those aspects are understood and marketed, the attendance level can increase tremendously.

Now that we have the message we want to send to our target market or markets, how can we effectively get into their brains to help them make the decision to attend the event? It has been shown that a message has to be seen at least three times before it is set in a person's memory. As such, repetition and consistency are key. Let us stick with the tennis tournament example we used previously. Taking our research that says our target markets are drawn to large events that showcase the best talent in a sport, our message should be, "The event that everyone is attending to see the very best talent in the world." Notice, there is no direct mention of the content, but since our research suggests that they just want to see the best of any sport, we seem to hit the mark. Also, we appealed to those who like to attend events. We do not want to forget the tennis aspect of the event, but that can be shown through images (if print media) or a quick mention of some of the players in the tournament (if broadcast media).

Most recently, the Internet has become a hot spot for event marketing and has proven a successful way to market. The 2006 Winter Olympics in Torino maintained the official site NBCOlympics.com; the site had 361 million page viewers, and 9.1 million streams of video were downloaded via the Internet. To reach that many people via a traditional marketing campaign, the financial commitment would be so large that it most likely would not be cost-effective. Conversely, the Internet provides an opportunity for fans to learn more of the event at their own leisure. As such, when marketing an event, it is easy to see why a well-designed Web site is an essential part of the marketing plan. Let us look at some examples of what can be displayed on a Web site to benefit the promoter from not only a viewer standpoint, but also from the revenue generation standpoint of the promoter.

First, how can you best utilize a Web site to help possible attendees and viewers? By creating a Web site that has both event information and marketing messages, a promoter is able to reach a vast audience, as was suggested earlier. Event information can include ticket prices, schedules, promotional opportunities, and merchandise. Many organizations are also including a merchandise page where event merchandise can be purchased ahead of time. Another bit of information that should be on an event Web site is up-to-date news about the event. This can be used as an avenue for not only updating attendees about what to look forward to, but it also serves as a great tool for public relations as well.

From a sponsor and hospitality standpoint, a Web site is also a critical piece of the puzzle. Here, we can include general demographic information so that a sponsor can analyze quickly if the event fits into its marketing scheme. Also, pricing and contact information along with photos illustrating sponsor activation should be included.

Some other ways of reaching the targeted attendee audience may not take much financial investment. First, we can look at public relations or local community involvement and appearances. An important point to remember for an event to appeal to the local community is that it must show support for that community. For example, a company could utilize the talents of theater performers in the local community to gain support and awareness. In most communities, there is some form of children's theater, whether it is organized by the local school system or a locally run organization. The performers can go to these local children's theaters and participate in their efforts, whether it is a rehearsal or some acting lessons. By giving back to the local community, an event gains tremendous favor and credibility in the minds of possible local attendees.

Staying within the local community, it is wise for any event to support a local charity. Many larger events will have a charity dinner where proceeds go to a local charity of choice. While at this dinner, items from the event can be auctioned off with proceeds going to the designated charity. Again, the focus on supporting the local community is a tremendous way to gain overall approval and support for an event.

A promoter can also utilize assets of the organizations that are sponsors of the event. Doing this, which is also termed sponsorship activation, can effectively reach the consumer base on a much larger scale. This time, let us look at a global sponsorship of an event: The Gillette Company's support of the 2006 FIFA World Cup. On its own, the World Cup is a spectacularly large event with over 3.3 million fans who attend and 1 billion who watch on television. However, it is difficult for an event such as the World Cup to reach fans on a more personal level. As Gillette is a product sold at retail locations throughout the world in various supermarkets, department stores, and other locations where hygiene products are sold, Gillette can fill the "personal" niche nicely. In the months leading up to the World Cup in addition to the duration of the 2006 World Cup, Gillette was running product promotions within the retail locations. This activation not only helped Gillette best utilize its sponsorship rights, but also provided the World Cup with added exposure without having to invest financially. To sum up this example, it is crucial for an event to support sponsors in any way possible to best activate their sponsorship, as it is a value-added effort for both the sponsor and the event.

MARKETING TO THE POTENTIAL SPONSOR

It is unusual for an event to be in such high demand that sponsors are begging to be a part of an event. As such, event organizers need to reach out to potential sponsoring companies with an appealing message that will illustrate clearly how being associated with an event will benefit them. It is not an easy thing to do, as companies are typically very tight when it comes to spending marketing money on special events. Let us look at what should make up a marketing plan when targeting potential sponsors.

First and foremost, the message should be focused completely on how the sponsoring company will benefit from a partnership with an event. Organizations are willing to spend money if they feel as though they are the ones benefiting from the expenditure. A good example of an effective marketing message to a potential sponsor emphasizes the assets of an event and how it can capitalize on the unique opportunity. For example, the Grand Prix of Houston, an international motorsports event held in Houston, Texas, promoted the event to sponsors with the message, "We offer a wide range of sponsorship opportunities that provide your brand with exposure to millions of consumers and businesses in Houston and around the world. Entertain clients, business associates and employees in a festive hospitality environment that is sure to impress. Promote your business with ticket promotions included in your sponsor package." This message is effective in communicating the different ways that a sponsor can benefit from being a partner with an international event held in the Houston market.

As we start to focus on particular sponsors, a marketing message needs to be catered specifically to a company's marketing message and needs. There are several ways to better understand what a company is looking for in a sponsorship. First and most simply, ask the company. Usually, an organization will be upfront in revealing what it hopes to accomplish and what message it hopes to convey. Other times, a little research in various forms of media will produce similar results. BP, the global oil empire, has changed the company acronym from standing for "British Petroleum" to "Beyond Petroleum," as it is pushing for an image of a more environmentally responsible company with developing technology that makes the world a cleaner place to live. As such, we could take this message and apply it to an event. Let us use a golf tournament as an example. How can we make the marriage between what BP is advertising and what the golf tournament can provide locally and internationally?

Locally, BP can utilize the attending spectators and show them hands-on what BP is doing to better the environment through interactive displays and demonstrations at the venue. Also, BP can have a presence in the community in the weeks leading up to the tournament, such as creating a small science fair for local high school students so they can understand how products of the future are being developed today. The key for BP is to be as visible in the marketplace as possible, associating the outdoor purity of golf with the development of "green" fuels that are friendly to the environment.

Internationally, we are assuming the tournament is covered on television and broadcast throughout the world. Although this is a more obvious approach to branding on a larger scale, television marketing is still tricky and needs to be addressed so that BP can understand how its message can effectively reach its intended market. First, BP should have television commercial time during the broadcast that explains what it is developing and how that will positively impact the global environment. Next, BP can promote segments of the show that not only focus on its efforts, but also how those developments relate to a golf course's environmental well-being. Moreover, the messages that are being communicated either locally or internationally must still remain consistent with each other.

The main point to understand when marketing to potential sponsors is that a promoter must be able to make the connection for the sponsor that shows how a sponsorship would be beneficial to them. Often sponsors rely completely on the promoter to assist them in making the most of a sponsorship and, as such, this process needs to begin with each marketing effort made to attract potential sponsoring organizations.

CONCLUSION

In conclusion, special events create a unique opportunity for organizations to reach attentive segments of their target markets. Whether the event is on a smaller local scale or on an international stage, we have discussed how an organization can effectively market through an event. We also touched on how an event can successfully market itself in order to ensure the overall profitability in the event promotion business. As organizations continue to spend money on sponsorships, which in turn fuels the event promotion industry, there must be an evolving understanding of how events can best be utilized to not only maximize the value of events for the sponsor, but also to increase profitability for the promoter.

CHAPTER 11

UNRAVELING THE WEB: SUCCESSFUL TOOLS FOR MARKETING ONLINE

Len Pagon and Paul Quigley

All business and consumer marketers of the 21st century need to extend themselves beyond traditional marketing channels to include the Internet in their go-to-market strategies. This demands that they be aware of the online channel and the unique challenges and opportunities created by it. The Internet is in a constant state of evolution and renewal, as consumers become more comfortable making purchases online, as high-speed (broadband) access and devices become more ubiquitous, and companies search for new and innovative ways to engage in a dialogue with their customers online. Need proof that it is a channel to be reckoned with? The numbers show that online sales are growing at a rate of 25–50 percent a year, and influencing 40–70 percent of all total retail sales. By the end of 2006, online sales are estimated to reach *$200 billion.*[1]

More importantly for marketers, though, is the driving force behind all business today—the shift in power from the company or the brand to the customer. Broadcast (Interruption) marketing strategies and techniques are creating so much noise for the consumer that postintroduction recognition rates have decreased. The Internet has opened a new channel to increase customer awareness, but it comes with a unique capacity—the user controls the information. Consumers not only decide what information they want to see, but how and when they want to see it. The power is now in the consumer's hands, and as marketers, the task is to adapt, and adapt quickly, to new ways of communicating information to a user group that is sometimes one (or many) steps ahead. This has created the demand for what is now called interactive or permission-based marketing.

One of the most alarming trends we see today in business is marketers who have not fully appreciated the need to modify their off-line tactics to adapt to the digital revolution. It is crucial, now more than ever, to develop relationships with your customers, keep up with the ever-changing online channel, and keep your brand and product offering consistent across channels to create success for your organization.

HOW THE EVOLUTION OF COMMUNICATION HAS AFFECTED THE END USER

The average American consumer gets inundated with nearly a million marketing messages a year—roughly 3,000 messages a day![2] As a human being, it is impossible to react to and register 3,000 calls for our attention a day. We are overwhelmed with messages: advertisements on billboards as we drive, calls from telemarketers as we eat dinner, commercials in our favorite television shows, "junk mail" in the mailbox, and now, pop-ups on the Web.

Users, particularly on the Web, have begun "filtering" their information. Why? The first reason is because they have to. Remember, 3,000 messages a day, coupled with the time constraints every person faces, make it impossible to take in all of that information. The second and more important reason is because they can. The Web has introduced an entirely new level of empowerment for the end user.

Let us use the news as a very compelling yet basic example. Before the Internet, if you wanted the news, you watched the evening programming on television or you read the newspaper. The television version of the news left no room for user input. You could watch it or turn it off. If you watched, you got the information the newscasters decided to provide you. With the newspaper the user has more control, being able to read only the articles or sections that you are interested in, but again, there are limitations on content, topics, and points of view. With the evolution of the Web, users can now go to CNN.com and sign up for breaking news alerts, or sign up for Really Simple Syndication feeds from favorite sports publications, and the information comes to you. Not only does it come to you, it comes in the format and frequency that you have deemed satisfactory, necessary even. The power is with the user. People are starting to ask the question, "Why should I sift through information that I'm not interested in, when I can have the exact information I want delivered to me, when I want, how I want?" That is empowerment.

Users can filter information any number of ways, which has given way to the birth of "permission-based" marketing. It operates on a premise of both sides giving a little. A company gives out a little bit of information about its services or products and the consumer gives a little information about himself or herself, like an e-mail address, and the permission-based relationship has begun. The challenge for marketers now is to get their customers to volunteer for the incoming information—to be chosen as a company or product valuable enough to let through a filter.

There are five primary areas we explore in this chapter that bring marketers a greater focus and understanding on using the Web for success:

- Web 2.0,
- Personalization: Relevancy and Navigation,
- Explosion of Broadband and Rich Media,
- Multi-Channel Experience, and
- Real-Time Data Integration for an Agile Enterprise.

WEB 2.0

A Brief History of the Web (1.0 through 2.0)

Just to get everyone on the same page, we provide a brief review of Internet facts. Lesson one: Al Gore did not really invent the Internet. It started in the 1960s as ARPANET (Advanced Research Projects Agency Network), a government-sponsored project with a few university campuses to find a way to communicate using asynchronous communication. The Internet, and its commercial separation (the .com we all know and love) did not really enter into the public consciousness until the early 1990s, when Netscape Communications Corporation and Microsoft Corporation brought Web browser technologies into the mass market. These were the predecessor versions of the World Wide Web, the first Web browser written on a NeXT computer by Tim Berners-Lee. This user interface combined with the technical concepts of HTML and packet switching supported dynamic content creation and asynchronous communication into what has come to be known as a Web site or, in marketing terms, a destination site to direct potential customers.

By the late 1990s, the Internet had taken off as a new frontier for average, everyday users to view, share, and store information globally. As the amount of content and information grew exponentially on the Web, the end user's new problem became finding what he or she wanted, so search capabilities were created, were improved, and were expanded. Companies took notice and saw this as a new channel of broadcast (push) communication to potential customers. Many of the early adopters, in what is now commonly referred to as Web 1.0, developed minimally interactive Web sites and started to push their messages out to customers, using the same broadcast tools with which they had succeeded in more traditional media channels.

These first generation Web sites were interactive and have been classified as "brochureware," which just means providing the same information that might appear in a paper-based brochure online. Sites were static and did not have a lot in the way of interactivity or depth of information. Companies knew they had to have an online presence, and that was translated into putting up "about us" and general product information. Soon everyone had a Web page, from General Electric Company to PetSweaters.com, and the "dot-com" era exploded. Investors were throwing money at any start-up company that had an idea, and business was booming. This led to the proliferation of the immeasurable advertising-based business model, which was heralded as the perpetrator of the dot-com meltdown.

Then, in 2000, the bottom fell out, the bubble burst, however you want to say it, and the "dot-com boom" became the "dot-com crash." Infrastructure investment exceeded capacity, and the economies of scale originally projected to occur with the rapid increase in online users did not materialize. Business models were not generating operating profit and were instead being sustained by new investment inflow. This led to investors pulling their money out of the market because they were not able to see real operating returns from companies and capital fled the market. Hence, the meltdown.

Slowly, we all recovered and companies began to refocus on the Internet and the Web as a legitimate business channel: we call this Web 1.5. The online user remained very active, the number of online users continued to grow, excess capacity was absorbed, and companies started cautiously spending on marketing in this channel again. This time, however, companies were demanding a level of measurability and accountability not seen in other media channels. Through this painful period of recalibration some companies learned to reach out and begin discussions with their customers. They came to realize that the customers with whom they had a relationship also spent more money with the company. More consumers started doing traditional business online, for instance, managing checking accounts, paying their bills, and shopping. On the heels of this renewed growth, the Internet and the Web also started to revitalize themselves into what is being termed Web 2.0.

What "Web 2.0" Really Means

As far as buzzwords go, Web 2.0 has exploded onto the scene as people continue to define the evolution of the Web. Yet as previously discussed, if you really look at the history and transformations of the Internet, this technically serves as version 3.0, because of the changes that occurred around 2000. Regardless of the technicalities, what is being called Web 2.0 is defined by a major shift toward user-focused and user-generated content. Let us look at a few of its features.

RSS Feeds

RSS feeds have been generating a lot of interest since early 2005 and are gradually being adopted by marketers as a serious tool for reaching customers. RSS is currently used or is planned to be used within the next 12 months by 63 percent of consumer product marketers, 65 percent of media and communications marketers, 37 percent of retail marketers, 37 percent of financial services marketers, and 38 percent of equipment and tech marketers.[3]

So what does RSS actually mean? Well, after a couple of variations, the acronym now stands for "Really Simple Syndication." It is a way to send information, both in text and multimedia files like video, to end users via a "feed." And once again, the power is in the hands of the users, because they "subscribe" to the feeds they want. The news media have been at the front of the adoption curve for using RSS to disseminate information, as users opt in for topics on which they want to receive updates. It allows the outlets to push out the information directly to the user, instead of the user having to go and search for it. Blogs commonly use RSS feeds to bring them information on the topics that they cover. RSS is a tool that responds to the new, savvy end user who wants personalized content, filtered by topics of interest, from sources that he or she trusts.

Bots

Yes, it comes from the term "Web robot," and, yes, it is designed to perform duties as requested by a Web user. Although your first thought probably goes to something like the robot-maid from the Jetsons, instead, think more in terms of the Web spiders search engines used to crawl Web pages. In the most simple of terms, bots can be used to go out and get information requested by a user. Some of the most popular bots in use include those that users can install to report the weather, sports scores, and movie show times. AOL Instant Messenger recently added bots to its program to allow users to more fully personalize their experiences. However, what robots would be complete without a dark side? Bots have been blamed for many malicious acts: bots that commit click fraud, systematically clicking through sites to deplete their keyword budget; bots that covertly install themselves on personal computers and are used as a remote attack tool; bots that exploit market imbalance for financial gain. In the long run, though, bots will serve as another tool that allows a user to customize his or her online experience and filter the information he or she is viewing.

Mashups

Mashups are much more sophisticated than their name sounds, and they are blazing new paths in putting information in the hands of end users. Mashups are a recent phenomenon that gained attention coming into 2006. The technology allows Web users to pull separate pieces of publicly available information from different sources and "mash" them together. One of the first, and most often noted by the media, mashups was the Google Chicago Crime map, which allowed users to see a map of Chicago, plotted with incidents of crime, to view the information in a totally new way. If the data have been compiled (for instance, if someone has had the time and energy to compile hometowns of soap opera stars), they can be mashed.

One caveat, however, is that mashups are permission based. The data need to be truly public, and there have been legal and ethical tussles over the availability and the use of some information. Some companies, like eBay Inc., for instance, go so far as to prohibit use of their information in mashups in all of their user agreements. Regardless of the ongoing resistance, this technology has opened doors for users to be able to create new views of existing data, empowering them even further to choose how they want their information presented to them.

Wikis

"Wiki-wiki" means "hurry quick" in Hawaiian, which is where this latest technology got its name. A wiki is a type of Web site that allows users to post content without having to be a site administrator, and it has become a popular tool that encourages collaborative writing. The most famous "wiki" to reach mass awareness is "Wikipedia," an online encyclopedia that allows users to post information on different topics. Wiki users do not have to know HTML and can easily add information to a public site. This is providing another outlet for users to share information across boundaries and has opened up the Internet to average users who do not know, or need to know, the ins and outs of Web programming.

Blogs

One of the hottest tools to come on the Web scene began as . . . an online diary. Blogs, short for "Weblogs," hit the Internet as early as 1994, when a college student started keeping a diary online. Since then, it has evolved from being a static, manually updated part of a Web site to a separate, dynamically updated tool that allows its creator to publish ongoing entries in chronological order. It may seem like a simple concept, but it cannot be dismissed by marketers. In 2002 blogs caught traditional media outlets "flat-footed" with the news that Senate Majority Leader Trent Lott made comments suggesting he supported policies of racial segregation, a story the mainstream news media had failed to pick up. The networks paid attention, though, once word got out, and they have stated that blogs are responsible for forcing the resignation of the leader of the U.S. Senate.

For marketers, this offers another tool at our disposal that, when used correctly, has the ability to impact millions of users. The technique is in understanding how to use it correctly. Companies currently use blogs in two ways: create their own or find existing blogs that their customers read and target them from a marketing perspective. On the issue of creating their own, companies should consider what types of information their customers really want to see, and need to see, in blog format. Is it an ongoing how-to manual for a product, or thought leadership from an expert? Putting up random information, just because it is in blog format, does not make it relevant to your end users. If your approach is to target existing blogs, find out which ones your customers are drawn to with both formal and informal surveys and begin a marketing "campaign" to get the blogs to notice you. Offer them relevant information they can include for their readers, and you may end up with exposure for your site/product to which you had not previously had access.

Online Social Networking

Call it the "myspace revolution." The Internet has become a global storehouse of information—and a bountiful target for viral marketing. Teenagers use it to set dates, gossip, and promote themselves among the high school set. Yet the technology behind "online social networking" stretches far beyond the world of Friday night football and proms. Business professionals have turned to the Web to expand their networks allowing them to develop new clients, stay in contact with past co-workers, and search for their next jobs. As the global workforce becomes more integrated and transcends the boundaries of time and distance, people will continue taking their "network" online, and both business-to-business and business-to-consumer marketers will see more new opportunities to tap into viral and word-of-mouth marketing. Think about it: a teenager adds his favorite band to his personal page and suddenly his 137 closest friends have heard of the band. If only 15 of those people add the band to their pages, their separate networks are exposed, and so on, and so on. Apply that reasoning to a new product, service, or event venue, and it can lead to very effective brand awareness and marketing within this channel. Online social networking will continue to break boundaries as a global, viral marketing tool for the first part of this century.

PERSONALIZATION: RELEVANCY AND NAVIGATION

Because users are so used to filtering information, they respond best to content that is customized for them. When marketers gather data for their mailing lists, they should be conscious of tagging customers with appropriate labels. This ability to slice and dice will create greater success in opt-in campaigns. In addition, the relevance of the content is important, and the basic marketing principles still apply. If you are a retailer of swimsuits, you would not run the same campaign in the month of January to those living in Arizona as in Minnesota. Remember, it cannot be repeated enough: customers respond best to content that is customized for them.

Search

The business of search has evolved very quickly in its relatively short life span; it has created an entirely new vocabulary for communication—SEO, SEM, organic, paid, keywords, and click fraud. What began in 1999 under the umbrella of Search Engine Optimization (SEO) has expanded to become known as a larger entity, Search Engine Marketing (SEM), which includes search engine optimization, as well as paid search advertising and paid inclusion. In short, this means getting visibility for your Web page within search engines. It is a big business. If you need proof that it is a force to be reckoned with, Internet users conducted 5.1 billion searches in December 2005.[4] In response, marketers in North America spent $5.75 billion on search in 2005.[5] There is a lot of money being spent as companies navigate the dynamic world of Internet search, as keywords (search terms) are purchased by the highest bidder, firms are hired to design complete SEM strategies, and some competitors even resort to "click fraud," the act of repeatedly clicking on your rivals' paid search links to deplete their budgets. The visibility in search engines will continue to be important to every marketer; however, every year between 2006 and 2010 will see at least another 10-percent growth in the industry.[6]

Analytics

Issac Asimov once said, "The most exciting phrase to hear in science, the one that heralds new discoveries, is not 'Eureka!' but 'That's funny. . .'"[7] Web analytics has created the ability of marketers everywhere to look at their online presence and explore the possibilities and their options of "hmm, that's funny" and get to the bottom of why things are happening and what their customers are doing. The ability in the past few years to get beyond the basic "number of visitors" statistics to see how your visitors get to your site, through your site, where they go, where they get stuck, and how long they stay has all become a crucial part of measuring marketing success. Web analytics allows a level of measurement rarely seen in other, more traditional media venues. If you run an e-mail campaign, for example, you can see how many people opened the e-mail. Then you can see how many people clicked through to your site. You can see where they went next from the page you brought them in on. You can see how long they stayed before they left. You can even test out site changes or campaigns to gauge which process is the most effective. All of this information allows greater insight into getting your visitors to convert, where you want them to and how you want them to.

Opt-In

E-mail marketing is a fundamental tool for marketers in the 21st century, but its short life includes an already spotted past. The term "opt-in" gained a hefty new level of respect in 2003 when President George W. Bush signed the CAN-SPAM Act, prohibiting e-mail marketing to be sent without the following criteria:

- An opt-out mechanism,
- A valid subject line and header (routing) information,
- The legitimate physical address of the mailer, and
- A label if the content is adult.

Marketers found it so difficult to navigate the roadblocks of the spam issues, as well as deliverability problems, that many pulled back on their e-mail marketing campaigns or stopped them altogether. However, now that new tools are in place to help navigate these issues, marketers are integrating e-mail marketing back into their overall marketing strategies, to complement their other online and off-line campaigns.

In online personalized marketing, the important thing is to tie all of your components together and measure, measure, measure. How many of your customers are clicking through your e-mail? How many are even opening it? Have your Web visitors gone up or down in response to a pay-per-click program? These are all answers marketers now have at their fingertips.

EXPLOSION OF BROADBAND AND RICH MEDIA

By the end of 2005–2006, with the recession far behind us, over 100 million users in North America have broadband Internet access at home, and 90 percent of online shoppers have access to broadband either at work or home. This continues to push even further growth behind the online channel, within new technologies that power what we call "rich media."

What Is Rich Media?

Rich media is an overarching term to describe the evolution of what users are able to view on the Web and refers to anything that has dynamic motion. In the past, images were static, in forms like GIFs and JPEGs. Today, users can watch video, walk through interactive product demos, or see what their new car would like in silver, red, or black. Often downloads of rich media "players" are required (Apple's QuickTime is a popular example) to allow users to access or play the information, but as the technology develops, look for less downloads to be necessary. The Web has taken enormous leaps in becoming a more interactive experience for users.

What Is Ajax?

What is old is new again, and so it goes with the Ajax technology. Though the technology was recently named in 2005, it was originally developed over ten years before as part of Microsoft's original Web scripting. The bottom line of the technology is that it superpowers Web applications and makes sites even easier for users to get the information they need. The days of having to download software for programs like Instant Messenger may soon be over, as Ajax takes the stage and allows users to run programs right on the Web, as opposed to on their computers. Instead of the old experience of "click-wait-load" on sites, it will now allow users to drag and drop information to create a dynamic interactive experience. For example, Ajax allows information to appear as Web site visitors roll over a list of items, like movies on Netflix, to see details of the movie without having to click into another page. Many people believe that Ajax is overhyped, but the idea behind giving users more information, in a more dynamic experience, is here to stay.

MULTI-CHANNEL EXPERIENCE

Multi-channel integration is at the forefront of where businesses are going today. It means companies can no longer afford to look at their Web sites as a separate silo, or channel, independent of their off-line brand. It means creating a consistent customer experience across stores, e-mail, Web, mobile, call center, and so forth. Promotions can be run online, in the store, through an e-mail campaign, and all must be consistent, which makes them all the more compelling. In the back-office operations, it is important that data be stored in the same places as well, independent of how the customer came to your brand. When someone calls into your call center, if he or she has visited the Web site and entered information onto the screens or forms, the customer rep should have that at his or her fingertips. The marketing ideal is one brand, consistent customer information, across all of your channels. Some companies are even going so far as to restructure organizationally, and, for example, putting a person in charge of customer retention across all channels rather than someone individually being responsible for Web, stores, and so forth, which shows how the business landscape is changing in response to this movement.

Branding through the Multi-Channel Experience

Marketers inherently understand the concept of brand. Yet there seems to be a lack of understanding as to how brand translates online. There is an important intersection of the traditional methods of building a brand with the new technologies available on the Web.

A brand will be only as strong as its consistency. Marketers must accept that the online channel is an extension of the off-line brand and another opportunity for a company to reinforce the qualities that make it unique. The high-end retailer Tiffany & Co. is a good example of brand across channels (www.tiffany.com).

When you enter a Tiffany store, you will not mistake it for anywhere else. Its brand is built around elegance, high-class, sophistication, personal attention, and a quality product. It even has its own trademark color, Tiffany Blue. When you have a moment, visit its Web site. It is clean, elegant, product focused, and, of course, accented with its trademark blue. Visitors can custom design jewelry, smoothly browse product selections, and get the "Tiffany experience" online. The store experience is the same as the online experience, which is critical for brand success.

Following is a brief overview of the primary traditional channels marketers must work through:

Stores/Branches

This is where a majority of traditional shoppers do their purchasing. Many people like the person-to-person interaction and still value the ability to see and feel a product firsthand. Even with the emergence of the online channel, many customers will use the Web site to browse and research and then come into the store/branch to purchase. This reinforces the importance that online and off-line marketing campaigns tie together.

Online

A company's Web site is now considered to be the most cost-effective and efficient channel. Companies that are using their online channel well allow customers to do everything they would do in person, in a store, or over the phone now online. Customers can open accounts, view product information, order and ship goods, get expert opinions, and talk to customer service. They can even initiate returns online. The Web even allows instant access to information that might not have appeared within other channels. I am sure you have had a similar experience, being on a site like Amazon.com and receiving a message like "Len, if you liked 'Business Driven Technology,' we also recommend 'Managing Business Process Flow.'" The online channel will continue to allow companies to provide enhanced customer personalization with low overhead costs. It is also the only channel where you can begin and continue a relationship with your customers over an extended period of time. You can learn of their likes and dislikes as well as their emerging interests. This creates opportunity to initiate pilots, expand existing products, and get rapid feedback from your customers about new product offerings.

Call Centers

Call centers remain a popular channel for many businesses, with the ability to handle a large volume of transactions. However, many are challenged with turnover rates as high as 35 percent and new employee training costs between

$8,000 and $12,000 per employee.[8] It is important to note that for those companies that do have a call center, it is essential to build the proper back-end systems to allow data to be shared with the other channels to avoid duplication and inefficiency.

Kiosks

Kiosks can be both electronic and traditional. Walk through any mall and you see dozens of traditional kiosks offering everything from personalized key chains to cell phones. The electronic kiosk, or computer kiosk, serves as an informational point for customers to access information online. Many have high tolerance features like touch screens and trackballs to help customers navigate the information. It allows users to browse at their own pace and view only the information in which they are interested.

Dealers/Distributors

In some businesses, products go through a dealer or distributor, which is another opportunity to create the same consistent customer experience. Lexus is a great example of this phenomenon, allowing customers to seamlessly work through the parent company (Toyota Motor Corporation), and from dealer to dealer, all with the same high-end experience.

In addition to the experience, it is important to leverage your customer intelligence across channels. The challenge is to use the Web by tracking conversion to drive traffic to the stores. Users will browse online, then purchase the product at a store. Some companies have smartly reacted by offering in-store pickup for items ordered online, so the consumer can still get the "product-in-hands" feel before the final purchase.

REAL-TIME DATA INTEGRATION FOR AN AGILE ENTERPRISE

Every function or online tool you interact with runs on an application. There is an application that is built to log you into your online checking. There is an application that allows companies to update content on their Web sites. In Web 2.0, the fundamentals of building an online presence, the "nuts and bolts," have started to undergo a fundamental change. In the past, different applications were built separately, sometimes with custom languages, which caused problems when they tried to communicate and interact with each other. Now that Service Oriented Architecture (SOA) is being adopted, different applications, services, solutions, and platforms are all working together in an interconnected way. SOA provides the environment and protocol for applications to be built so that they can be reused, communicated with, and have a higher level of performance. Now instead of creating an application from scratch, the process is like a set of Legos, using blocks of existing information to build on each other. Business users can now react not only more quickly, but more cost-effectively, to the ever-changing market.

CONCLUSION: SO WHAT DOES ALL THIS MEAN TO A MARKETER?

All of these new tools, these current evolutions of the Web, all drive toward one important lesson: the power of the end users has changed significantly and the role of the marketer has increased considerably. Change is no longer an option.

In this chapter, we have reviewed where the Web is in its current state of evolution, as well as what new tools are available to marketers. In summary, let us review the most important takeaways for successfully using the Web as a marketer.

- *Remember that this is the era of user-controlled information:* This is the single most important thing to remember from the discussion around using the Web for marketing. People have become overwhelmed with marketing messages and time constraints and have become empowered with the amount of tools at their disposal to "filter" information. A company must understand and navigate this new relationship in order to be successful in the years ahead.

- *Understand and segment your customer:* Do not assume anything about consumers. For example, conventional thought would say that the Baby-Boomer generation, because it is older, is one of the least Internet-savvy demographics. Wrong. One of the lowest groups is actually 35–45-year-olds, and the Baby Boomers rank way above average in their use of the Internet. Understand your customers. Figure out how they should be grouped, whether it is by age, or interest, or geography, and so forth, and then. . . .

- *Make your information relevant:* You would not try to sell a pair of Manolo Blahnik shoes to a shrimp fisherman in Louisiana who consistently buys steel-toed work boots. Remember, users are overwhelmed with information, and they are going to respond best to content that is customized to them. When they do enter into the permission-based relationship with your company, respond always with relevant, timely information. The consumer needs to get value out of the relationship, or he or she will quickly leave you in the dust for another relationship, and maybe competitor, that can.

- *Measure, measure, measure:* The technology is available today to take out much of the "guesswork" that can factor into marketing. Are you wondering whether adding a "forward to a friend" feature increases your click-through rates on an e-mail campaign? Your analytics will tell you. Understanding the tools you have at your disposal, and what they are telling you about your online presence, will only increase your chances of success. The biggest failure companies face in analytics is that they fail to devote the proper resources to understanding and analyzing the data. It should be an integrated part of your overall marketing strategy.

- *Pay attention to what others are doing:* Always watch the market. Visit other companies' sites, see what they are doing well in transitioning their brand experience online. There will always be those that are ahead of the curve in the technologies they are using and the different tactics they take in reaching customers. Listen to "buzz" you might hear around a certain product or company and what they are doing online. Nike, Inc., Mini Cooper, and The Coca-Cola Company are three of many sites that effectively translate their brands online.

Technology will continue to change. New tools will be created to address an unmet need and will intentionally or unintentionally impact the way your message is communicated—for instance, the future is in mobile technologies and how companies will address getting their online presence translated once again to a new form of media. You need to be ever vigilant. As a marketer it is critical to adjust, and adjust quickly, as the marketplace and end users change. This era of user-controlled information is also an era where innovation is rewarded. Those who will be most successful are those who understand the guiding principles and are introducing new and exciting ways to navigate the digital revolution.

NOTES

1. Shop.org's annual "2006 State of Retailing Online Report."
2. Seth Godin, "Permission-Based Marketing."
3. AdAge 2006 Interactive Marketing and Media Factpack.
4. 2005 Nielsen/Net Ratings.
5. Search Engine Marketing Professional Organization.
6. Jupiter Research.
7. www.brainyquote.com/quotes/quotes/i/isaacasimo109758.html.
8. Call Center News.

CHAPTER 12

PROMOTING PROFESSIONAL SERVICES: THE EXCITING WORLD OF ACCOUNTANCY

Elizabeth A. Galambos

"Have you been in an accident? Have you been to a doctor recently? Is your child stuck on the bench at Little League? Someone ought to pay for your pain. We're the ones who can get you the result you think you deserve. Call Dewey, Cheetum and Howe at 1-555-SHY-STERS today."

This might be the first thought that comes to mind when you think of marketing professional services—a laughable TV commercial for personal injury lawyers. This is simply advertising, and at that, it is professional services advertising at its worst. Today's marketing for professional services includes promotion, public relations, and selling, as well as advertising—all done tastefully. These services build brands, attempt to instill a positive image of both the service and the organization that offers the service, and serve as a means to attract new clients and enhance relationships with current clients.

Services marketing is a relatively new venture for accounting firms in the last decade. Past codes of ethics instated by the American Institute of Certified Public Accountants (AICPA) and a general negative attitude toward advertising on the part of professionals in the service industry together hindered marketing efforts until the mid 1980s. The study of marketing has seen slow, but steady growth over the last 20 years, as accounting firms across the country began to advertise in the Yellow Pages and engage in direct mail campaigns for new business. Today, many small and mid-sized accounting firms are beginning to see the benefits of establishing a marketing program—that includes more than just advertising—within their firms.

CURRENT CLIMATE

Marketing is a relatively new practice in professional services firms in fields such as law, medicine, and accounting. In the past, the prevailing attitude toward marketing activities within these professionals was that marketing was synonymous with advertising and that advertising was an inappropriate medium over which to send a message about professional services to clients and prospects. Even today, many accountants, attorneys, and physicians misunderstand what marketing really is and its overall goal for an organization. Many professionals think that marketing means using "hard-sell" techniques, and they feel that they are above doing that.[1]

Many professionals are just beginning to realize that something is missing in their business growth strategy. In response, the professional services industry has taken the approach to "try out" marketing either by engaging an outside provider to formulate and implement marketing strategy or by hiring an in-house professional to take on these responsibilities. Professional service marketers are just beginning to understand what works and what does not. Best practices guides simply cannot encompass all the facets of brand-building and business development, because there is still so much to learn about the industry and about clients' needs and desires. Every marketing initiative is an experiment—a chance to be creative and analytical at the same time. Professional services marketing is evolving so rapidly that, contrary to popular belief, even accounting can be fun!

HOW DID WE GET HERE FROM THERE?

Beginning in 1922, all forms of paid advertising were banned by the AICPA. A council established by the organization instituted the ban in reaction to similar prohibitions against advertising in the legal and medical professions. This professional code of ethics regarding advertising came to include competitive bidding and direct solicitation of potential clients in later years. In response to pressure from CPAs, the AICPA loosened its definition of "advertising" in 1975 to allow firms to publish press releases regarding changes in partnership status, admissions of new partners, mergers, office relocations, and changes in telephone numbers. The next year, an AICPA task force was set up to reevaluate the reasons behind and the implications of the advertising ban.[2]

Change arrived in 1977 when John R. Bates, a partner in a law firm in Arizona, took the State Bar of Arizona to the Supreme Court of the United States after he chose to advertise his services in a daily newspaper. Bates's law firm wanted to market its practice of providing low-cost legal services to middle-income individuals who did not qualify for public legal aid. The majority of Supreme Court justices found that allowing attorneys to advertise their services in printed media would not harm the legal profession or the administration of justice. The

Supreme Court actually favored this kind of advertising, agreeing that consumers would be supplied with valuable information about the availability and cost of legal services.

The ripple effects from this case hit the industry with great force as accountants were faced with three significant challenges, including assaults on professional codes of ethics (especially involving the Bates decision), changing expectations of clients, and increased competition.[3] In addition to these forces, the threat of government intervention also contributed to the pressure for the accounting profession to adapt. During this time, the accounting industry was under investigation by the United States Department of Justice for antitrust violations and by the Federal Trade Commission for anticompetitive practices.

Accountants in the late 1970s were having much difficulty in coping with all of these environmental changes because of three other reasons: their dislike of commercialism as they did not see themselves as "businesspeople," their reliance on and trust in the professional code of ethics outlined by the AICPA, and their belief that marketing meant only selling and advertising.[4]

The AICPA noted this turmoil and on March 31, 1978, Rule 502 went into effect, officially lifting the ban on advertising within the industry. The rule states, "A member shall not seek to obtain clients by advertising or other forms of solicitation in a manner that is false, misleading, or deceptive. The direct uninvited solicitation of a specific potential client is prohibited." The last line was deleted from the rule one year later in response to changing attitudes and fears of violating laws.[5]

Accounting firms were very slow to engage in any new marketing activities as the influence of the original ban on advertising lingered, and they feared that potential clients would see advertising as unprofessional, which might reflect poorly on the firm. Consumers' responses to advertising on the part of professionals was generally favorable, according to a survey conducted by Robert E. Hite and Joseph A. Bellizzi for the *Journal of Advertising Research* in 1986. The study found that consumers believed that advertising would not lower professional image, could be used tastefully, and would convey useful information. Interestingly, the survey results showed evidence that consumers believed it was more appropriate for CPAs to use advertising than it was for lawyers or physicians.[6]

In 1992—15 years after the Bates decision—a group of marketing consultants conducted a survey of over 240 accountants to gauge their attitudes toward advertising. The survey uncovered the following notable results:

- Over 55 percent of the accountants believed that ethical codes against advertising exist to maintain and increase practicing accountants' incomes.
- There is much disagreement as to whether large, established firms would prosper while smaller firms would suffer if advertising were widely used. Almost 36 percent said that would happen, nearly 42 percent said that it would not, and 22 percent had no opinion on the matter.

- Almost half believed that advertising would help to provide more positions for new accountants entering the profession.

- Sixty-two percent thought that prices for services would drop, and almost 70 percent believed that the quality of services would improve if advertising were widely used.

- While only 34 percent believed that advertising would help to inform the public as to situations when an accountant is needed, 49 percent believe that it would help the public in its selection of an accountant.

- Just over 29 percent believed that public confidence in the accounting profession would be impaired by advertising, but nearly 49 percent disagreed.

- More than twice the number of those surveyed who agreed that stringent regulations for accounting services advertising would have to imposed also believed that these regulations would be unnecessary.[7]

WHAT IS DIFFERENT? THE NEW PARADIGM

Now, 20 years after that survey, the services marketing environment has evolved. The most important thing to understand is that clients buy benefits—not just the features of the product. The key is to distinguish your benefits from those your competition offers. When accountants saw themselves less as business-people, the firms were thought to be more product oriented. Now, the thought is that they are service oriented. Clients' beliefs have shifted in the same way. They are more influenced by how the firm can satisfy their needs rather than just by what qualifications and resources the firm boasts.

With a good, marketers can tout its special features to position the product differently than its competition. With a service, consumers cannot evaluate the product directly. Instead, the quality of the service and the relationship built between the company and the client helps to distinguish its service from its competitors. For example, a CPA would not explain to his or her client the ins and outs of a 1040 individual tax return. Instead, the CPA focuses on selling accuracy and convenience to the client, relaying a message that the client will not have to be bothered by preparing his own tax return or worrying about making mistakes.

A survey conducted by Thomas D. Wood and Donald A. Ball for the *Journal of Accountancy* in 1978 identified the six most important factors in selecting an accounting firm used by corporate clients. In order, they were (1) technical expertise in the client's field (benefit) (2) general technical competence as evidenced by being a CPA (feature), (3) sufficient size to provide backup when necessary and specialists if needed (benefit), (4) reputation based on recommendations of business associates, attorneys, and bankers (feature), (5) ability to get along with clients (benefit), and (6) price (feature). Some features, such as being licensed as a CPA for example, could be spun by the accounting firm as a benefit. Licensing would permit clients to worry less about the accuracy of their financial statements because they could be assured of the expertise of the firm.[8]

A follow-up survey in 1980 showed that benefits—such as a better understanding of specific business practices due to the firm's specialized knowledge, one-stop shopping for similar services (for example, taxes, financial planning, and employee benefits), and long-lasting client relationship—were very important. This same survey also showed the some features were still very important to potential clients, such as the firm's reputation (strong influence from referrals), the firm's client list, its size, and also the location of office(s). Location (convenient access for the customer) is a major factor in the selection of an accounting firm.[9] In this sense, location is not truly seen as a feature in this case, but instead as a benefit.

TODAY'S COMPETITIVE ENVIRONMENT

Nowadays, the accounting industry is a highly competitive environment, as firms strive to gain more clients, more awareness, and more revenue. Although most firms coexist with their competitors by specializing in particular industries or services, local firms tend to submit bids for the same prospects and attempt to lure clients away from their competitors. Accountants are very keen to this practice and are oftentimes very protective of the firm's client list, staff members, and marketing growth strategies. Accounting professionals typically do not share information about best practices, successes, and failures among themselves unless they are not competing directly in the same market.

Accounting marketers are more open in communicating with other accounting marketers. They exchange all types of information from campaign strategies and artwork to proposal templates and big ideas. Even within the same market, accounting marketers are generally more willing than accountants to communicate with competitors. Marketers understand that the methodology employed by one firm may not necessarily work for another firm. There is an understanding that client lists are confidential, but the camaraderie generated by sharing of knowledge is useful in keeping up-to-date on the state of the local market and the industry. Keeping in touch with other local accounting marketers also helps firms to track how each firm fits into the local marketplace. The best way to organize and record information about your competitors is to perform a systematic analysis. Using a simple spreadsheet, marketers can track useful competitive information such as the following:

- Competitive rankings,
- Outcomes of bids,
- Services offered,
- Strengths and weaknesses,
- Contact information and office location(s),
- Major clients (those known),
- Niches (both advertised and known),

- Resources (including national alliance memberships),
- Their staff members with whom you have preexisting relationships,
- Your clients who know them,
- Slogan or tag line,
- Marketing practices (media advertising, Web site, and so forth),
- Community involvement, and
- Word-of-mouth information.

A competitive analysis should be used as a tool when planning for the future of the firm. Generally, an internal marketer begins the process of collecting information that becomes confidential to the firm and should not be seen outside the firm. Once the spreadsheet has been populated with a significant amount of information, the spreadsheet should be passed along to management team members to add their comments about experiences in working with other firms, their contacts at competitors, and their general impressions. Management and marketing should meet to discuss and review this information on a yearly basis to reevaluate internal goals. However, the competitive analysis should not serve as the sole criterion for establishing goals; quantifiable internal data reports on results and qualitative data like opinions of the staff and management should also be factors in planning for future endeavors.

CAN ACCOUNTING BE FUN?

Getting these opinions from the staff and working with management means that the marketers have to interact with the accounting professionals. Accountants are generally perceived to be number-crunching introverts with little personality who speak an entirely different technical language. To some extent, this is true. Accountants tend to be shy rather than outgoing, more cautious than risk taking, more left-brained than right-brained. However, with the demand for accounting services on the rise in a highly competitive environment, accountants need to develop better "people skills," which have become more important than ever.

In the industry of professional services, relationships are the key to winning and losing new business. Without a base of trust, mutual respect, and shared value, no bids can be won. Because marketing is such a new concept for accounting firms, vast opportunity exists for marketing professionals to assist accountants in their pursuits for practice growth. Marketers can offer partners and other staff members opportunities for sales coaching and training, strategic growth planning methods, enhanced public speaking skills, networking skills, collateral support for prospect meetings, and much more marketing-related assistance to help professionals achieve their personal and career goals.

To a certain extent, accountants, attorneys, and bankers are stigmatized as being uptight. The stereotypical accountant is a man in his 60s who is wearing a blue, black, or gray suit, carrying a briefcase in one hand and a 10-key (or adding machine for those who do not speak accounting) in the other. His hair is graying, he looks uninteresting, and he keeps saying things like "unrealized gains," "amortization schedule," and "net income."

This traditional professional image is what clients and the general public have come to expect when they think of an accountant. In fact, to a certain extent, clients want their accountants to be very professional, precise, frugal, and maybe even slightly robotic. Accountants are paper-pushing, number-crunching, bean counters—and clients expect them to behave this way even though this may not always be the case.

In an industry heavy with uniformity, rules, and standards, a firm's biggest challenge is to pinpoint its competitive differentiators and promote them in a way so that clients and prospects will hear them. It is a struggle to maintain a professional image while taking risks to be "different" from others. Firms must challenge themselves to strike a balance between what clients expect (professionalism) and what they want (a difference). However, it is crucial to consider how far is too far before your clients think you are not professional anymore.

If all the accountants at XYZ CPAs rode Harleys to work everyday, would clients think of them as different from their competitors? Maybe, but riding motorcycles to work is not meaningful to clients. Perhaps some clients would see the firm's people as "fun loving" or as "risk takers," but is that the perception you want your clients to have?

Because each firm's values vary, the things that make firms different should vary as well. A firm could make arrangements between clients to offer perquisites, "perks," like a discounted gym membership to a client's facility or free golf passes to a client's golf course. Practices could send birthday cards and anniversary gifts to executives of A-level clients or use a customer relationship management (CRM) software to track a client's preferences from communication methods to favorite beverage to be sure you always customize your service to each client.

Another way firms tend to differentiate themselves is to say, "Our people make us different." This is overused, so it has essentially lost its meaning. What is it about your people that makes them different? Have they been with the firm for a long time? Are they older/younger? Have many of them earned advanced degrees and certifications? Are they very personable and friendly? Whom do they know? What do they do besides accounting? Where have they worked before? Where did they attend college?

The answers to these questions become more and more important to clients as they begin to develop relationships with their service providers. Again, clients know that most firms have the same qualifications, experience, and fees, and they want a provider who offers them something that they can obtain only with a particular firm—a relationship with their accountant. It is true that what makes each firm different is its people, but it is the personalities of the individual accountants assigned to the client that win bids, sell additional services to existing clients, and retain current engagements. Perks, incentives, and personalized service are easy to advertise and can get your foot in the door, but relationships are the real substance that distinguishes a firm and keeps clients satisfied.

MARKETING STRATEGY

Traditional management of marketing strategy involves four main facets that are often referred to as the 4 Ps: product, price, promotion, and place (distribution channels). More recently researchers and consultants have defined as many as 16 Ps for the accounting industry. Philip Kotler promoted his idea of 6 Ps—a much more manageable number—in a 1984 publication where he added public opinion and political power to the original 4 Ps. In Kotler's view, the 4 Ps include the following elements and sample dimensions: product (for example, auditing, taxes, and compilations), price (cash-and-carry only and delayed billing), promotion (advertising specialty items, Yellow Pages, and direct mail), place (fax machines and travel to client), public opinion (customer relations program and seminars for clients), and political power/issues (community involvement and Chamber of Commerce).[10]

In today's accounting firms, marketing serves a number of purposes that revolve around the goals of staying in business and growing financially and structurally. According to long-time management and marketing consultant William J. Winston, the top ten roles and uses for marketing in accounting firms are as follows:

- Informing clients about services,
- Educating the community about specific issues impacting it,
- Attracting new clients,
- Retaining existing clients,
- Identifying potential clients,
- Keeping up-to-date on marketplace changes,
- Nurturing professional networks,
- Being part of an overall strategic planning process,
- Enhancing customer service and quality, and
- Enhancing the professional image of the firm.[11]

This was reinforced in a 1990 survey conducted by three marketing consultants for the *Journal of Professional Services Marketing* in which over 200 randomly selected CPAs were asked to list the marketing activities of their firms. The top ten marketing activities in order were personal contact, reputation of the firm, going to the client's office, community involvement, office location, professional memberships, competitive pricing, controlling expenses, newsletters and brochures, and client meeting rooms.[12]

Institutional marketing plays a major role in the marketing activities of accounting firms, as the reputation of the firm and community involvement are both in the top five responses, while professional memberships along with newsletters and brochures round out the top ten. Location is also a major consideration, as accountants are concerned with visiting clients, establishing offices near their clients, and providing a pleasant atmosphere for clients when they visit the firm's office(s).

BRANDING

Branding in a word is image. It is creating and maintaining a perception in the minds of clients, prospects, current and potential employees, the local business community, and even the general public. Firms accomplish branding goals through various methods including advertising, Web presence, newsletters, donations and sponsorships of charitable, social, and business initiatives, media relations, public speaking engagements, community involvement, promotional activities, and even nontraditional methods like TV advertising and blogging (keeping an online Weblog or journal).

With this integrated marketing approach in which these methods work together to build a branding campaign, they must all have a consistent message and theme to help the firm create a unique identity in its marketplace. Using the same logo, colors, wording, and slogan gives the audience a better opportunity to develop a clear understanding of what the firm's message is. When you keep hearing things like "I see you guys everywhere!" it is an indicator that the firm's branding campaign is a success!

Advertising

Advertising for the professional services industry serves two purposes—name recognition and image building. Accountants, attorneys, and physicians do not generally benefit in any direct way from advertising. In fact, depending on the tone of the advertisement, these initiatives may hinder growth and cast a negative image on a firm.

Advertising is often perceived by target audiences (those who are seeking a professional service) as not being truly insightful as to a firm's reputation. It is the firm telling you the audience what it wants you to hear about it. However, advertising regularly in publications that reach the right audience can help a firm to send a message about its image. This can help introduce the firm to a new audience or maintain a preexisting positive image for the firm. Advertising should always be used in appropriate media that match the reason for the advertisement.

For larger firms looking to gain greater name recognition, advertising can be successful in achieving this goal.

Web Site

One specialty area of branding for a firm is its Web site. The site's overall appearance and its functionality are crucial to managing a Web site that is valuable to the firm's clients, prospects, and other contacts. The firm must commit to a goal for the site—a purpose for its existence. In today's business environment, it is mandatory to have a Web presence. However, the quality of the site will reflect on the firm and, therefore, building and maintaining a user-friendly Web site is an important element of a branding campaign.

A Web site can be used for several different purposes: a source for those seeking more information about the firm, a recruitment tool for young talent, a staff directory, a platform by which to exchange electronic files with clients (using a portal system), a center for newsletter archives, and even a vehicle by which to accept registrations for upcoming events like seminars. The site should be designed and populated with information in such a way that it attracts visitors to return to the site regularly. Be sure not to bury important information under paragraph after paragraph of text.

For the best use of resources, working with a Web design firm to create, maintain, and update a Web site is often the best choice. Professional photographs, graphics, formatting, style, and design all help to convey the image of a professional services firm. Web design firms can also help to build a Web site that is optimized for search engines so that the site will be at the top of the list when customers are searching for services using particular phrases or topics. Appropriate Web design can include tools that track visitors to a Web site and their behavior there. Reviewing these reports and comparing the results to the firm's goals for its Web site will provide insight into whether the firm is on track or whether it needs to rethink its Web strategy.

Newsletters

A newsletter is a great awareness tool that helps maintain regular communication with clients, prospects, referral sources, and other contacts. It should serve as a vehicle for conveying important information about new laws, rules, and regulations, industry trends, and hot topics, but it should also communicate announcements and news from within the firm, including new employees, promotions, awards received, public speaking engagements, upcoming firm events, new services offered, major sponsorships and donations, and any other newsworthy topics.

The tone of the newsletter, along with the delivery, will determine the degree of success in achieving high readership levels. The general appearance of the newsletter should reflect the firm's image. It should look professional, clean, and simple, but be sure that it is customized to your audience. Preprinted newsletters, canned articles, and logo-it-and-go templates do not demonstrate value to readers, and typically, they are disregarded. Generally, when a staff member's byline is attached to an article, it is better read. Standard content is available to be purchased, and a mixture of canned articles and bylined articles is the best approach to using resources most effectively while meeting the goal of a successful level of readership.

Readers infer lots of information from a firm's newsletter. If there are spelling or grammatical errors, inconsistent fonts, or even missing hyperlinks, readers may believe that the firm lacks attention to detail. For paper versions, the weight and "feel" of the paper, the colors used (or lack of color), the length, and whether it has a printed or labeled mailing address are all clues in developing the readers' perception about the firm. For electronic versions, readers pay attention to the "From" and "To" addresses, the e-mail's similarity to unwanted e-mail (spam), the day and time of delivery, and the ease of use in obtaining more information.

Consistency is also key. Choose a color scheme, format, and style prior to publishing and stick with it. Any major changes to the newsletter should be done at the beginning of the year or at the beginning of another notable time period. Readers like to know what to expect when they open a newsletter, and this also helps to ensure that the intended message will reach its audience.

Some important decisions to make when publishing a newsletter include the method and the frequency. Paper newsletters are falling by the wayside of their electronic counterparts. However, some firms still believe in the "power of paper." People will open their regular mail, enjoy having the "touch" of a physical item, and it results in better readership. On the other hand, e-mail newsletters can be sent to contacts in real time and, depending on the service used for publishing, can be more cost-effective than paper versions especially for color, photographs, and even sound and motion.

Planning for newsletter content is crucial in determining the right frequency. What kind of information should be included? How often should this information be communicated? For more frequent publications, it is important to have enough meaningful and newsworthy information to share on a regular basis and to schedule articles when the topics are relevant to the readers.

Especially for electronic newsletters, readers must always be given a choice to either opt in to receive or opt out of receiving the newsletter. Many firms take the opt-out approach where they collect e-mail contact information from staff members' networking efforts and add them to their mailing list. These people begin receiving the newsletter and can opt to no longer receive it if they choose. New contacts are simply added by default. Other firms take the opt-in approach where they specifically ask new contacts whether they would like to receive their newsletter and add them only if they respond in the affirmative. In today's environment, many firms using e-mail newsletters utilize a combination approach by adding e-mail addresses as they are collected, but also asking for interest at the time of the personal contact or through the firm's e-mail newsletter sign-up area on the firm's Web site.

Donations and Sponsorships

Another way to boost name recognition and build an image is to give donations to community organizations and sponsor charitable, social, and business events. The benefits of donations and sponsorships come in the power of association. By supporting charitable, social, and business events like a wine auction, a theatrical production, or an awards presentation, a firm creates an image of itself as an associate of that organization. It gains name recognition with those who attend the event and changes from a "nobody" to a "somebody."

One example of institutional marketing can be seen through the hosting of informational seminars for attorneys, bankers, and other accountants where continuing legal education (CLE) or continuing professional education (CPE) credit is offered. The material in these meetings can be very technical, but the purpose is to create an image in the mind of the attendants that the firm is experienced, knowledgeable of the most up-to-date issues, and trustworthy. When attorneys and bankers perceive the firm in this manner, they are open to building mutually beneficial relationships with the accounting firm and are more willing to serve as referral sources to the firm. The actual services offered by the accounting firms are not mentioned, but the attendants infer from the topics discussed that the firm performs services related to the material.

Professional and Civic Memberships

Another way to capitalize on the power of association is to encourage staff members to volunteer for professional and charitable endeavors and then tell people about it without bragging. Community involvement through serving on boards and committees, plus donating time to participate in programs and fundraisers, helps staff members with individual professional development and helps the firm with image building. Professionals also meet new contacts and strengthen preexisting relationships through volunteering. Both professional organizations, such as Rotary International, Kiwanis International, and the Chamber of Commerce, and civic organizations, such as the United Way or the American Red Cross, provide opportunities for involvement. The perception of the firm is enhanced as it gains a reputation for being "one of the good guys" in the marketplace.

Having this kind of reputation helps in business development efforts because prospects will already have an opinion about the firm before they know anything about the firm's service approach. Prospects will tend to swing the door open for a firm they already know about through branding efforts rather than a firm that is a stranger to them.

Media Relations

Media relations efforts help a firm to build credibility in its marketplace and within its community. Through submitting articles to trade publications and business journals, pitching stories about trends and developments, and sending press releases about firm news, a firm can benefit from a third party's influence over the public audience. Simply having the firm name published in a local newspaper can result in thousands of impressions. However, those impressions may not come from the audience with whom you wish to communicate.

Press releases are the simplest and easiest form of communication with the media. After sending a short press release about firm news like a new hire or promotion, or an industry trend like the demand for fraud investigation services, a follow-up call to the reporter is always helpful to offer more information about the topic, including the availability of personal interviews and even images to support the story. Pitching story ideas to reporters is more complicated and may involve some research. Oftentimes, you can borrow story ideas from other markets and apply them to your local market. Marketers can also offer an accountant's advice and expertise to business reporters when they write their stories. Ideally, the firm could become "the voice" for accounting-related issues for a local publication.

Media relations efforts are time-consuming in nature because they rely on careful wording and timing of information releases, diligent follow-up, and extensive market and industry research. In return, there are no guarantees of control over the placement or tone of what is published. Oftentimes a small marketing department cannot justify the time that is necessary to manage these communications. Many firms have taken the approach to outsource the public relations function, which can be a costly, but worthwhile endeavor if the firm can afford to do so.

Public Speaking

Marketers can assist staff members in scheduling public speaking engagements. This component of a public relations strategy affords professionals an opportunity to "sell" their experience and expertise to an attentive audience. Presentations to small groups at morning Kiwanis meetings and to larger crowds at a conference, for example, can allow the demonstration of talent in front of an audience with potential clients.

Not everyone is skilled in public speaking, but with some training, accountants and other service professionals who are nervous in front of crowds can learn to be more comfortable as a speaker. In the long run, by developing these people skills, they will become better service providers and communicators with their clients. Scheduling speaking engagements may be difficult at first, but smaller organizations like Rotary Clubs and Kiwanis meetings are more willing to invite first-time speakers to present. Before contacting organizations, determine the topics that the speaker is comfortable and knowledgeable about presenting.

Giveaways /"Logoing"

Logoing is a term sometimes used to describe the practice of branding in which a company places its logo on an item that is used by its staff or given away as a gift. Most businesses have a signature item that they brand with their logo to pass out at events like seminars or trade shows, or to give to clients, prospects, and other contacts as gifts. The purpose of logoing items (or distributing premiums or advertising specialties) is to leave something behind by which people can remember the firm. Ideally, you want the person to value the item enough to keep it so that each time he or she uses it, he or she thinks of the firm. Pens, portfolios, mugs, picture frames, desk sets, and notepads are all common logoed giveaways.

It is best to tie in the logoed gift with a characteristic unique to the firm. Moore Stephens Apple in Akron, Ohio, plays on its name by giving its top clients a chocolate in the shape of an apple with its logo impression on it as a holiday gift. Giving gifts for holidays and momentous occasions, or as a thank you for doing business with the firm, is appreciated by the recipients and serves as a goodwill effort to build better rapport.

Recruiting

In the accounting industry, professionals are in high demand and staffing is a continuing issue among firms across the nation. By developing a mutually beneficial relationship with local universities, firms can use this name recognition and goodwill in the community to recruit the best talent and develop an image as a premier firm.

Funding scholarships, serving on advisory boards, and speaking to student groups are ways to make an impression with students and university officials. The best way to get the attention of the students, the faculty, and the leadership is to offer a greatly desired opportunity for students such as a scholarship or internship. The firm would generate interest with highly skilled students (potential employees) who can help with the workload, and the student interns would get desirable real-world experience. In the process, the firm builds name recognition.

Nontraditional Methods

Nontraditional methods of brand marketing, such as radio and TV advertising and blogging, are gaining momentum with the professional services industry. With the passage of two solid decades of trial-and-error marketing, accountants and lawyers are dabbling in radio sponsorship on National Public Radio stations and even 30-second television branding ads. For firms in some major metropolitan areas, television advertising accomplishes the goal of creating a distinction from the competition. Firms take a risk in engaging in these kinds of branding methods, as it is unclear whether the benefits outweigh the risk involved. Will the business community accept TV as an appropriate medium by which a professional firm can communicate its message?

Another way some firms are communicating their message to the public is through blogging. Blogging is a kind of online journal where a person can post messages and others can add comments, which can sometimes lead to an open forum discussion. Few service professionals are using blogs as a communication tool, but their influence is clear. Blogs are like a person's favorite magazine: they just cannot put it down. Two examples are Philadelphia attorney Peter B. Nordberg, who discusses expert witness issues through his blog at www.daubertontheweb.com, and Arkansas CPA Kerry M. Kerstetter, who answers tax questions and posts tax-related cartoons and links to stories on his blog, *Tax Guru,* at www.taxguru.net.

Pitfalls

Overall, branding must be carefully approached so as to groom the firm in the public eye as a provider of quality services that benefits the community by its presence in the market and dedication to economic growth. This has to be accomplished without crossing the invisible line to levels perceived as distasteful by the target audience. Even if a firm has a shining reputation and great brand awareness, the firm may not necessarily prosper without the follow-up steps to branding. The biggest pitfall with any branding campaign is disregarding the sales activities.

BUSINESS DEVELOPMENT

Every business wants to grow and to prosper, and the businesses of accountants, lawyers, physicians, and bankers are no different. Whereas branding plays a lead role in building the foundation, business development activities are aimed at boosting revenue and, ultimately, growing the practice. Firms vary on the way in which they conduct sales activities like networking, prospect meetings, direct mail campaigns, seminars, and telemarketing. At some firms, the marketing director plays a larger role in the sales process by participating in everything from networking to prospect meetings and proposal writing. At other firms, marketers play more of a supportive role by providing coaching and training for accountants through the sales process. And some firms have tackled sales by hiring a business developer whose sole responsibility is to generate leads and follow through with them to a close.

Networking

Strategically socializing or networking at business, social, and charitable functions is a great way to meet prospective clients and contacts who could potentially refer work to the firm. It also serves a purpose by creating a "buzz" for the firm by getting people to talk about the firm and its employees. Professionals can keep up-to-date with the latest local business issues, create a bigger network of personal contacts, and even generate leads for new client opportunities.

Chamber of Commerce events, business organizations, and charity fund-raisers are great opportunities for networking. Similarly, golf can bridge the gap between strangers and strengthen relationships between colleagues. Golf outings provide a perfect setting for open discussion and deals to be made. It seems that in the public accounting industry, playing golf is second only to earning a CPA license. Networking on the golf course gives professionals one-on-one time to listen to and learn about others while building mutually beneficial relationships.

Each professional should keep a personal database of his or her contacts, but the marketer for the firm should also maintain a centralized database of contacts. This list should also include information about how the contact was developed, his or her business sector, what he or she may be interested in as far as the firm's services, and who from the firm knows him or her. Many software applications are available to help organize this information, but the most helpful software tool is a CRM application. With so many options to choose from, a firm should determine its goals for using the software before even looking at available options. CRM solutions range from very affordable to very expensive, depending on which features the firm is interested in having available.

Direct Mail Campaigns

Direct mail campaigns are commonplace for accounting firms and are used in a variety of ways. Overall, direct mail campaigns can be successful if the right message is delivered to the right audience. Some firms develop full-circle campaigns that include mailers, e-mails, Web site integration, and follow-up calls for a particular service targeted at a special niche group or minimarket. Other firms use direct mail for seminar invitations or even for branding campaigns. The goal for any direct mail campaign is to entice the recipient to take some kind of action —either make a phone call, visit a Web site, or register for a firm-hosted seminar. For the most successful direct mail campaign, the firm should follow up with the prospects with phone calls or customized e-mails. Calls to prospects to discuss previously mailed materials can be considered a telemarketing effort. With a positive approach and a message prospects are interested in hearing, direct mail campaigns can be worthwhile endeavors, resulting in the generation of new leads.

Seminars

Face-to-face interaction with prospects is one of the best ways to make an impression and begin to build relationships with prospects or their colleagues who may be willing to refer business to the firm. Services professionals have a wealth of knowledge in their field and sharing that knowledge—especially for free—helps to build goodwill and fosters confidence among the firm's contacts, introduces the firm to prospective clients, and provides the firm's professionals with an opportunity to develop their marketing skills.

Firms often offer CPE and CLE credit to draw in larger crowds for seminars on issues beneficial to a range of businesspeople. Inviting current clients and potential clients to seminars adds value to current services and enables the cross-selling of additional services.

When presenting at a seminar, the firm's professionals have the undivided attention of the audience, and they are able to communicate the marketing message and obtain feedback from the audience. Marketing's role in presenting seminars is to plan carefully for all aspects of the presentation, always thinking from both the perspective of the attendee and the firm. A flawless seminar will leave the impression that the firm is well organized, knowledgeable, and successful, but a seminar with a dull speaker, cold coffee, and inferior handout materials will leave an imprint that is nearly impossible to forget.

Referrals

Through networking, seminars, and working with current clients, service professionals meet other service professionals, including accountants, attorneys, and bankers, who have the ability to refer their clients and contacts to you and vice versa. In order for this kind of exchange to occur, you must first establish credibility and a foundation of trust and mutual respect with the referral source. No one will be willing to refer business to you without having a positive opinion of the firm's service quality.

Invitations to lunch and events like golf outings and presentations help professionals get to know other professionals. After-hours "mixers" between professional services firms—like accountants and attorneys—also provide a relationship-developing opportunity. Referral sources can provide some of the most qualified leads, as many of the referrals are for their clients, with whom they have chosen to work. Current and former clients who are willing can also provide referrals to the firm, and their firsthand knowledge of working with the firm is oftentimes the best sales pitch you can use to close a deal.

Sales Calls/Prospect Meetings

The next step beyond meeting people and developing relationships through networking, direct mail campaigns, seminars, and referrals is the prospect meeting. This is the time when the firm will leave a lasting impression on the prospect. The key to a successful prospect meeting is to arrive prepared, knowing a substantial amount of information about the prospect already, and to listen carefully to the prospect. Many deals are lost and clients turned into unsatisfied customers when the professional does not listen to the prospect's needs.

Not every prospect is a good match for the firm. Often this is discovered when meeting directly with the prospect. In these cases, it is best to refer the prospect to another firm that may be more suitable for meeting his needs.

Keeping track of numerous business development opportunities can be challenging, and a firm should use a process to be sure that accountants are following up on leads in a timely manner. The simplest method to track prospect status is to build a Pipeline, which is an Excel spreadsheet where prospect information is keyed and sorted based on its current stage in the sale process.

1. *Suspects (in accounting language, these are similar to footnotes)* are prospects that fit the firm's parameters for being a client. In other words, based on what you know about him or her, you would like that person to be a client. No interest has been shown on the part of the prospect.

2. *Unqualified Leads (similar to long-term assets)* are prospects who might be interested in the firm's services. You may have heard that they were looking for a new firm, or based on your discussion with them, it is your understanding that they have a need.

3. *Qualified Leads (similar to current assets)* are prospects with whom you have had a clear discussion to know that they have a need, along with the authority to resolve it, and that there is potential for the firm to assist them. You must reasonably believe that the prospect will buy from you.

4. *Proposal Stage* is the step where the firm is preparing a proposal to provide services to a prospect. The prospect is clearly interested in using the firm as its service provider.

5. *Final Stage* is the last step in the sales process where the prospect is reviewing the proposal and the firm is awaiting the decision. Follow-up is crucial at this step, as with every step, to be sure that the prospect thoroughly understands the contents of the proposal and that the firm has developed a solution that meets the prospect's needs.

Wins and losses should be tallied on the Pipeline in addition to the estimated revenue won or lost. The Pipeline promotes accountability among staff members to keep in contact with leads and uncover any trends as to the firm's opportunity win rate.

Proposals

A proposal is seen by many firms—and also by many clients—as a necessary evil. A proposal is the paperwork involved in making a decision to use professional services. However, despite their reputation for being standard drag-and-drop information documents, proposals play a significant role in the selection process.

A proposal demonstrates to a prospect that the salesperson was truly listening to his needs, understood his position, and has put forth genuine effort to solve the prospect's problems. A good proposal focuses on the benefits to the potential client and highlights the most important points of previous discussions about the prospect's needs. The proposal should avoid lengthy content about the firm as a service provider. By the time a prospect has a proposal in his or her hands, he or she already knows a great deal about the firm.

When proposing on a project that is out for bid, the first firm to submit a proposal is the one with which all others are compared. Even if electronic copies were specified, hard copy is often appreciated. Follow-up hand delivery with a call or visit to answer questions ensures a positive impression. By taking these extra steps, the prospect will see that the firm has a strong desire to be chosen and will feel that the firm will truly value the business.

Whether or not the firm wins the business, a person not directly involved in the sales process (many times the firm's marketer) should call the prospect to ask for feedback about the firm's sales process and why the firm did or did not win the bid. These conversations are oftentimes enlightening as they provide another perspective and can help the firm with both its branding and sales strategies.

Client Ownership

Incentive plans influence staff members to close sales, and afterward, they want to know that they will be rewarded by being solely responsible for their clients. Many lower-level professionals fear that they will not have ownership of the new clients they bring in and may begin to act very protectively toward them.

Management team members struggle with a similar issue. They want to see that their clients receive the best service—which generally means that they want to personally perform the services for their clients. For management, relinquishing some control by passing down work to senior- and staff-level accountants is challenging.

Because time is billable in professional services, time management is crucial to practice growth. Partners and other managers are oftentimes the best salespeople for the firm because they are highly regarded in their industry due to their experience. If staff members have been well trained in their field, management should feel confident in its ability to provide top-quality service to the firm's clients.

Nontraditional Methods

Some professional service firms have seen success in their sales process with untraditional methods such as telemarketing and trade shows. Larger firms with greater resources have attempted to attract leads through follow-up calls for direct mail campaigns and cold-calling on prospects.

Trade shows give service professionals an opportunity to speak directly with prospects in a sales setting. Setting up a trade show booth is very costly, as larger, more technology intense displays and nicer premiums attract more attention to the booth, one major goal. Trade shows tend to result in a higher volume of prospects, but not necessarily the quality of prospects desired. This method is best implemented when a firm has a specific service to offer prospects guaranteed to be attending the trade show. For smaller firms, trade shows are not a feasible option, but larger firms are beginning to show their wares at these conferences.

Taboos

Despite its use in some markets, telemarketing is considered more of a taboo than an acceptable practice. In the 2004 Accounting Marketing/Sales Responsibility and Compensation Survey conducted by the Association for Accounting Marketing, 29 percent of firms reported having used telemarketing techniques. Thirty-four percent conducted these calls internally, 40 percent outsourced the function, and 26 percent used a combination of both.[13]

Other business development methods that are generally thought of as inappropriate for the industry include direct solicitation (as in door-to-door sales) and any quick-sell methods. Showing up uninvited at a prospect's office without an appointment is never a good way to build a credible reputation, and using sales techniques that focus on a quick and easy close would make prospects look for another provider or leave them in a whirlwind of doubt about their decision to do business with the firm.

Professional services are sold based on relationships and trust, and not on special coupon offers or quick-sell pitches. One rule of thumb proposes that it takes six "touches" before a prospect will seriously consider working with a professional service firm. That means that selling professional services takes time, and methods that revolve around quick turnaround will not be successful in the professional services industry.

CLIENT SATISFACTION AND RETENTION

Because professional services are sold on relationships, client retention is also dependent upon the relationship. Clients want to feel that they are special to the firm. They want to feel that the firm values their business and would inconvenience itself to assist them. For these reasons clients need to be coddled, to some extent, by the professionals assigned to their accounts. This attention to satisfaction should be a priority within the firm from the top down.

Birthday and holiday cards, gifts for special occasions and milestones, and invitations to recreational activities like a baseball game or concert are all simple gestures that give clients the special attention they desire. Surveying clients on an annual or biannual basis is a good way to keep discussion going about their needs, wants, goals, and fears over which the firm has influence. Clients recognize and appreciate that the firm is making an investment in their satisfaction.

The client satisfaction survey is an opportune time to introduce the client to other services that may be of benefit to them. This cross-selling strategy helps to create "multiservice customers" who rely on the firm greatly for many of their needs. In today's marketplace, clients are turned off by the hassle of switching firms, and the more services a firm provides to a client, the more difficult it is to leave the firm.

An example of cross-selling is to begin by completing a client's tax return and then offer tax-planning services to help him or her save money. Next, a firm can bid competitively on another service to that client, which will lead to consulting work on a larger scale, and possibly even personal financial planning for the client's executives. Investing time into cross-selling strategies is worthwhile, as it is less expensive to keep a current client than it is to acquire a new one.

Today's industry trend is for firms to have the capability to offer more and more services to their clients and essentially become a "one-stop shop" for all their clients' needs. These full-service firms are incorporating consulting practices for human resources, information technology, and even marketing. In addition, through memberships in national and global alliances and associations, firms are working together across competitive markets to provide a plethora of services to their clients, thereby growing revenue and reliance on the firm.

The Rehmann Group in Saginaw, Michigan, is an example of a firm that is successfully integrating a diversification marketing strategy into its practice. It arranged a deal with InfoQuest, a provider of a client satisfaction survey tool that claims to elicit a higher response rate than any other survey method. Rehmann Group employees dedicated to selling this product call on marketers at other accounting firms across the nation to sell the system to its colleagues. This diversification strategy involves a great deal of risk, but as it expands the scope of the firm and draws in clients from new market segments, it often has the largest growth potential.

BUDGET

When establishing a budget for marketing expenses, management and marketers must collaborate on the firm's goals and prioritize expenses based on project importance. The anticipated cost of each task should be estimated and summed to develop the overall budget. Typically, a firm's marketing budget encompasses 2–4 percent of the firm's gross annual revenue, and the majority of firm's do not include marketing or sales salaries in the budget.[14] This is a guideline only; the budget should be set based on the tasks to be undertaken and the results that are expected.

The budget should include expenses for any advertising or promotional activities like the firm's newsletter, Web site, promotional giveaway items, or print advertisement placement. Some firms choose to include some, but not all, sales activities. Direct mail campaigns are generally included, but sometimes gifts to clients, business lunches, networking function expenses, and mixers with other local business professionals are not included. Marketing and sales training for staff including outside speakers, training materials, conferences, and continuing education may or may not be included in the budget.

A good rule of thumb is to establish initial goals for marketing at the beginning of the fiscal year and apply expenses to the budget only if they help marketers and staff to work directly toward those goals. Arguing over the budget is a poor use of time, and planning at the beginning of the year will help to alleviate some tension down the road. There will undoubtedly be some unexpected expenses so, while planning, be conservative with the figures. In obtaining approval for the budget, work with management team members to help them see the value in designating dollars to the budget by creating projections of results for marketing efforts. Translating concepts into numbers helps accountants to see the value of marketing activities, which can be expensive.

WHEN IS THE PAYOFF?

Many partners get anxious about the investment in time and dollars allocated to marketing at the firm. All marketing efforts are centralized around supporting and providing a venue for building relationships, and doing so can take a significant amount of time. Reporting the results in both a quantitative and a qualitative manner will help management to see progress directly related to marketing initiatives. Marketers prepare yearly, quarterly, and sometimes even monthly reports, collecting all data from branding campaigns and sales activities—information such as the response rate for a direct mail piece, the number of column inches (translated to dollars) resulting from media relations efforts, the number of attendees at a recent seminar, and the opportunity win rate for proposals.

Regular reviews of marketing initiatives are helpful to assess specific campaigns, evaluate staff performance, and reallocate dollars within the budget as necessary. Each year, management and marketers should use this information to create an overall marketing plan and budget for the year.

PARTNER BUY-IN AND STAFF SUPPORT

Many accountants hold on to the belief that marketing is not a worthwhile pursuit for their firms and that the costs to implement such a program would exceed the benefit. They are skeptical of marketing and its potential benefits. It is true that setting up a marketing program within a firm can be a costly and time-consuming endeavor. However, when partners' time begins to free up and a working plan is in motion, partners see the justification for such an investment. When a firm has established a positive marketing culture within its own corporate culture, marketing initiatives are supported in an indirect and direct manner, and they tend to result in greater professional growth for individuals and practice growth for the firm as a whole. The struggle for internal marketers in these situations is to prove their worth to the firm's leadership.

Building support for marketing activities among nonmanagement staff can be a difficult process, as many staff- and senior-level accountants view marketing as a separate function that simply coexists—rather than interacts—with their client service function. Many firms—like RINA Accountancy Corporation in Walnut Creek, California—have engaged in lunchtime Rainmaker Roundtables to coach staff about the benefits of learning marketing skills and integrating them into their professional goals.

Some firms have taken the approach to develop personal marketing plans with each staff member to coincide their personal goals with the firm's goals and set realistic objectives. Some firms also offer incentive or bonus plans to encourage staff members to take the initiative with marketing efforts. Burkett, Burkett & Burkett Certified Public Accountants in West Columbia, South Carolina, developed a point system where accountants are awarded a predesignated number of points based on the type of activity accomplished.

The overall goal is to get all staff members on the bandwagon for marketing efforts. Especially if marketing is new to a firm, some staff members will not understand that marketing will directly involve them and achieving success will require a significant amount of effort and support on their part. Job descriptions will change to reflect the new focus of marketing, and some staff members may be reluctant or even refuse to participate. Once the professional understands his or her unique role in the marketing process and in achieving the firm's goals, he or she has a stake in the outcome and so feels included as part of the process.

SUMMARY AND CONCLUSION: THE BOTTOM LINE

Throughout the industry, marketing for accounting firms is seeing slow, but steady growth as accountants are beginning to view their firms as service-oriented businesses.[15] Increasingly, marketers are approaching professional service firms to offer their talents. The growth can also be attributed to partners' dissatisfaction when billable time is lost as they engage in marketing activities themselves. They recognize that publishing newsletters, placing advertisements, preparing seminars, and many other marketing-related tasks may be best left to others.

The trend for smaller and mid-sized accounting firms over the last decade has been to either outsource to another service provider or hire an internal marketing director to coordinate these activities and relieve partners and other accountants in firms from these responsibilities. In a survey conducted in 2004 by the Association for Accounting Marketing, 26 percent of the participants worked at firms that had had an internal marketer only for three or fewer years. More than half of the participants worked at firms that had an internal marketer for six or fewer years. According to the same survey, 63 percent of the respondents were the only marketers at their firm, and 31 percent of the respondents supervise just one to three people. Only 6 percent of the respondents work with more than three people on the marketing/sales staff. Also, 46 percent stated that they were the first-ever marketer at their current firm.[16]

Once viewed as unseemly and borderline unethical, marketing is becoming a new lifeblood for professional services firms. The identification of a firm's strengths and weaknesses compared to its marketing, and positioning that firm versus its competition, enables senior management to direct the tasks of professional marketers. The marketers then organize the efforts of the firm's other professionals to offer their skills to clients and work to retain those clients. Properly executed, these marketing strategies can lead to a long life for the firm and harmonious interactions among its professionals.

NOTES

1. Honeycutt, Earl D. Jr., and John A. Marts, "Marketing by Professionals as Applied to CPA Firms: Room for Improvement?" *Journal of Professional Services Marketing,* 6 (January 1990).

2. Hite, Robert E., and Norman O. Schultz, "A Survey of the Utilization of Advertising by CPA Firms," *Journal of Professional Services Marketing,* 3 (January/February1987).

3. Kotler, Philip, and Richard A. Connor, Jr., "Marketing Professional Services," *Journal of Marketing* (January 1977), 71–76.

4. Ibid.

5. Hite and Schultz, "A Survey of the Utilization of Advertising by CPA Firms."

6. Hite, Robert E., and Joseph A. Bellizzi, "Consumers' Attitudes toward Accountants, Lawyers and Physicians with Respect to Advertising Professional Services," *Journal of Advertising Research* (June/July 1986), 45–54.

7. Stevens, Robert E., C. W. McConkey, D. L. Loudon, and P. Dunn, "Accountants' Attitudes toward Advertising and Their Use of Marketing Tools," *Journal of Professional Services Marketing,* 10 (February 1993).

8. Wood, Thomas, and Donald A. Ball, "New Rule 502 and Effective Advertising by CPAs," *Journal of Accountancy* 145 (June 1978), 65–70.

9. George, William R., and Paul J. Solomon, "Marketing Strategies for Improving Practice Development," *Journal of Accountancy* 149 (February 1980), 79–88.

10. Kotler, Philip, *Marketing Management—Analysis, Planning, Implementation and Control* (1991), Englewood Cliffs, NJ: Prentice Hall.

11. Winston, William J., *Marketing for CPAs, Accountants, and Tax Professionals* (1995), Binghamton, NY: Haworth Press.

12. Gillett, John W., A.A. Hiltner, and D.J. Elbert, "Marketing: Are Accountants Responding to the Challenge of Change?" *Journal of Professional Services Marketing*, 8 (February 1993).

13. Association for Accounting Marketing, "2004 Accounting Marketing/ Sales Responsibilities and Compensation Survey Results," http://www .accountingmarketing.org.

14. Ibid.

15. Gillett et al., "Marketing: Are Accountants Responding to the Challenge of Change?"

16. Association for Accounting Marketing, "2004 Accounting Marketing/Sales Responsibilities and Compensation Survey Results."

CHAPTER 13

CELEBRITY BRANDING: PERILS AND PAYOFFS

Christopher Gebhardt

Personal beauty is a better introduction than any letter.
> —Diogenes Laertius. Circa A.D. 200

CELEBRITY ENDORSERS: AN OLD, AND EFFECTIVE, APPROACH

The use of celebrities to promote products has been a long-standing strategy for many companies. One of the earliest examples is the association of Queen Victoria with Cadbury Schweppes's cocoa in Great Britain.[1] While estimates vary, all agree that the use of celebrity endorsers has risen dramatically, not only in the United States, but across the globe. It has been suggested that in the early 1980s approximately one in six advertisements utilized a well-known figure and that it may be as high as one in three advertisements today.

Why do marketers choose celebrity-based advertising and communication strategies? Does associating a product or service with a well-known actor, athlete, or model lead to more positive attitudes, greater purchase intent, and ultimately purchase? Does anyone really purchase a Canon PowerShot digital camera just because it is endorsed in advertisements by tennis ace Maria Sharapova? Even better yet, do any companies or CEO's contact Accenture to arrange for technology consulting services due to the fact that golf great Tiger Woods is shown in Accenture Ads? Advertisers seem to think so, and the results suggest they are correct. This chapter reviews the reasons behind this star-struck phenomenon and how celebrity endorsements fit within the larger context of building a brand. These and other related topics are the subject of this chapter.

THE CELEBRITY: NOT A SILVER BULLET

While using celebrities is an often-utilized strategy, it is not a silver bullet to building a brand. It does have tremendous potential to short-cut the process of building brands, which can be a laborious and frankly somewhat random process. How does celebrity endorsement fit into the brand-building process? What are the advantages and disadvantages? How can celebrities best fit into our strategic marketing process?

THE BRAND-BUILDING PROCESS

First, what is a brand? A brand is an intangible summation of a set of perceptions about a good or service or company. As such, a brand is the embodied representation of a product or service in the mind of the buyer. A brand is

- A representation,
- A short hand,
- The essence of a larger concept,
- An implied relationship,
- The elevator pitch,
- The gut feeling,
- A statement of to whom...for what.

Interestingly, a brand does not happen in a vacuum and is only partially driven by marketing, as brands occur within a culture that has great influence as well. A great brand has a sense of place, purpose, and progression. In building brands, marketing management must focus on defining a unique space and building it for the long haul. As shown in Figure 13.1, the Brand Pyramid creates the brand essence, through a combination of product attributes, functional benefits, rational benefits, and emotional benefits. The use of a celebrity, if well chosen, can create linkages at each of these levels in the brand creation pyramid.

THE PROMISE AND PERILS OF PARIS (HILTON)

While it is certainly one of the oldest brand tricks, there is as much peril as promise in the use of a celebrity-based strategy. Attaching a brand to a well-known celebrity exposes the brand to external risk, associated with the vagaries of celebrity behavior that is outside the control of the brand manager. Sometimes a celebrity can just be a bright shiny object to get attention and break through the clutter. In this case, the only real branding element is a possible cool factor.

A recent example is Paris Hilton writhing on a car, ostensibly washing it, but really just getting wet and slippery while wearing a small bikini, and, of all things, eating a burger from Carl's Jr., the West Coast fast-food burger chain. While Paris

Figure 13.1
The Brand Pyramid

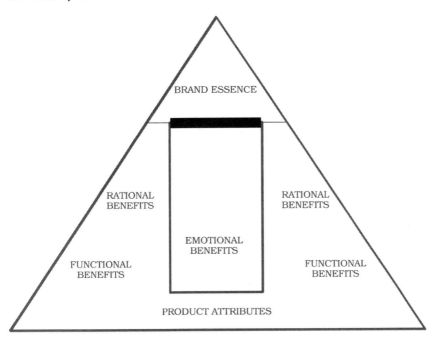

Hilton may be great eye candy, associating a family-oriented burger chain with an edgy, unpredictable, rich, globe-trotting icon may be risky business. Paris Hilton reached a plea agreement with prosecutors stemming from her September 7, 2006, arrest in Hollywood on suspicion of DUI after failing a field sobriety test.[2] Thus pinning a brand's personality with a real, live celebrity may create risks that are totally outside the control of the firm.

A more extreme example is O.J. Simpson, running back and star of Hertz Rent a Car commercials. The football icon seemed like a perfect fit to demonstrate fast and reliable service offered by Hertz—perfect until the football star was accused of killing. While he was eventually found not guilty of the crime in a legal sense, the court of public opinion issued a different verdict. O.J. Simpson became a liability, too hot and too controversial to ever again endorse any serious product or service. A more recent celebrity misstep was the allegation that waif model Kate Moss was sniffing cocaine at a recording session with her partner's (Pete Doherty) band, Babyshambles. After the cocaine story broke, Ms. Moss was dropped from a tentative multi-million-dollar contract with Swedish clothing retailer Hennes & Mauritz and received a nonrenewal notice from Chanel. While perhaps isolated, these instances point out the perils of attaching a brand's image to a star's image.

It is also interesting to note that, while Kate Moss was dropped from these two brands, other brands retained her and even increased her compensation. Indeed Kate Moss is earning more today (£30 million) than before the cocaine scandal broke.[3] How is this possible? One suggestion is that Kate Moss's brand recognition increased after the allegation, creating even more opportunity for her to cut through the clutter, a topic that is discussed further in this chapter. Another explanation is that Kate Moss was retained and added as an endorser for brands that had a matchup with her new edgier, cool brand image. This may help to explain her endorsement of brands such as Versace, Christian Dior, Roberto Cavalli, and David Yurman, which are positioning themselves to appeal to the globe-trotting jet-setters, or the Generation Y consumers who emulate this group.

CREATIVE CRUTCH?

In addition, use of a celebrity to jump-start a brand may be a poor substitute for an integrated brand strategy. Use of a well-known celebrity is not necessarily a bad thing, but may be an example of substituting celebrity for creativity in the communications process—in other words, celebrity branding can be a crutch for a brand team that has run out of ideas. If the endorser rings untrue, it will actually hurt rather than help the brand.

For example, Cadillac picking Cindy Crawford to revamp the brand about ten years ago is an example of a poor brand-celebrity matchup.

GLOBAL USE OF CELEBRITIES

This celebrity phenomenon is not unique to the American culture, as celebrity endorsements are significantly utilized in British, European, and Asian cultures as well. For example, in the Philippines, the obsession with celebrities endorsing products is widespread across brand categories, with actors as likely to endorse hamburgers as telecommunication services.[4] According to Nestor Cuartero, editor of a Manilla-based celebrity tabloid, the celebrity craze in the Philippines is such that "if you are even related in some way to the celebrity—whether you are her brother or driver—then by association you can get yourself [an advertising] deal.[5] Research by media giant Universal McCann found that 35 percent of Asian consumers admitted they would likely agree that they would purchase brands endorsed by celebrities. Thus global celebrities are one means for anchoring a truly global campaign strategy. Stars with global appeal, such as David Beckham (soccer star), Britney Spears (pop star), and most recently Christina Aguilera (pop star), can be utilized across a number of cultures to create a consistent global brand image.[6]

Celebrities with worldwide appeal can minimize cultural differences and position the brand as a truly global player. Successful examples include Pizza Hut,

Inc.'s use of supermodels Cindy Crawford and Linda Evangelista, and PepsiCo's use of Michael Jackson and Britney Spears. Therefore celebrities with worldwide appeal may successfully position brands as being truly global, achieve economies of scope and scale, and reduce barriers such as time, space, and cultural differences.

This broad-based appeal for celebrity-based advertising explains their increased use, but not the underlying mechanisms for their success. The reasons that celebrity-based appeals can be successful are the subject of the next section.

WHY USE CELEBRITIES?

The reality is that star power gets us looking. Indeed it not only attracts consumer attention, but media attention, and thus free publicity as well. Research has documented that use of a well-known celebrity in advertising was a key to obtaining media coverage.[7] For example, the July 16, 2006, issue of *Star* magazine carried a multipage spread showcasing the new global ad campaign being rolled out for Pepsi, featuring Christina Aguilera in a "Pepsi Passport Campaign." Thus, there is the direct advantage to companies when consumers are attracted by the celebrity in the advertisement and the indirect advantage when their ad is discussed in the media. This indirect appeal, due to nonpaid publicity generated by the campaign, offers a secondary, but very useful incentive to consider a celebrity-based strategy.

CUTTING THROUGH THE CLUTTER

The motivation behind celebrity endorsers includes cutting through the clutter to obtain attention, aiding brand recall, and increasing ad effectiveness due to the source credibility of many celebrities.[8] A frequently cited reason for using celebrities is their ability to attract immediate attention. As noted by Zafer Erdogan, "Increasing competition for consumer's consciousness and new product proliferation have encouraged marketers to use attention creating media stars to assist product marketing."[9] Coupled with technologies such as remote controls, TiVo, and programming on demand, more control is taken away from media sources and placed in the hands and hearts of consumers. Thus one of the primary reasons that celebrities are effective is their ability, quite simply, to obtain the customers' attention. In an age when entire magazines such as *People, Teen People,* and *Us Weekly* follow the weddings, breakups, shopping trips, and vacation travels of celebs, it is easy to see why marketers turn to well-known actors, athletes, and models to rev up their marketing and attract attention to their brand.

In today's media-cluttered environment, where the average American consumer is exposed to over 1,000 ad images daily, it is not surprising that the use of well-known figures is a particularly popular promotional strategy. The widespread fascination that the public has with well-known actors, sports figures, musicians, and models helps to bring attraction and additional talk value to a product or a brand, and while their endorsements are not cheap, they may offer impressive results. For example, when international telecom force Vodafone Group was struggling to get a foothold in the Australian market, it turned to a celebrity who, while not widely used in the U.S. market, has been a prolific product endorser in South Korea: Michael Richards. The well-known transvestite actor, Michael Richards, who played Kramer in *Seinfeld,* brought increased profits to telecom giant Vodafone. After featuring the *Seinfeld* star in a $40 million series of humorous ads, sales in Australia jumped by 1.3 million customers over three years.[10]

BRINGING MEANING TO A BRAND: A POSITIONING STRATEGY

Celebrity endorsement is increasing as companies seek not only effective methods that gain national headlines and cut through the clutter, but as a means for effectively communicating competitive differential advantage, bringing culturally related meanings to promotion and aiding consumer recall.[11] As shown in step 3 of the Strategic Marketing Process (Figure 13.2), choosing the best positioning strategy is critical. Celebrities with already established brand personas can assist in creating strong brand positioning strategies that bring meaning to a brand in the consumer's mind.

When compared to non-celebrity-based strategies, for example, a created icon, such as the Pillsbury Doughboy, for muffins, or Tony the Tiger, for cereal, research suggests that celebrity endorsers were more effective at creating positive attitudes toward the brand and greater purchase intentions.[12] Past research has suggested that celebrities provide additional information to consumers by providing clues to the product's effectiveness. For example, Carmen Electra was recently featured in a campaign for Max Factor makeup, focusing on a new Max Factor product called Lash Perfection. The sultry eyes of this well-known and sexy star gave visual meaning to communicate the brand attributes of stand-out eyes that give maximum impact through long, lush eye lashes, which were the product attributes that Max Factor wanted to communicate to potential buyers.

Another very effective brand positioning strategy using a well-known celebrity is the Canon PowerShot campaign, featuring well-known tennis star Maria Sharapova. The PowerShot campaign features a focused and intent-looking Sharapova getting ready to execute a powerful serve. The ad copy reads as follows:

> PowerShot: It's not every day that style and substance combine to form a single source of power and beauty. With its sleek exterior and DIGIC Image Processor, each Power Shot digital camera does exactly that. And just like Maria Sharapova, this combination is a force to be reckoned with.

> (www.powershot.com).

Figure 13.2
The Strategic Marketing Process

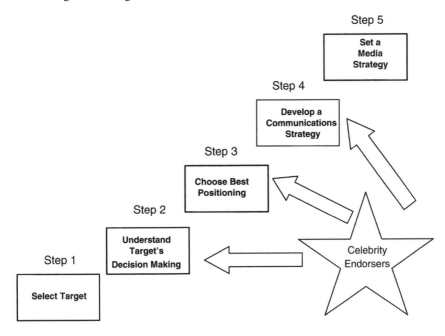

Source: Adapted from Percy, Larry, and Richard Elliott, *Strategic Advertising Management,* 2nd edition, Oxford University Press, Oxford, New York, 2005, p. 106.

The juxtaposition of an attractive Wimbledon tennis star with a power serve and the Canon camera creates an effective positioning strategy and strong brand image, serving as an excellent example of an effective strategic use of a celebrity.

It seems pretty much like a slam-dunk strategy. Hire a well-known celebrity and a company has a guarantee of product success. Not so. This chapter further explores the nuances of selecting and implementing an effective celebrity endorsement campaign.

Let us first look at several examples.

GOT MILK? AN EXAMPLE OF AN EFFECTIVE CELEBRITY AD CAMPAIGN

One of the most long-running and widely known celebrity endorsement campaigns is the "Got Milk?" Milk Mustache campaign, begun in 1994 by the Milk-PEP (Milk Processing Promotion Board) to increase the consumption of milk products by both children, adolescents, and adults in the United States.[13]

In 1994, the Milk Processors of California launched an advertising campaign, starting with print advertising, using pictures of celebrities with milk mustaches. Why use a milk mustache? It is not a new idea. Neither is using a celebrity for advertisement. However, using a celebrity sporting a milk mustache was a new and very big idea. But that was not all. At the bottom of every print was a short, four-line copy that reflected the personality of the celebrity, and in between was surprising new information about milk and its benefits to health. The idea was that if the visual had stopping power and if the copy was charmingly and engagingly written and made a person smile, then there was a very good chance of getting the message across.[14]

Spending only one-tenth of the promotional budget of a traditional competitive beverage product, the popular milk mustache campaign regularly shows up on lists of most favorite ads among children and teens. The long-standing campaign finds its appeal in a common theme using a broad range of celebrities drawn from the worlds of fashion, sports, entertainment, and music. The campaign was voted one of the ten best ad campaigns of 1998 by *USA Today,* the *New York Times,* and Video Storyboard Tests. The campaign was so widely known that celebrities called requesting to be in an ad, and kids collect the ads and frequent the interactive Web site www.whymilk.com.

This maybe new celebrity marketing campaign has been credited with improving the overall image of milk and slowing the 30-year decline of milk consumption overall, with studies suggesting that consumption would have dropped an additional 4.5 percent without the celebrity-studded campaign. Most impressive is the increasing milk consumption among teens, which grew from 21.4 gallons per person per year in 2000 to 24.1 gallons per person in 2003.[15]

WHAT MAKES FOR AN EFFECTIVE CELEBRITY ENDORSER?

Generally, to be an effective product endorser the celebrity must first and foremost be credible. Unfortunately, several individuals are no longer effective as celebrity endorsers due to their loss of credibility. As previously discussed, this would include football star O.J. Simpson, who previously promoted Hertz rental cars, pop icon Michael Jackson, who appeared in endorsements for Pepsi-Cola, and the stylishly thin model Kate Moss, who was dropped by both Chanel and Burberry after she was photographed sniffing cocaine by a British tabloid.[16] Similarly, Dell Inc. did not renew golfer Benjamin Curtis's contract after he was arrested for allegedly trying to buy marijuana.[17]

The importance of source credibility as a main driver of effective celebrity endorsers has been well documented. As outlined in Table 13.1, Dimensions of Source Credibility past research has found that there are three primary dimensions to source credibility, namely, (1) expertise, (2) trustworthiness, and (3) attractiveness. Research suggests that each of these three dimensions makes an independent

Table 13.1
Dimensions of Source Credibility

Dimension	Definition	Source
Expertise	Extent to which a communicator is perceived to be a source of valid assertions	Hoviland, Janis, Kelley[18]
Trustworthiness	The consumer's confidence in the source as objective and honest	Ohanian[19]
Attractiveness	Communicator's perceived physical attractiveness	Chaiken[20]

contribution to source effectiveness. Extending this to the arena of celebrity endorsers suggests that to be most effective, celebrity endorsers should be perceived as knowledgeable in the product category and be perceived as honest and unbiased in their recommendations. Not surprisingly, most products are endorsed by individuals that are not only well known within their field, but are great looking as well.

Research has documented that attractive individuals are, in general, more likely to be perceived as more persuasive than unattractive communicators. As a result attractive individuals are more likely to be hired for a job, make more successful salespeople, and are more likely to be voted into political office. The attractiveness dimension is perhaps even more relevant to the celebrity-endorser domain, as opposed to executive spokesman or consumer testimonials. Celebrities are traditionally photographed and portrayed in a manner that accentuates their positive attributes, through the use of lighting, makeup, fashion, and scenery. The draw of celebrities is the fact that they are not like the rest of us; indeed, it is the stars' personification of a fantasy ideal that sets them apart.

TIGER WOODS AND ACCENTURE: AN EXAMPLE OF SOURCE CREDIBILITY

Using the three-dimensional approach to celebrity endorsers, we consider the use of Tiger Woods as an endorser for American Express credit cards. At the age of 30 Tiger Woods is arguably the world's greatest golfer playing on the tour today (2006). As the youngest winner of all major golf championships, he is recognized throughout the globe as a world-class athlete. A recent print advertisement[21] for Accenture, a recognized leader in technology and outsourcing consulting services, carried a picture of Tiger Woods finishing his golf swing, with the following ad copy:

Do you see the forest?
    Or the trees?
    High performers see both.

Go on. Be a Tiger
    accenture
    High performance. Delivered

Fortune magazine, July 12, 2006

Is Tiger Woods an effective celebrity endorser for Accenture's worldwide consulting services? According to the source credibility model of celebrity endorsers, the answer would be a resounding yes for celebrity endorser in general, and for Accenture consulting services in particular. First, is Tiger considered an expert in the area of performance, the attribute targeted by this campaign? Indeed yes. Next, is Tiger Woods considered to be trustworthy as an athlete and an individual? Yes. He has consistently proven he is trustworthy in a sport that is considered by many to be a true gentleman's game. Golf is the only major sport in which the athletes are expected to, and actually do, assess penalties on themselves. And, of course, with his broad smile, trim athletic build, classic black attire, and likeable persona, Tiger is considered to be a very attractive person as well. Thus using the tricomponent model of source credibility, Tiger Woods would be expected to be an effective celebrity endorser for many products and services, including Accenture consulting services. This probably explains why Tiger Woods has been hired to endorse a variety of well-known products and brands, including Nike golf attire and equipment, American Express credit cards, and Buick cars, among others.

WHEN BEAUTY MAY BE ONLY SKIN DEEP

While the research on the three-prong dimension of celebrity endorsers and the dimensions of expertise, trustworthiness, and attractiveness has been fairly consistent and well received, several studies have delved more deeply into the issue of endorser attractiveness. For example, a 1990 study by Michael Kamins found that "beauty may be only skin deep," as their research suggested that attractiveness may be relevant only when the product being promoted is related to attractiveness.[22] The researchers found, for example, that celebrity attractiveness was relevant for an attractiveness-related product or a beauty-oriented product, which good-looking Tom Selleck promoted. In contrast, balding, and perhaps unattractive, Telly Savalas was perceived to be an effective endorser for a computer that was not related to attractiveness, but not a good endorser for a luxury car.

Research has, in many cases, focused on the hypothesized and disproportionate impact of celebrity-endorser attractiveness on ad effectiveness, a topic that is analyzed in more detail later in this chapter. What about successful celebrity endorsers that are not particularly attractive? What theory will explain why Dennis Rodman is chosen to endorse a product? While it may be true that many celebrities are attractive, it is also true that many successful celebrities may not be generally perceived to be more attractive than the general public. For example, Dennis Rodman, Donald Trump, Rosie O'Donnell, and Jerry Springer, among others, are not exceedingly attractive, but have been successful endorsers for many products.

WHEN CREDIBILITY IS NOT PRESENT

Sometimes celebrities do not appear to be very credible, but also do very well as a spokesperson for a brand. For example, in 1998 William Shatner became the spokesperson for "priceline.com." Shatner has been an effective endorser for the Priceline brand for over eight years. As a sign of the increased integration of traditional and new media, Shatner's new commercial aired on June 30, 2006, appearing online before it appeared on TV.[23]

Shatner has been an excellent priceline.com pitchman, but not because he has a ton of credibility as a brand. Rather, his somewhat campy persona—really the opposite of credibility—has worked because the brand embraced his tongue-in-cheek nature and thus infused itself with this same personality and life. The ads make you smile, create a connection, and help you feel part of a "I get the joke" crowd. It certainly is not based on Shatner's credibility as a warp speed traveler or starship captain. In this case the celeb brand helps set up a joke that otherwise cannot be told in 30 seconds, which makes the creative more effective—it is not about his knowledge at all, and that is okay.

How do we explain this? It is better explained using the matchup hypothesis, detailed in the next section.

MATCHUP HYPOTHESIS

The matchup hypothesis suggests that the message conveyed by the celebrity endorser and the message conveyed by the product should converge to maximize advertising effectiveness. The matchup hypothesis suggests that the visual imagery of the celebrity conveys information above the explicit verbal information contained in the ads.[24] Past examples of well-matched celebrities and products include Maria Sharapova, Wimbledon Champion and endorser for the Power-Shot camera by Cannon, great golfer Tiger Woods and Accenture consulting services, and classical-looking actress Uma Thurman who promotes exclusive and sophisticated TAG Heuer watches and timepieces.

ATTRACTIVENESS-RELATED PRODUCTS AND THE MATCHUP HYPOTHESIS

Researchers have hypothesized that according to the matchup hypothesis there should be congruence between the image of the celebrity and the image of the product. Thus products that are meant to enhance beauty, and sexuality, such as makeup, cologne, jewelry, and clothing should match up their products with an equally attractive celebrity endorser to achieve the greatest impact on product evaluations. Appropriate examples of matchups between a celebrity's physical attractiveness and attractiveness-related products would include actresses Penélope Cruz and L'Oreal Bare Naturale makeup, Eva Mendes and Revlon ColorStay makeup collection, and Sarah Jessica Parker and her Lovely fragrance brand.

In line with past research and hypotheses, the Kamins study found that spokesperson attractiveness enhanced attitude toward the ad, when the advertised product was related to attractiveness (a luxury car).[25] In contrast, there was no difference in attitude toward the ad between the physically attractive and physically unattractive spokesperson when the product being promoted was unrelated to attractiveness, for example, a computer. The takeaway from this research is that a company promoting an attractiveness-enhancing product, such as clothing, high-end jewelry, cologne, or makeup, will need to carefully select celebrity endorsers who are perceived to be attractive by the target group; whereas companies promoting products that have more utilitarian uses, such as computers, appliances, and luggage, may not have to pay as much attention to the attractiveness of their celebrities and may rely more heavily on the more traditional "Q" fare quotient ratings, which measure a star's popularity and recognizability.

THE AIDA MODEL OF ADVERTISING: MOTIVATIONS FOR USE OF CELEBRITY ENDORSEMENTS

Much research in the effectiveness of celebrities has focused on the ability and impact of celebrities to change consumer beliefs and positively impact consumers' attention to purchase.[26] Perhaps today the single biggest reason to use a celebrity is to help your promotional message get noticed. Let us face it. A message that never gets processed is not going to change anyone's purchase intention.

One of the oldest models of advertising, the AIDA Model (Figure 13.3), proposes a hierarchy of effects model for use of advertising as follows:

1. Attention,
2. Interest,
3. Desire, and
4. Action.

Figure 13.3
The AIDA Model of Advertising

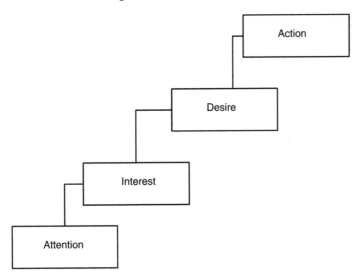

Within this model the goal of advertising changes based upon the stage that an individual consumer is on the continuum. Advertisers must consider that different consumers will be at different stages along this continuum, making it imperative to have ads targeted at the various stages. For example, at the earliest stages the goal is to obtain the consumer's attention, which is increasingly difficult in the new business environment. New digital technologies make it more difficult to get the attention of consumers through the traditional media channels of print, radio, and television. These new technologies include Web-enabled PDAs (personal digital assistants), cell phones with GPS (global positioning systems), Web-based online consumer communities, high-definition TVs with two-way communication, and satellite radio and television. One advantage of using a well-known celebrity is to attract the consumer's attention, but this alone is not sufficient. The use of celebrity endorsers must be across mediums, to provide an integrated message and create a unified image in the mind of consumers. To emphasize the integrated nature of today's marketing environment consider that research by Forrester Research found that the influence of the Web goes far beyond Internet purchases, estimating that over $126 billion in off-line sales were directly influenced by the Web.[27]

Within this more fragmented environment the customer has much more information and control than ever before, making it increasingly difficult to create an impression in the consumer's mind. Within this new advertising landscape the celebrity endorser gives the consumer a reason to look, pay *attention,* and move the consumer to the *interest* stage of the AIDA model. In addition the characteristics of the well-known celeb may increase the *desire* of the consumer to the action stage of purchasing the brand, in order to emulate his or her style, position, or personality. Thus the use of a celebrity endorser may be consistent with the AIDA model of advertising and help the brand to achieve the desired action as the consumer climbs the staircase to action.

CELEBRITY AND BRAND PERSONALITY

Consumers evaluate brands through human personality characteristics. Brands have personalities, whether it is the rebellious nature of Harley-Davidson motorcycles or the conservative personality of Talbot's, a clothing store for women. In many cases, individuals want brands with personalities that match their own, and in other instances consumers may want to purchase brands that have specific personality characteristics, for particular situations.

Why is there a relationship between celebrities and the brands they promote? One theory is that brands take on the personality of the celebrities who endorse them. Consistent with the theory of brand personality, brands take on human characteristics that engage buyers and connect them to particular brands. "Consumers evaluate brands through human personality traits, whether you've imputed traits to the brand or they've done so because you haven't. Of course, this is largely an unconscious evaluation."[28]

The research in brand personality assigns dimensions, such as sincere, sophisticated, and rugged to brand personality in much the same way as sociologists assign personality traits to humans.[29] Using the framework developed by Jennifer Aaker, the five distinct core dimensions of brand personality are listed in Table 13.2.

For example, in 2003 Tiger Woods, golf's leading money winner, became the centerpiece of Accenture's advertising campaign, by using a metaphor for high

Table 13.2
Aaker's Five Core Dimensions and Facets of Brand Personality

CORE DIMENSION	Sincerity	Excitement	Competence	Sophistication	Ruggedness
	Down to earth	Daring	Reliable	Upper Class	Outdoorsy
	Honest	Spirited	Intelligent	Charming	Tough
	Wholesome	Imaginative	Successful	Good-Looking	Masculine
	Cheerful	Up-to-Date	Leader		Western

performance.[30] Clearly this ad is using the Aaker's brand personality dimension of competence and related facets (reliable, successful, leader) to assign the human characteristics of Tiger Woods to the Accenture brand. Combining the theory of brand personality with the matchup hypothesis suggests that brand managers should carefully select celebrity endorsers who exhibit personality characteristics that align with the brand image and the personality they are hoping to form in the minds of consumers.

CELEBRITY ENDORSERS, BRAND PERSONALITY, AND MARKETING STRATEGY

A key step in developing marketing strategy is determining the best positioning strategy. In the traditional strategic planning process there are five key steps as shown previously in Figure 13.2, "The Strategic Marketing Process." The five key steps are as follows:

Step 1: Select the target,

Step 2: Understand the Target's Motivation and Decision Making,

Step 3: Choose Best Positioning,

Step 4: Develop a Communications Strategy, and

Step 5: Set a Media Strategy

Select the Target

The first initial step is, of course, to select the target market or more likely multiple target markets for your product, as well as an understanding of the motivations of each group. PepsiCo, for example, has multiple distinct target markets, ranging from Generation Y teens who are attracted to rap music and reality television, as well as Baby Boomers who are likely to listen to country tunes and Fox News.

Understand the Target's Motivation and Decision Making

The next step, understanding the target market motivations and decision making, requires a deep understanding of the nuances of the interests, opinions, lifestyles, and values of each group. For instance, within the Generation Y market, the subset of kids ages 8–14 constitutes the *tween* market. The tween market has unique motivations, shopping, and communication patterns. Generation Y consumers visit the malls more than any other age group, spending nearly $50.00 per mall visit, and are the largest users of cell phone text messaging and downloading of ring tones.[31] In addition, the profile of the Y Generation suggests that this group is not motivated by traditional media and is more likely to share buying decisions with its social group, while using the Web to make friends, find product information, and communicate with other teens throughout the globe.[32] Selected motivations and behaviors of the Generation Y, tween market are shown in the following list about the Motivations and Behaviors of Generation Y:

Tween Market of 8- to 14-Year-Olds[33]

1. Brand-Image Conscious: Know brand images better than an advertising expert.
2. Use Non-Traditional Media: No longer expect to be informed by traditional media of TV and radio.
3. New Definition of Loyalty: Individual brand loyalty is being replaced by group brand loyalty of tweens and their social group peers.
4. Global Communicators: nearly 24 percent of tweens communicate weekly with teens in other countries.
5. Internet Savvy: nearly one-quarter of all tweens worldwide use the Internet as their primary communication tool.

Selecting the appropriate celebrity endorser requires a deep understanding of stage two in the process: Understand the Target Audience Decision Making. This stage involves understanding the wants and needs of the target audience, including its motivations to purchase. These motivations are likely to be a combination of both cognitive and emotional motivations to purchase a cola beverage due to the cognitions, "I am thirsty," but he or she is likely to purchase a specific brand of cola, for example, Pepsi, due to the emotional attachment of the association between Mariah Carey and the upbeat music in the Pepsi ads.[34]

INTEGRATION IS KEY

Consumers are receiving media in new ways, due in large part to the increased access of broadband capabilities and the increasing demand for personal video recorders and video-on-demand systems. As a direct result of this shift, brand builders will need to create messages that are interesting and entertaining, encouraging consumers to opt in. "They need to smuggle brands into the content in a strategic way...by development of proprietary content that consumers willingly opt into and messaging that is wrapped around content."[35] While some industry executives are hesitant to support new models, executives at Integrated Entertainment Partners see integration of entertainment and brand building as one method for addressing the attack on traditional advertising methods. The traditional 30-second TV spot may no longer reach the intended target market as more consumers use technology to bypass commercials, time shift programming, and pay for commercial-free options. As a direct result brand building in the future will rely more on delivering messages through integration of content with brand messaging. Ideally, this integration will be across media and in manners that engage and entertain our targeted consumers.

One path for accomplishing this is imbedding brands within story lines, blurring the line between celebrity as product promoter and product user, for example, James Bond driving an Aston Martin and Tom Cruise wearing Ray-Ban sunglasses in the movie *Risky Business*. In the future, we might see movie scenes taking place in Starbucks, or Dunkin' Donuts, while lovable actress Reese Witherspoon may be shot driving in her cherry red Acura TL, and perhaps we can cast heartthrob Tom Cruise in a role where he and steady Angelina Jolie are cruising along Highway One in a silver Maserati. The ability to imbed brand messages within a story line will deepen consumer involvement and blur even more the distinction between promotion and product as celebrities of all forms become more entrenched in our culture.

EXAMPLE: CHRISTINA AGUILERA

An excellent example of an integrated campaign that uses multiple media channels to effectively integrate a brand personality with a particular brand image is the 2006 Pepsi campaign featuring pop superstar[36] Christina Aguilera. In these trendy television spots under the title *Downloaded,* the 25-year-old pop star, who formally pitched for The Coca-Cola Company, travels around the world wearing location appropriate scanty costumes, suggestive of the local culture. In these trendy ads fans around the world are shown downloading her song "Here to Stay" onto their cell phones. Each time the fans push the button to download, they get to see a picture of the sexy star transported to various exotic locations including Brazil, Tokyo, and the Arabian dessert, where the toned and tanned pop star is dressed or undressed in costumes ranging from a belly dancing costume to a Kabuki-style geisha outfit.[37]

This promotional campaign successfully integrated Christina Aguilera's personality with the personality of the Pepsi brand. According to Aaker's brand personality framework, Ms. Aguilera's personality might be classified as daring (daring = daring, trendy, and exciting)[38] and thus mesh nicely with the characteristics of many Generation Y consumers. This promotional campaign also crossed multiple media channels, furthering the integration of the brand and the pop diva. This ad creatively encouraged multiple media domains and involved the audience by encouraging cell phone downloads, music downloads, and increased traffic to the Web, where the television commercial could be viewed. In addition the novelty of the campaign resulted in coverage in celebrity-oriented magazines such as *Star.*[39]

Returning to the development of the brand essence, discussed earlier in this chapter, understanding the target market needs also includes selecting the set of brand benefits that are most important to the audience and that will allow you to differentiate your brand from the competition. As previously outlined, these benefits may be related to functional attributes of the brand (nail polish that dries faster), rational benefits (cheaper than the competition), or emotional benefits, using a well-known song, such as "Happy Birthday," to bring emotion to a radio commercial. The celebrity can directly relate to brand benefits that are at any of these levels in our brand pyramid, discussed earlier in this chapter.

The firm must focus on these brand benefits in a way that taps into the buyer's motivation to purchase. These motivations are often unconscious and at times hidden. It is common, for example, for a consumer to state that he or she bought a Rolex watch because it kept good time—which is not likely the case. A consumer is motivated to purchase an expensive Rolex watch because he or she can. The motivation is much more closely aligned with the motivation to impress, and to show status, than with any cognition about keeping good time. The third stage requires determining the best positioning.

CONCLUSION

In conclusion, celebrity endorsers should be considered as one potential element in our brand-building toolbox. When a celebrity is well known, has a matchup with the brand personality, and is used to make multiple connections with the brand-building pyramid, it can be an effective approach. William Shatner has been an excellent example of an effective link and matchup with a brand, priceline.com. Shatner's somewhat "campy" personality has worked because the brand embraces his tongue-in-cheek nature and thus infused a brand—really imparting the brand essence with some life and personality. The ads made you smile, creating an emotional connection in the brand pyramid. Too often celebrity endorsers are used to short-cut the brand-building process, and while they may create some short-term buzz, they are not a substitute for long-term building of a brand personality.

NOTES

1. Erdogan, Zafer, "Celebrity Endorsement: A Literature Review," Journal of Marketing Management, 15 (1995): 291–314.
2. Lee, Ken, "Paris Hilton Accepts Plea Deal in DUI Case," January 22, 2007, http://www.people.com/people/article/0,,20009307,00.html.
3. Kate Moss, http://www.forbes.com/lists/2006/53/BMGU.html (accessed April 18, 2007).
4. Hargrave-Silk, Atifa, "A Star Struck Obsession," Media Asia, 2003, pages 44–47.
5. Ibid., page 44
6. Ibid.
7. Erdogan, "Celebrity Endorsement: A Literature Review."

8. Ohanian, R. "Construction and Validation of a Scale to Measure Celebrity Endorsers Perceived Expertise, Trustworthiness and Attractiveness," Journal of Advertising 19, no. 3 (1990): 39–52.

9. Erdogan, "Celebrity Endorsement: A Literature Review."

10. Hargrave-Silk, "A Star Struck Obsession."

11. Erdogan, "Celebrity Endorsement: A Literature Review."

12. Atkin, C., and Block, M., "Effectiveness of Celebrity Endorsers," Journal of Advertising Research, 23 (March 1983): 57–61.

13. Food Marketing to Children and Adolescents Report to Congress—Comment Project No. PO64504, by Milk-PEP to the Federal Trade Commission, April 3, 2006.

14. Shulberg, Jay et al., *The Milk Mustache Book: A Behind the Scenes Look at America's Favorite Advertising Campaign.* The Ballantine Publishing Group, New York, 1998.

15. Ibid.

16. Duncan, Apryl, "The Good the Bad and the Ugly: Celebrity Endorsements of 2005," as found in http://advertising.about.com (accessed July 23, 2006).

17. Ibid.

18. Hovland, Carl I., Irving L. Janis, and Harold H. Kelley, *Communication and Persuasion.* Yale University, New Haven, CT, 1953.

19. Ohanian, "Construction and Validation of a Scale to Measure Celebrity Endorsers Perceived Expertise, Trustworthiness and Attractiveness."

20. Chaiken, Shelly, "Communicator Physical Attractiveness and Persuasion," Journal of Personality and Social Psychology, 37, no. 2 (1979): 1387–1397.

21. *Fortune* magazine, July 12, 2006.

22. Kamins, Michael, "An Investigation into the 'Match-up' Hypothesis in Celebrity Advertising: When Beauty May Be Only Skin Deep," Journal of Advertising, 19, no. 1 (1990).

23. See www.williamshatner.com (accessed September 25, 2006).

24. Rossiter, John R., and L. Percy, "Attitude Change through Visual Imagery in Advertising," Journal of Advertising, 9, no. 2 (1980): 10–16.

25. Kamins, "An Investigation into the 'Match-up' Hypothesis in Celebrity Advertising."

26. Ohanian, "Construction and Validation of a Scale to Measure Celebrity Endorsers Perceived Expertise, Trustworthiness and Attractiveness."

27. Forrester, "Did You Know?" Forrester Research online newsletter July 25, 2006, Sucharita Mulpuru (Forrester Research) (Forrester@en25.com).

28. Wolfe, David B., and Snyder Robert, *Ageless Marketing: Strategies for Reaching the Hearts and Minds of the New Customer Majority,* Dearborn Trade Publishing, a Kaplan Professional Company, 2003.

29. Aaker, Jennifer, "Brand Personality Dimensions Framework," Journal of Marketing Research, August 1997, pp. 347–356.

30. Accenture.com; http://www.accenture.com/Global/About_Accenture/Company_Overview/Advertising/default.html.

31. "Teen Market Profiles," Mediamark Research Inc., http://www.magazine.org/content/files/teenprofile04.pdf.

32. Adapted from Martin Lindstrom, "Branding Is No Longer Child's Play!" *Journal of Consumer Marketing*, 21, no. 3 (2004): 175–182.

33. Ibid.

34. http://www.pepsi.com/ads_and_history/, July 31, 2006.

35. Myers, Jack, "Ad Agencies' Day of Reckoning Is Coming," *Jack Myers Entertainment Report,* April 9, 2003.

36. Christina's Pepsi Passport, *Star,* July 16, 2006, pages 6–8.

37. Ibid.

38. Aaker, "Brand Personality Dimensions Framework."

39. Christina's Pepsi Passport.

CHAPTER 14

SPONSORSHIP-LINKED MARKETING: OPENING THE BLACK BOX

T. Bettina Cornwell, Clinton S. Weeks, and Donald P. Roy

Research on sponsorship-linked marketing spans several literatures, including the marketing subdiscipline areas of advertising, consumer behavior and strategy, as well as sports management, human movement sciences, and the social sciences. Sponsorship of sports, causes, the arts, and events forms a major portion of the so-called "unmeasured media" spending for many firms. Unmeasured media is the catchall category for the various other promotional expenditures of firms and nonprofits outside the major media such as television, radio, print, and outdoor (for example, billboards and transit cards). Moreover, sponsorship spending [estimated to reach $28 billion worldwide in 2004 (IEG, 2003)] for some firms is now the "tail that wags the dog" with more and more advertising (measured media) being thematically tied to sponsorship investments.

Despite broad-based acceptance and dependence on sponsorship-linked marketing programs as a communications tool, little is known about how individuals process these fragments of information (Pham and Vanhuele, 1997). Following a review of corporate sponsorship literature, Cornwell and Maignan (1998) and Cornwell (1999) criticized research in the area for lacking explanatory theoretical frameworks of how sponsorship works in the minds of consumers. Since then, a number of theoretically grounded studies of corporate sponsorship have been published, but the black box of sponsorship information processing is only just being opened. With this in mind, this chapter has three goals. The first is to provide a meaningful summary of theoretical progress to date regarding how consumer-focused sponsorship works. The aim here is not to provide a comprehensive review of all recent sponsorship research, but to focus specifically on those papers forwarding theoretically grounded research. The second goal is to critically examine this research with an emphasis on psychological processing and measurement. Finally, it is the goal of this chapter to integrate disparate research into a theoretical framework to guide future research and to assist in the management of sponsorship outcomes.

CONSUMER-FOCUSED SPONSORSHIP-LINKED MARKETING

Sponsorship has been defined as "a cash and/or in-kind fee paid to a property (typically a sports, entertainment, non-profit event or organization) in return for access to the exploitable commercial potential associated with that property" (IEG, 2000). Sponsorship-linked marketing is then "the orchestration and implementation of marketing activities for the purpose of building and communicating an association to a sponsorship" (Cornwell, 1995, p. 15). These two definitions together highlight central differences between advertising and sponsorship. Whereas sponsorship involves a fee paid in advance for future potential communication values, advertising offers a more knowable and more controlled communication. Further, while sponsorship requires leveraging (promotional spending in addition to the sponsorship fee) to obtain the greatest value, advertising is often sponsorship's most valuable leverage.

Sponsorships may be directed toward consumers, channel members, financial institutions, government, community, and employees (Gardner and Shuman, 1988). The sponsorships themselves may entail sports, arts, causes, and combinations of these, such as the FedEx St. Jude (children's research hospital) Classic. While nonconsumer outcomes can range from the interest of potential investors to esprit de corps, consumer-focused sponsorships typically seek to improve some aspect of awareness, attitude, image, or behavioral intention to purchase products, utilize services (for example, have a mammogram), or give donations (for example, time to a cause and money to a nonprofit). The processes by which these outcomes are achieved and theoretical explanations for them have only recently received considerable researcher attention. Figure 14.1 shows a model of Consumer-Focused Sponsorship-Linked Marketing Communications that brings together current theoretical understanding. This model does not consider business-to-business focused sponsorship or sponsorship-stakeholder communications such as those directed at financial institutions or nonconsumer audiences. The model does consider (1) individual and group level factors that influence processing of sponsorship messages and responses, (2) market factors that impact sponsorship outcomes and are largely uncontrollable, at least in the short term, (3) management factors that are controllable and can strongly influence both processing and outcomes, (4) mechanics of processing, and (5) consumer-focused outcomes of sponsorship. Uncharacteristically, perhaps, we start our discussion with the middle of the model.

Figure 14.1
Model of Consumer-Focused Sponsorship-Linked Marketing Communications

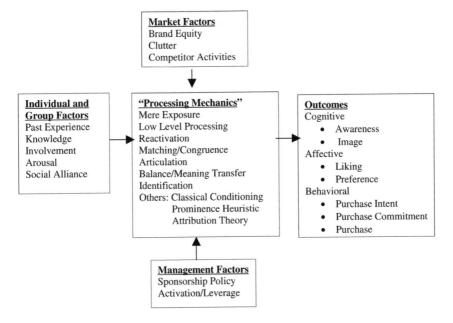

THEORIES OF HOW SPONSORSHIP WORKS

Many investigations of sponsorship effects have not posited any theoretical explanation of how sponsorship works in the mind of the consumer (for example, Cornwell et al., 2000) or have posited a theoretical process but have not directly investigated it per se (for example, Speed and Thompson, 2000); instead they examine individual and environmental factors believed to influence recall and recognition of sponsorship stimuli. Still, most research on consumer-focused sponsorship states or assumes an associative memory model, as discussed in the marketing literature by Keller (1993). In conceptualizing brand knowledge (in sponsorship we would also be concerned with corporate or firm knowledge), Keller uses a definition based on brand awareness and brand image. "Brand awareness relates to brand recall and recognition performance by consumers. Brand image refers to the set of associations linked to the brand that consumers hold in memory" (p. 2). Brand associations include all types of perceptions held in memory, even those from the distant past. Attributes, benefits, and attitudes developed over time—essentially other informational nodes linked to the brand and containing meaning—can be considered to be brand associations.

Thus, with the above memory model stated or assumed, most sponsorship research has focused on improving the recall, recognition, or brand associations held in memory. Selected research exploring theoretical explanations related to the improved processing of sponsorship stimuli is reviewed in the following sections. The center of Figure 14.1 lists the theoretical "mechanics" of consumer-focused sponsorship communications and Table 14.1 briefly summarizes these research contributions. It should be noted that, in the main, these are not competing theories, but could be understood as complementary concepts from a management perspective.

Mere Exposure, Low-Level Processing, and Reactivation

The mere exposure hypothesis introduced by Zajonc (1968, 1980) suggests that repeated exposure to a stimulus will engender an affective response. Liking and subsequent preference formation is accomplished without awareness of the preference formation process and has been found across a wide range of stimuli including words, pictures, and figures (Bornstein, 1989). Impoverished communication stimuli such as simple brand logos, which are minimal by nature and cannot carry the wealth or quality of information that more complex communications can, are commonplace in sponsorship-linked marketing situations, and exposure to them may be one way sponsors benefit from this process. Bennett (1999) reported finding mere exposure effects in a field study of U.K. football (soccer) supporters, who had just viewed a football match where sponsor information was present. Unfortunately, the lack of exposure control (fans entering games and exiting games were queried for recall of sponsors) did not result in a strong test of mere exposure since any number of extraneous communications may have influenced responses.

Mere exposure was also studied by Olson and Thjømøe (2003) and was contrasted to central and peripheral processing in a controlled setting. Central route processing refers to high-involvement situations requiring in-depth consideration that leads to brand attitude formation or change (Petty, Cacioppo, and Schumann, 1983). In opposition to this, the peripheral route refers to low-involvement situations where individuals form or change attitudes without active deliberation or consideration (Petty, Cacioppo, and Schumann, 1983). Olson and Thjømøe (2003) examined sponsorship-like conditions with low involvement and limited processing and contrasted mere exposure (brand name only) conditions to peripheral route conditions (brand plus some brand information). Findings supported the mere exposure effect, in that participants appeared to form favorable evaluations simply as a result of exposure to brands (particularly for fictitious brands). Their results with regard to low-involvement processing found that individuals having processed additional brand information did have greater attitude change than those exposed but having not processed the information (those in the brand plus information condition who did not read the additional information). While this study did explore the low-involvement processing of

Table 14.1
Summary of Literature Supporting Possible Processing Mechanics of Sponsorship

Possible Mechanics	Study Description	Findings
Mere Exposure		
Bennett, 1999	Measured brand recall from spectators entering and exiting sporting venues.	Mere exposure and false consensus effects were found.
Olson and Thjømøe, 2003	Compared mere exposure of a brand with varying levels of cognitive processing of brands.	Mere exposure enhanced preference for the brand name. Exposure to additional, but unprocessed information did not affect preference.
Low-Level Processing		
Olson and Thjømøe, 2003	AS BEFORE.	
Petty, Cacioppo, and Schumann, 1983	Manipulated level of product involvement, strength of argument, and type of endorser in a magazine advertisement for a product.	Two routes to persuasion were found: central and peripheral. High-involvement consumers were influenced by strength of argument, and low-involvement consumers by type of product endorser.
Reactivation		
Pham and Vanhuele, 1997	Experimentally tested for the effects of advertising fragments.	Established brand associations were reactivated by advertising fragments, regardless of whether the fragments were directly attended to, or otherwise.
Matching/Congruence		
Becker-Olsen and Simmons, 2002	Examined participant responses to high- versus low-native fit sponsorships involving social causes.	Low-fit sponsorships resulted in less favorable thoughts and attitudes toward the sponsor and generated less affective and behavioral responses from participants than high-fit sponsorships.

(continued)

Table 14.1 (continued)

Possible Mechanics	Study Description	Findings
Cornwell, Humphreys, Maguire, and Tellegen, 2003	Manipulated congruence and level of sponsor-sponsee relationship explanation (articulation) via press releases, and assessed cued recall.	Recall was better for congruent sponsors than for incongruent sponsors. Recall for incongruent sponsors improved with articulation.
Cornwell, Pruitt, and Van Ness, 2001	Examined share price changes of motorsport sponsors. Compared the worth of sponsoring a winner versus just participating in a sponsorship.	Significant gains in share prices were found when congruent sponsors sponsored a winner, but there was little effect on share price for incongruent sponsors.
Ferrand and Pages, 1996	A sample of participants produced lists of adjectives describing both an event and a product. These were examined for similarities to assess effectiveness of image sponsoring.	A number of similarities were found across adjectives used to describe a tennis event and a brand of mineral water. Event/product specific elements were also identified.
Gwinner, 1997	Outlined a model of how sponsorship can impact brand image. Explained that image transfer is aided by factors such as sponsor-sponsee similarity.	
Gwinner and Eaton, 1999	Assessed the extent to which image transfer occurs from brand to event, through event sponsorship depictions.	Participants tended to rate events and brands similarly in terms of "personality," particularly when they were matched on either image or functional bases.
Johar and Pham, 1999	Manipulated congruence and perceived market prominence of sponsor, and measured sponsor identification.	Consumers (mis)identified sponsors as being those companies congruent with the event being sponsored and more prominent in the marketplace.
McDaniel, 1999	Examined how consumers' reactions to advertisements leveraging sports sponsorships can be influenced by preexisting advertising schemas.	Brand-event matchup was suggested to significantly improve attitude toward the advertisement.

Possible Mechanics	Study Description	Findings
Musante, Milne, and McDonald, 1999	Outlined a methodology to assess the level of perceived fit between the image of a brand and that of a sponsor.	Sponsors that were functionally related to the sport were found to have the best levels of perceived fit.
Pracejus and Olsen, 2002	Two studies examined how brand-cause fit in cause-related marketing campaigns impacts consumer choice.	High fit between a brand and a cause was more effective in influencing consumer choice behavior than was low fit.
Rifon, Choi, Trimble, and Li, 2004	Examined how consumer attributions of sponsor motives influence the effects of sponsor-cause congruence on ratings of sponsor attitude and sponsor credibility.	Sponsor-cause congruence was associated with attributions of altruistic motives, greater sponsor credibility, and positive attitudes about sponsors. Congruence effects on attitudes about sponsors were mediated by sponsor credibility.
Speed and Thompson, 2000	Used a classical conditioning framework to examine consumers' attitudes about sponsors and events, and perceptions of sponsor-event fit.	Consumers' responses were influenced by attitudes toward the sponsor, perceived sponsor-event fit, and the perceived sincerity and ubiquity of the sponsor.
Articulation		
Cornwell, Humphreys, Maguire, and Tellegen, 2003	AS BEFORE.	
Balance/Meaning Transfer		
Dean, 2002	Examined balance theory and attribution theory in relation to sponsorship.	Sponsorship of a well-liked charitable event resulted in enhanced corporate community relations, and in both positive and negative attributions.
Gwinner, 1997 Keller, 1993	AS BEFORE. A conceptual model of brand equity was presented. An associative memory model was used to explain how brand awareness and brand image may affect brand knowledge.	

(continued)

Table 14.1 (continued)

Possible Mechanics	Study Description	Findings
McCracken, 1989	Presented a conceptual model of how celebrity-endorser advertising operates. Suggested meaning is transferred from celebrity to product to consumer.	
Identification		
Cornwell and Coote, 2005	Social Identity Theory was used to examine peoples' willingness to purchase the products of the firms that sponsor nonprofit organizations.	There was a positive relationship between consumers' identification with the nonprofit organization and their intention to purchase its sponsor's products.
Madrigal, 2000	Examined how social alliances between sports fans and preferred sports teams influence purchase intentions of a sponsor's products.	Purchase intentions were greater among those who identified with the team being sponsored and when such intentions were perceived to be the group norm.
Madrigal, 2001	Examined how consumers' levels of team identification can influence their attitudes toward a sponsor, and their purchase intentions.	Team identification was found to moderate the effect of attitude on intention to purchase.
Other		
—Classical Conditioning		
Speed and Thompson, 2000	AS BEFORE.	
—Prominence Heuristic		
Johar and Pham, 1999	AS BEFORE.	
Pham and Johar, 2001	Extension of the work of Johar and Pham (1999), examining the congruence and prominence heuristics of sponsor identification.	Prominence bias arose when consumers were unable to retrieve the sponsor's name directly from memory and instead relied on a constructive memory process.
—Attribution Theory		
Rifon, Choi, Trimble, and Li, 2004	AS BEFORE.	
Dean, 2002	AS BEFORE.	

brand information in addition to brand name, the results are essentially a comparison of the central processing route to mere exposure. Since it used advertisements containing only text without logos, or pictures, the study did not have the typical cues used in peripheral processing, and so we still know little about peripheral processing in sponsorship.

Communication associated with sponsoring, while impoverished in nature, is also embedded, by design, in some event or activity, which is intended to be of interest to the individual. Thus, in the main, individuals are not expected to be highly involved with sponsorship communications relative to the event experience. Moreover, sponsorship contexts are not capable in their use of signage, title sponsorship announcements, logos, and the like to carry involving messages. These messages have been termed advertising fragments (Pham and Vanhuele, 1997). This is very similar to the situation where advertising is embedded in televised communications and thus theory from advertising has been borrowed. In a study of the potential of advertising fragments to reactivate established brand associations, Pham and Vanhuele (1997) used response time as an indication of the ability to access brand associations stored in memory. Individuals receiving exposures to target brand fragments took less time to verify a statement of a core brand association than those who did not receive target brand exposure. While the substantive difference between conditions was arguably small (300–400 milliseconds), the authors state that this reduced response latency was meaningful given the minimal manipulation undertaken in the experimental context.

While mere exposure effects are relevant to particular sponsorship situations (and may be influential in the individual's prior experience with the brand), it is perhaps low-level processing and the reactivation of previously held brand associations that have the broadest application in sponsorship communication processes. For example, arena exposures to sponsor messages have been shown to influence memory for sponsors (Cornwell et al., 2000), but the field study in which this was found lacked control for corresponding advertising exposures. From a practitioner's perspective the broadcast audience (rather than the attending audience) and its exposure to peripheral event signage (for example, location based, scoreboard, and uniform sponsor identification) and computer-generated graphics (for example, presenting sponsor logo) may be even more important. Interestingly, media exposure to computer-generated logos holds more promise for controlled experiments, but processing of these peripheral cues has not received researcher attention.

Exploration of low-level processing seems fruitful since peripheral cues constitute the mainstay of sponsorship communications. Moreover, most brand managers would not introduce a new brand with the impoverished stimuli of the sponsorship context (note the parallel here to the value of mere exposure for fictitious brands). Rather, they might use sponsorship as a reminder for an established brand; therefore, most sponsor processing will potentially have a reactivation of memory component.

Matching and Congruence

The most frequently investigated theoretical concept related to the improved processing of sponsorship stimuli is undoubtedly the idea of match or congruence (also called fit, relatedness, and similarity) between the sponsor and event or activity (for example, Cornwell, 1995; Cornwell, Pruitt, and Van Ness, 2001; Ferrand and Pages, 1996; Gwinner, 1997; Gwinner and Eaton, 1999; Johar and Pham, 1999; McDaniel, 1999; Musante, Milne, and McDonald, 1999; Rifon et al., 2004; Speed and Thompson, 2000). Congruence theory suggests that storage in memory and retrieval of information are influenced by relatedness or similarity, such that viewing a running event that is sponsored by a running shoe brand seems appropriate and is easily remembered.

One conceptualization of congruence finds that people best remember information that is congruent with prior expectations (Srull, 1981), whereas the competing theory is that incongruent information requires more elaborate processing and results in greater recall (Hastie, 1980). Thus, finding the running event sponsored by an insurance company might be remembered for its lack of congruence. Researchers in sponsorship have used schema congruity theory (Musante, Milne, and McDonald, 1999) and the idea of advertising schemas (McDaniel, 1999) to explain matchup effects. While the memory effects of matching have been supported, the effects of incongruence have only been seen as a lack of fit and have not been investigated in their own right.

Across a range of field and experimental studies, congruence is typically found to hold a significant positive relationship with memory for sponsorship stimuli and other sponsorship outcomes (see Table 14.1). The only potentially negative consequences of congruence suggested thus far relate to heuristics used in recollection. For small brands, a market prominence bias may operate against the true congruent sponsor when a competitor with a large market share is more readily recalled and therefore thought to be the sponsor (Johar and Pham, 1999). Although not as yet discussed in the literature, brands at parity, those notably similar in the consumer's mind, may be particularly vulnerable to confusion and misattributions when both major competitors are engaged in similar sponsorship activities. However, given the weight of evidence currently supporting the value of perceived congruence between sponsor and event in supporting memory for the relationship, advantages decidedly outweigh disadvantages.

Articulation

The vast majority of sponsorship literature on matching considers the communication value of sponsor-event pairings and suggests that the theoretical development of brand image depends on establishing a link between the two. From a management perspective, the goal has been to establish the best match via examining the overlap in existing images (Ferrand and Pages, 1999). Sponsorship research on articulation departs from past studies by moving beyond simple pairing of sponsor and event as under the matchup hypothesis. Here, research considers the relational context and meaning (for example, Bain and Humphreys, 1988) between sponsor and event and how articulation of this relationship influences memory. This is not a new concept from the perspective of the practitioner. For instance, Texaco's sponsorship of the 1992 Olympic Games was explained by stating in advertisements that the oil company strives for excellence in what it does, just as an athlete strives for excellence in his or her sport. There has also been research attempting to measure how program elements collateral to the sponsorship relationship might "create fit" (Becker-Olsen and Simmons, 2002). Research is now showing that communicating a link makes sense from an advertising or leverage perspective, but that articulation may also be developed within the basic sponsorship relationship.

Preliminary results of an experimental study of fictitious press releases found memory for sponsorship relationships to be influenced by the nature of the articulated link (Cornwell et al., 2003). In particular, under conditions of an incongruent relationship between sponsor and event, articulation of the reasons for the sponsorship relationship resulted in improved recall for the relationship. These results are in accordance with recent research in psychology by Prior and Bentin (2003), which showed that incidental learning of the pairing of two unrelated nouns was better when these were linked in a meaningful sentence than when presented in isolation.

Additionally, although our focus here is on consumers, it is worthwhile to note that articulation of sponsorship relationships may also be beneficial for firms whose target audiences are nonconsumer. Research concerning the reactions of financial community members to information regarding new advertising agency–client relations (Mathur and Mathur, 1996) and financial-relations advertising (Bobinski and Ramirez, 1994) suggests that investors are constantly seeking to find information that better informs their decision making. Thus, articulation of a sponsorship relationship might work to improve consumer memory while at the same time serving as a signal to the financial community of the role and value of the sponsorship to the firm. Sponsorship articulation, if eventually supported by subsequent empirical work, could be a valuable management tool for firms marketing products that do not have logically sanctioned links to popular sports, arts, and charity events and activities.

Balance Theory and Meaning Transfer

In the investigation of image change in sponsorship, balance theory has been utilized to explain attitude change. Heider's (1958) balance theory argues that individuals strive for consistency and avoid perceived inconsistency in behavior and attitude. In sponsorship, the individual will seek a balanced relationship between the event and the sponsor. For example, an imbalance is created when a preexisting positive attitude toward a charitable organization and a neutral or even negative attitude toward a firm are combined in a sponsorship. In such a case, the individual may seek harmony by reconsidering the attitude toward the firm and adjusting it in a positive direction (the desired outcome), or the individual could reconsider his or her attitude toward the charity and adjust this in a negative direction. Balance theory has been utilized by Dean (2002) in the sponsorship context, similar to that just described, to explain attitude change due to sponsorship.

Another approach seeking to explain image effects in sponsorship considers meaning transfer and follows McCracken's (1989) model of the celebrity-endorsement process. This implies for sponsorship that "meaning" moves from the event to the sponsor's product when the two are paired during an event, and then to the consumer in his or her role as spectator or participant. McCracken's model was concerned less with the mechanism of the pairing process and more with the movement of meaning. Likewise, Gwinner's (1997) adaptation of McCracken's work to sponsorship does not specify how the event image transfers to the brand image. Subsequent empirical work, however (Gwinner and Eaton, 1999), does posit an associative memory process (Keller, 1993) where brand associations are formed during sponsorship activities.

No example of potential image transfer effects could be more pronounced than those sought by sponsors of the X Games developed by ESPN. Combining new, perhaps once-outlawed sports such as snowboarding, sky surfing, cliff diving, skateboarding, and mountain biking; the X Games target a youth market with an "in your face attitude" (Morris, 1998, p. 8). The list of sponsors seeking an image transfer effect from such action sports include Taco Bell Corp., Disneyland, Burger King, Levi Strauss & Co., PepsiCo/Mountain Dew, The Coca-Cola Company, Kellogg Company, Gatorade, Schick, Reebok International, and Activision, Inc. (Pearson, 2003). Corporate sponsors seeking a more youthful image with the X Games seem to follow the image transfer model of McCracken as outlined: meaning moves from event to sponsor's product to consumer.

Identification

Social identity theory, as found in management, argues that people will place themselves and others into social categories such as sports participant, organizational member, or political group (Tajfel and Turner, 1985). Research on identification, as an individual level process, suggests that people tend to make social classifications because it provides a systematic way to define others and to locate oneself in the social environment. Moreover, when an individual identifies with an organization, he or she becomes vested in its successes and failures (Ashforth and Mael, 1989). In their study of college alumni, Mael and Ashforth (1992) showed how organizational and individual antecedents influence organizational identification with the alma mater and how in turn, organizational identification is linked to support for the organization. Following the work of Mael and Ashforth, Cornwell and Coote (2005) found a similar relationship in the sponsorship of a cause. Antecedents led to organizational identification with the cause and this in turn led to purchase commitment for the products of sponsors.

Outside the sponsorship context but within sport, social identity theory has been utilized to explain sports team identification and its positive social and self-concept consequences (for example, Branscombe and Wann, 1991). Following this research, Madrigal (2000), in a study of adults attending a college football game, found that favorable purchase intentions were positively related to team identification and were more common when such intentions were perceived as a group norm. In a subsequent study utilizing a random telephone survey, Madrigal (2001) found that "team identification moderates the effect of attitude on intention to purchase" (p. 157). In similar research, perceived prestige of a sports team was shown to influence one's identification with that team and in turn influence key sponsorship outcomes such as sponsor recognition, attitude toward sponsor, sponsor patronage, and satisfaction with sponsors (Gwinner and Swanson, 2003). In sum, social identification as an explanatory construct has received support across several areas of application and is deserving of additional research. Again, while the current writing is concerned with consumer-focused sponsorship, it is worth noting that identification would also be of central interest in any study of employees as an audience for corporate sponsorship.

Other Theoretical Building Blocks

Numerous other theoretical building blocks can be identified in the literature. For example, Speed and Thompson (2000) utilized classical conditioning as a theoretical framework for sponsorship, but did not examine classical conditioning effects per se. Researchers Johar and Pham (1999) utilized, among several theoretical concepts, relatedness, semantic overlap, market prominence, and information economics to develop propositions regarding the use of heuristics in sponsor identification. In the context of cause sponsorships, Dean (2002) and Rifon et al. (2004), used attribution theory to explain consumers' causal inferences of sponsors' motives.

What these and other studies previously discussed suggest is that in addition to simple explicit memory, various other influential variables must be considered depending on the sponsorship context (for example, attribution theory may be more important for cause sponsorships, whereas the role of prominence may be more important for large-scale sports). Implicit memory also plays a major role in the processing of sponsorship information. As such, greater consideration in future research must be given to investigating implicit memory for sponsorship information, rather than just using studies involving sponsor recall and recognition tasks tapping explicit memory. Implicit learning in relation to sponsorship may result from classical conditioning as suggested by Speed and Thompson (2000), or perhaps from repetition or perceptual learning (Squire, 1987). Implicit memories, which are typically not available to conscious recollection, may nonetheless influence outcomes such as brand awareness, attitudes toward companies and products, and purchase behavior.

MEASURING SPONSORSHIP OUTCOMES

Despite the acceptance and proliferation of sponsorship-linked marketing programs, gross approximations to traditional advertising spending (for example, second-by-second tallies of clear and in focus logo exposure during auto racing) are still the main means used by practitioners for measuring sponsorship effectiveness (for example, consider the "Sponsor's Report" offered by Joyce Julius, http://www.joycejulius.com/index.html). These measures are still, as previously noted by Cornwell (1995), "of apples and oranges": 30 seconds of in-focus logo exposure does not equal a 30-second advertising message detailing brand attributes and benefits and providing a toll-free number for immediate response. Although one can understand the industry's need for measurement (and quantification) of some kind, these experiences are qualitatively different and thus work differently in the consumer's mind.

What communication effects are sought when utilizing sponsorship-linked marketing to communicate with consumers and how are they realized? Consumer-focused sponsorship outcomes, as studied using field surveys or experimental designs, can be classified as cognitive, affective, and behavioral. Examples of studies investigating each of these are discussed in the following text and provide a representative (although not comprehensive) picture of the way sponsorship effects are often assessed. While field studies, due to their quasiexperimental nature, do not make strong contributions to our understanding of sponsorship-information processing, they are discussed to demonstrate how they might be improved by a better understanding of psychological processes and to support overall model development.

Field Work

Cognitive Outcomes

The focus of cognitive measures in sponsorship is typically on awareness. Bennett (1999) measured consumer awareness of sponsorship information, both before and after the viewing of a soccer match. On exit, awareness was based on a measure of free recall for "any firms or brands advertised on perimeter posters" (p. 301). Subsequently, awareness was cued by product category and then by a "fully aided" cue, which asked if attendees recalled specific brands (including foils). Similarly, Nicholls, Roslow, and Dublish (1999) cued tennis and golf event attendees with product category information and sought their top-of-mind brand awareness. Pope and Voges (1999) sought to measure the relationship between the belief that a company was involved in sponsorship and corporate image. They provided the name of a possible sponsor and asked respondents whether the company was involved in sponsorship and also asked them to rate dimensions of the company's image.

Perhaps the most comprehensive field work study specifically considering the use of cognitive measures is that of Tripodi et al. (2003). Using telephone survey data collected around the time of the 2000 Olympics, they considered four approaches to measuring recall (p. 447): (1) event sponsorship prompt ("When you think of [Event Z], which sponsors come to mind?"), (2) brand sponsorship prompt ("When you think of [Brand X], what sponsorships come to mind?"), (3) category sponsorship prompt ("When you think of [Category Y, e.g., banks], what sponsorships come to mind?"), and (4) brand recognition recall ("I am going to tell you some of Brand X's current or recent sponsorships. For each one, could you tell me whether you were aware, before today, of Brand X sponsoring that event?"). Not surprisingly, Tripodi et al. found that these different approaches to measurement yielded different estimates of recall.

Affective Outcomes

Affective measures often consider liking, preference, particular attitudes, or favorable thoughts. Examining brand preference, Nicholls, Roslow, and Dublish (1999) provided a list of leading brands to event spectators and asked, "Which of the following brands of [category] do you prefer?" (p. 372). Madrigal (2001) used a telephone survey to ask people about their attitudes toward purchasing products from sponsors of a university sports team. When considering the effects of fit for a cause sponsorship, Becker-Olsen and Simmons (2002) measured favorable thoughts and attitudes toward the sponsorship. Clearly affective outcomes may be even more important for cause sponsorships at the brand and corporate levels.

Behavioral Outcomes

Behavior, or intended behavior, has typically been measured with semantic differential or Likert scales. For example, in considering the influence of the act of sponsoring on intention to purchase, Madrigal (2000) used a three-point scale to query attendees at a football game, asking them about their likelihood of buying the products of a hypothetical sponsor. In a later study, Madrigal (2001) used a five-point scale and asked people about their likelihood of purchasing a sponsor's products within a three-month period, and about the amount of effort they put into buying a sponsor's products.

In field studies, it is assumed that indicators of cognitive processing like correct recall of sponsors are measures of sponsorship communication success. For affective and behavioral outcomes it is often assumed that people have insight into specific attitudes and intentions about future behavior and that their responses reflect the influence of sponsorship exposure. If one assumes that a hierarchical information-processing model of advertising applies to sponsorship (for example, see Shimp and Gresham, 1983), then exposure to, and comprehension of, marketing communications are foundational to higher-order effects such as preference and purchase intent and may therefore be relied upon when studies are focused at higher levels. These studies, however, tell us very little about the mechanisms underlying sponsorship information processing and are poor at validly isolating cognitive and affective responses, or behavioral outcomes. Moreover, their simplicity and lack of control may count as effective as those sponsorships with outcomes that are suboptimal for, or even counter to, long-term marketing objectives.

Experimental Work

Cognitive Outcomes

In experimental designs a number of recall and recognition measures have typically been utilized as outcome measures of sponsorship. For example, in order to examine the influence of sponsor relatedness and prominence on memory, Johar and Pham (1999) asked respondents to match an event with one of two possible sponsors (an actual sponsor and a foil) after exposure to a number of event-sponsor relationships. Pham and Vanhuele (1997) used weak cues in their study of response latency. Here, individuals were asked to verify if statements regarding a brand were true or false. In their study of the role of articulation in supporting recall for event-sponsor pairings, Cornwell et al. (2003) cued individuals with the sponsor and asked for the event, after having previously exposed them to a series of fictitious sponsorship press releases. Each of these studies has been able to identify variables that influence recall and recognition.

Affective Outcomes

A number of affective outcomes related to sponsorships, such as attitude, preference, and liking, have also been examined experimentally. Olson and Thjømøe (2003) compared the attitudinal influences of varying levels of brand information processing by using two experimental groups that differed in the number of exposures they received to specific types of brand information. The researchers then queried participants with statements like "I feel that [brand name] is appealing to me," and provided a seven-point scale for responding (p. 255). In an experiment comparing native high- and low-fit sponsorships, Becker-Olsen and Simmons (2002) found that participants exposed to sponsorships with low fit "generated less favorable thoughts, formed a less favorable attitude toward the sponsorship, saw the firm's positioning as less clear, and generated less favorable affective and behavioral responses to the firm" (p. 287). McDaniel (1999) administered pre- and post-test attitudinal measures around exposing participants to variations of advertisements depicting sponsorship information. In this way changes in the participants' attitudes (toward the brand, for example) could be attributed to viewing the sponsorship information in the advertisement. Attitudes toward not only a specific sponsor, but also co-sponsors and toward the event being sponsored, were investigated by Ruth and Simonin (2003) in an effort to better understand processing in relation to multiple-sponsor events, as is typical of many sponsorship situations. Clearly research considering both cognition and affect is preferable, especially when the potential for high recall but negative affect is possible.

Behavioral Outcomes

Measurement of behavioral effects of experimental sponsorship manipulations has also been attempted. As part of an experiment examining the effects of sponsors' usage of varying degrees of promotional efforts, McCarville, Flood, and Froats (1998) questioned participants about their intentions to purchase a sponsor's products. Pracejus and Olsen (2002) provided consumers with information about cause-related marketing campaigns, similar to sponsorships, and examined how consumers' choice of service was influenced by whether the campaign involved high or low congruence between brand and cause.

Although experimental designs like these provide greater control than field studies, several issues regarding the nature of the dependent measures used have yet to be examined. For example, there has not been a specific analysis of the nature or direction of cued recall. In what circumstances would cuing with the sponsor for the event be appropriate and in what circumstances would cuing with the event for the sponsor be appropriate? As mentioned, Tripodi et al. (2003) found radical differences based on cues, but these results may be context dependent. In what instances is free recall or category-cued recall preferred?

It is argued here that directional cuing is appropriate for corporate or brand image (for example, that created in corporate sponsorship of charity events) in that the marketing manager is concerned that individuals know the event-sponsor relationship. Accepting an associative symmetry hypothesis of memory (Asch and Lindner, 1963), where each member of a pair is suggested as being capable of recovering the entire pattern or relationship; knowing that "this type of event is sponsored by this firm" or that "this firm sponsors this type of event" is equally valuable to the marketing manager.

In examining brand awareness, as is typically sought by fast-moving consumer goods in their sponsorship of popular sports, free recall or category-cued recall would be appropriate. However, field studies and some experimental designs have an implicit cuing direction from the event or event exposure to the sponsor. For example, this happens when top-of-mind awareness, immediately following exposure to an event, is sought by supplying product categories and measuring sponsor mentions. Further, in such situations, the potential for demand characteristics is high, as is the potential for a market prominence bias, as suggested by Pham and Johar (2001).

Eventually, measures of sponsorship outcomes must also deal with the age-old problem of isolating effects or as Keller (2001) describes it, locating the "main effects" of a marketing communication's contribution (p. 832). This is true for all three types of sponsorship outcomes: cognitive, affective, and behavioral. Some studies have attempted to control for or explicitly consider the influence of both prior product and event knowledge before assessing sponsorship effects (for example, Roy and Cornwell, 2004), and, as is discussed in greater detail in the section on leveraging, a few studies (for example, Lardinoit and Derbaix, 2001; McCarville, Flood, and Froats, 1998) have also considered collateral promotions and communications. However, no study as yet has considered either the incremental effect of sponsorship over existing advertising or the synergistic potential of sponsorship and concurrent advertising. This is an area where future sponsorship research will undoubtedly prove useful.

In addition, as suggested previously, if implicit learning is engendered in sponsorship exposures, alternative measures not requiring conscious recollecting must be devised. These could incorporate word fragment (Duke and Carlson, 1993) and word-stem completion tasks (Tulving, Schacter, and Stark, 1982) or include a divided attention task to measure the respective contributions of explicit and implicit memory (for details, see Jacoby, Toth, and Yonelinas, 1993).

INDIVIDUAL AND GROUP FACTORS

An increasing amount of attention is being given to the mechanics of processing sponsorship messages and resulting outcomes (Crimmins and Horn, 1996; Gwinner and Eaton, 1999; McDaniel, 1999; Speed and Thompson, 2000). However, a great number of individual factors also influence information processing of sponsorships. Four individual factors typically of interest in sponsorship research are presented here, namely, arousal, prior experience, knowledge, and involvement. In addition, for many types of sponsorships, group level variables such as social alliances are relevant. This list is used only to illustrate the role of individual- and group-level factors in the processing of sponsorship stimuli, since a full treatment of such variables is beyond the scope of this chapter.

Arousal

The extent to which a target audience processes a brand-event linkage created via sponsorship may be influenced by the level of arousal elicited by the sponsor or event, or both. When a person experiences increased arousal, processing of stimulus-related information increases, and in turn, increased attention to processing results in greater acquisition and storage of information (Kroebe-Riel, 1979). This is called the processing efficiency principle. In contrast, the intensity principle suggests that increased arousal focuses so much attention on the arousal-inducing stimulus that processing of peripheral information is inhibited (Pavel-chak, Antil, and Munch, 1988). Studies of television viewing support this perspective. In a study of advertisement recall for Super Bowl XXXIV, a game in which the outcome was not decided until the last play, recall was greater during the first half than the more intense second half (Newell, Henderson, and Wu, 2001). It is argued that the intensity created during the second half led viewers to attend more to the game and less to the embedded commercials. In other studies, arousal created by a television program has even been found to impair processing of stimuli subsequent to the program (Mundorf, Zillman, and Drew 1991; Scott and Goff, 1988).

Another view is that arousal and consumer responses should be examined in terms of an inverted U rather than a linear relationship. Low levels of intensity are insufficient to create desired consumer responses, while high levels of intensity result in a focus on the stimulus driving the intensity (Park and McClung, 1986). Thus, a moderate level of intensity is thought to be optimal for creating arousal and has been found to result in greater advertisement memory and more favorable attitudes toward advertisements (Tavassoli, Schultz, and Fitzsimmons, 1995). In the sponsorship context, Pham (1992) found that arousal related to viewing an exciting event significantly decreased the recognition of embedded sponsorship stimuli.

Thus presenting individuals with marketing messages when they are in an aroused state could detract from communication goals or could result in an assimilation effect, where peripheral cues become assimilated with the central cues, and thus, associated with the arousal (Broach, Page, and Wilson, 1995). In the case of sponsorship, an assimilation effect could occur if the positive association one holds for an event becomes related to the associated sponsor. In sum, arousal seems an important individual level variable, but we still have a poor understanding of its potential influence related to various sponsorship contexts (for example, sports, arts, and causes).

Prior Experience

A consumer's prior experience with a sponsor or event, or both, can trigger cognitive and affective responses that can impact on the processing of sponsorship messages. In marketing, Alba and Hutchinson (1987) propose that increased product familiarity enables consumers to remember brand and product information and develop more refined cognitive structures. The benefit provided by familiarity is that more elaborate cognitive structures emerge from an increasing number of product-related experiences (Söderlund, 2002). In turn, more elaborate cognitive structures enable more efficient processing of product-related stimuli to occur when the product is encountered in the future. The tendency is for new associations to be of the same valence as existing associations (Grush, 1976). Thus, familiarity not only increases the number of associations held in memory, but it positively impacts the perceived relations between new stimuli and existing associations.

High levels of familiarity with a product or brand have been found to result in more positive consumer reactions such as satisfaction, word of mouth, and repurchase intentions (Söderlund, 2002). Several studies have found that one of the primary objectives firms have for entering into a sponsorship is to increase brand awareness, or familiarity (for example, Marshall and Cook, 1992; Quester, 1997; Shanklin and Kuzma, 1992). A positive effect associated with an event can transfer to a sponsor, thus creating the possibility that future exposures to the brand will be positively influenced.

Despite the obvious importance of prior experience in the processing of additional information regarding the brand, few studies in sponsorship have considered it, and none directly. Dean (2002) considered the ability of sponsoring a cause (Special Olympics) to enhance perceptions of a local food store chain (Food Lion) and found that differing prior attitudes toward the firm influence the magnitude of attitude change. More extensive consideration of past experience is warranted within the sponsorship context.

Consumer Knowledge

A cognitive-based individual level variable that can influence information processing of a brand-event linkage presented via sponsorship is knowledge. In the case of event sponsorship, this is examined in terms of a consumer's knowledge of the product category of the sponsoring brand as well as of the event being sponsored. In a study of the influence of consumer knowledge on consumer behavior, Sujan (1985) examined how experts and novices differ in the processing of product information. When information consistent with product knowledge is encountered, both experts and novices engage in category-based processing. However, when presented with information that is discrepant from category-based knowledge, experts engaged in longer, more analytical thought processes, referred to as piecemeal processing, while novices relied on category-based processing. Also, expertise has an impact on comprehension processes and the stimulation of product-related inferences (Celsi and Olson, 1988). That is, as a consumer goes from relatively automatic processing to more focused processing, his or her knowledge level of the product category becomes increasingly influential in the types of thoughts stimulated.

Consumer knowledge is argued to influence the development of consumer responses to event sponsorships through its impact on information processing. Roy (2000) and Roy and Cornwell (2004) have found that consumers with higher levels of knowledge about the product category of the sponsoring brand, the sporting event, or both, have the ability to make more judgments about sponsor-event congruence and elicit more thoughts pertaining to the sponsorship than consumers with less knowledge in those areas. For example, individuals with expertise in golf might know about past sponsors of golf events and about the expense of sponsoring such events and bring this knowledge to their assessment of any new sponsor.

Involvement

Mitchell (1979, 1981) views involvement as "an individual level, internal state variable that indicates the amount of arousal, interest, or drive evoked by a particular stimulus or situation" (1979, p. 194). Involvement is often conceptualized as a two-dimensional construct comprised of cognitive and affective dimensions (Park and McClung, 1986; Zaichkowsky, 1994). In a consumer behavior context, the cognitive dimension reflects personal relevance of the message content based on functional performance, while the affective dimension reflects personal relevance of the message based on emotional or aesthetic appeals to a person's desire to express an actual or ideal self-image (Zaichkowsky, 1994). Due to the limited message content of sponsorship communications, the affective dimension is of most interest here.

Research into the nature of the involvement-behavior relationship for advertising messages suggests an inverted-U relationship, similar to findings in research on arousal (Park and McClung, 1986). According to Pham (1992), an inverted-U relationship exists between felt involvement and recognition of embedded sponsorship stimuli (for example, billboards lining the fence of a soccer field). Lardinoit and Derbaix (2001) found a significant influence on unaided recall among those with high enduring involvement (with the game of basketball).

Involvement has been theorized to moderate the persuasion effectiveness of advertising messages (Petty and Cacioppo, 1981). Of particular interest to sponsorship, Petty, Cacioppo, and Schumann (1983) found that under low-involvement conditions, the presence of peripheral cues, like celebrity endorsers, was an important determinant of product evaluations. Interestingly, additional research has shown that high-involvement consumers hold more favorable brand attitudes when they perceive a match between endorser and brand (Schaefer and Keillor, 1997).

In a study of the effects of matchup between a brand and an event on responses toward sponsorship advertising, McDaniel (1999) explained the importance of considering involvement. This study used advertisement stimuli depicting sponsor-event pairings that differed in terms of perceived level of matchup and the form of media vehicle (genre of magazine) in which they were presented. Event involvement differed across the three events tested, and the sponsor's product category was considered high involvement for the participant sample. Results suggested that matchup effects were present, in that more positive attitudes toward the sponsorship advertisements were reported when there was a greater perceived matchup between the sponsor and the event. Although perceived matchup varied with involvement, McDaniel noted that involvement is likely to be an important moderator in the relationship between sponsor-event matchup and sponsorship advertising responses.

In sum, since sponsorships have few central messages, most of what is communicated can be considered peripheral cues. With this in mind, felt involvement (in general) and enduring involvement with the sponsored event are variables that may influence the information processing of a sponsorship and are expected to influence consumers' perceived congruence between sponsor and event. It seems reasonable that other forms of involvement (for example, with the product category of the sponsor) warrant further investigation; however, at least one study examining purchase decision involvement found that this did not co-vary with corporate image effects stemming from sponsorship (Pope and Voges, 1999).

Social Alliances

We must also recognize that sponsorship audiences at a group level can be expected to have any number of preexisting social alliances that will influence receptivity to sponsorship-linked marketing communications and that these social alliances can vary greatly in their importance, duration, and influence. Social alliances are considered here as social categories (Tajfel and Turner, 1985). With respect to the current discussion, the most obvious and perhaps well-researched social alliances would relate to fans in sports contexts (for example, Gwinner and Swanson, 2003; Madrigal, 2000; McDonald, Milne, and Hong, 2002; Wann and Dolan, 1994), but even here, a great deal of variability exists when one evaluates the role of sponsorship. For example, consider the nature of the fan relationship with a team like the Dallas Cowboys (www.dallascowboys.com) and contrast this with the fan relationship with an America's Cup team like Oracle BMW Racing (www.oraclebmwracing.com). The Dallas Cowboys have sponsors including the Ford Motor Company, MasterCard, and Miller Lite beer, just to name a few. The fan relationship, however, is held with the Dallas Cowboys, not the sponsors. In contrast, America's Cup teams tend to be one with their sponsors because many of the competing teams in each race are established through sponsorship. Naturally, social alliances are also found in the arts and with causes and with similarly varying degrees of importance.

The goal here is not simply to offer again already established social group theories (even though they may apply), but rather to say that whether fan behavior in arenas or cohesiveness of private arts groups is considered, social alliances can play a potential role in motivating individual variables such as involvement and arousal and in swaying "group think" regarding sponsorship response. Moreover, many sponsorships come with particular social alliances that must be considered, especially when sponsorship deals are contrary to the desires of established groups as was seen in a number of stadium-naming sponsorships in the 1990s (Clark, Cornwell, and Pruitt, 2002). On the positive side, existing strong alliances may support sponsorship goals when sponsors are accepted via the identification process and fan loyalty is translated to brand loyalty.

In summary, four individual level variables are presented as influences on how consumers evaluate sponsorship messages: arousal, prior experience, involvement, and knowledge. It is individual differences such as these that impact how a consumer processes a brand-event stimulus in a sponsorship context. In addition, the potential influence of group level variables, like social alliances, was also discussed. There are, additionally, market and situational factors that may also influence an individual's processing. Examples of these follow.

MARKET AND SITUATIONAL FACTORS

Brand Equity

Brand equity refers to how a brand is perceived or positioned in the marketplace. Both sponsors and properties hold equity of a sort and while this might be developed by sponsorship, in the short run, the various brand equities of concern are given and are thus considered here as market or situational factors for a firm. At least eight brand equity measures (drawn from Aaker, 1996) have been investigated in the sponsorship context and were reported by managers as being supported by sponsorship (Cornwell, Roy, and Steinard, 2001). While sponsorship was perceived to make a greater contribution to general elements of brand equity (brand awareness, corporate image, and brand image) than to distinctive elements (brand personality, differentiating the brand from competition, image of quality, and brand loyalty) both general and distinctive elements were ranked above the midpoint on average. Thus, experience with sponsorship-linked marketing communications is argued to develop brand equity in the mind of the consumer; however, the brand equity a sponsor brings into an association influences information processing of that association. Substantial investments in marketing communications can serve as a signal of brand quality (Kirmani and Wright, 1989). Differences in processing sponsorship stimuli between events with high-equity sponsors and low-equity sponsors are attributed to consumers having more accessible brand associations for high-equity brands than low-equity brands.

The effect of a sponsor's brand equity on consumer memory for sponsorships has been termed a prominence bias (Johar and Pham, 1999). This implies that low-equity sponsors may not reap the benefits (for example, sponsor recognition and more positive brand image) that high-equity sponsors of similar events enjoy (Pham and Johar, 2001), with this being more pronounced for sponsorships of major events (Johar and Pham, 1999). The role of brand equity in sponsorship response has also been examined in terms of its effect on perceptions of sponsor-event congruence (Roy, 2000). High-equity sponsors in three different product categories were perceived as being more congruent sponsors than low-equity competitors for major events such as the Summer Olympics, the United States Open Championship men's golf tournament, and the National Basketball Association All-Star Game. In turn, persons with a high level of perceived sponsor-event congruence had a more positive attitude toward the sponsor and a stronger relationship between event attitude and brand attitude than persons having a low level of perceived congruence. High-equity sponsors enjoy an advantage over their low-equity counterparts in terms of greater cognitive responses (for example, recognition and recall), but not greater levels of attitudinal change (Lardinoit and Quester, 2001). Many benefits of brand equity are afforded a firm when it has a strong brand. Among these benefits is increased effectiveness of marketing communications (Keller, 1998) including sponsorships. The advantages enjoyed by high-equity sponsors, together with disadvantages, deserve additional researcher attention.

Clutter

In early discussions of the managerial value of sponsorship, communication within a low-clutter environment (that is, one where there is a low level of competing communications) was cited as an advantage (Gardner and Shuman, 1987). As the popularity of sponsorship has increased, so too has clutter. One study has attempted to model the influence of individuals' perceptions of sponsorship clutter on consumer response to sponsorship (Cornwell et al., 2000). The measure used in the field setting was not an objective measure of messages observed or remembered, but was instead derived from self-reported perceptions. Despite having only a two-item measure of clutter, results indicated a negative influence of the perception of clutter on recall and recognition of sponsors.

Recent research on the influence of multiple sponsors for an event goes beyond simple consideration of a cluttered environment and examines consumers attitudes related to the specific characteristics of sponsors for the same event (Ruth and Simonin, 2003). Arguing that the pairing of products and events is a reciprocal relationship where events influence the perception of sponsors and sponsors influence perceptions of events, Ruth and Simonin (2003) show, for example, that the presence of a controversial product (for example, tobacco) can negatively impact event impressions. Thus, not only can the presence of other sponsors influence communication processing, it can influence image and potentially image transfer. While the number and visibility of sponsors and advertisers for a particular event are set largely by financial and media requirements of the sport, art, or cause seeking sponsorship, clutter resulting in an oversubscribed event can at least be avoided by managers, as can controversial cosponsors.

Competitor Activities

While any number of actions by rival competitors could influence the sponsorship mechanics of a true sponsor, one of the most discussed behaviors of competitors in sponsorship is ambushing (for a review, see Crow and Hoek, 2003). Sandler and Shani (1989) discuss ambushing as the efforts of an organization to associate itself indirectly with an event in the hope of reaping the same benefits as an official sponsor. As observers of sponsorship note, this has become an art form with all manner of high jinx being used to attract attention (for example, streakers with competitors' names tattooed on their buttocks and competitor hot air balloons drifting over stadiums). The specifics of ambush marketing, what is and is not ambushing from a legal perspective, are still debated (Hoek, 2004), but from an information-processing perspective, the potential interference is all that matters. The intrusion of competitor information will likely have detrimental effects on memory for the true sponsor. Moreover, since most of the ambushing tactics are whimsical or fun, few, except the true sponsors, are likely to hold negative opinions of the ambusher. This observation is, however, open to empirical investigation.

MANAGEMENT FACTORS

Effectiveness of sponsorship-linked marketing communications is largely dependent upon the response processes of consumers. Sponsorship managers, however, are able to influence the outcome of a sponsorship program, and some preliminary observations regarding managerial influence on sponsorship mechanics can be made.

Creating an environment of proactive sponsorship management is essential in ensuring that all activities ultimately contribute to enhancing clear memorable communications. A commitment to managing sponsorships in such a manner is consistent with the view that sponsorship is a resource that can be a source of competitive advantage for a firm (Amis, Slack, and Berrett, 1999). Sponsorship managers who actively manage their sponsorships believe that they have succeeded in differentiating their brands from the competition and have added financial value to their brands (Cornwell, Roy, and Steinard, 2001). Two management factors known to play a role in the outcome of sponsorships are a firm's sponsorship policy and the extent to which a sponsorship is leveraged once rights to commercial association have been obtained.

Sponsorship Policy

Establishment of a comprehensive sponsorship policy for potential and existing sponsorships is necessary to ensure that consumers are able to build a web of connectivity among a firm's various sponsorship activities. This is done through determining what types of events should be sponsored, which audiences should be targeted, the number of sponsorships that should be undertaken, and the level of sponsorship that should be sought for given events.

Often events are chosen because of significant overlap between the target audience for the event and the target market of the brand, or because of functional similarity between the brand and event (for example, a swimming event and a brand of swimwear). With this in mind, managers undertake sponsorships with the expectation that mechanics like mere exposure and low-level processing will play a role in promoting consumer-focused outcomes such as brand awareness, preference, or purchase intent. Research on event-sponsor congruence and balance theory suggests that memory will be facilitated and image transfer enhanced for those pairings that seem more logically sanctioned to consumers and that managers should thus aim to sponsor those events perceived to be related to their field of business (for example, Cornwell, Pruitt, and Van Ness, 2001; Gwinner, 1997; Gwinner and Eaton, 1999; Johar and Pham, 1999; McDaniel, 1999; Speed and Thompson, 2000). Articulation research, however, also reveals that incongruent event-sponsor pairings may be used to achieve desirable sponsorship outcomes, provided that a reason for the sponsorship is explained by the sponsor (Cornwell et al., 2003).

The research by Johar and Pham (1999) and Pham and Johar (2001) on the prominence bias is pertinent in deciding which events to sponsor. This bias suggests that companies perceived to be more prominent in the marketplace can often be credited with a sponsorship regardless of whether they are an actual sponsor. Pham and Johar recommend that prominent brands should take advantage of this, but be wary when evaluating the effectiveness of a sponsorship through measures of memory, in that consumer recollections may be based on prominence rather than actual sponsorship exposure. They advise that nonprominent brands may find sponsoring prominent events less effective in enhancing brand awareness and that greater value may be obtained through sponsoring less prominent events.

Policy must also address the portfolio of sponsorships a firm holds. Multiple sponsorships have the potential to reach more consumers, such as Gatorade's sponsorship of football (NFL), basketball (NBA), Major League Baseball, golf

(PGA), stockcar racing (NASCAR), and U.S. soccer; however, there are risks involved with a portfolio of sponsorships (Ruth and Simonin, 2003). From the consumer perspective there is the risk of being associated with too many events, which can lead to confusion, diverse and unsupported memory networks, and potentially negative sponsorship response (Speed and Thompson, 2000).

The level of sponsorship undertaken may also impact on the various cognitive, affective, and behavioral outcomes that sponsors might seek. Sponsors can take on a variety of forms: title sponsor, presenting sponsor, category exclusive sponsor, or sponsor with no special rights, with each form dictating how prominent the sponsor will be at the event. Mere exposure, low-level processing, and memory reactivation may be more relevant to those sponsors relying on on-site signage alone, while processes such as identification may be more relevant to those with exclusive or title contracts. Exclusive sponsorships, which often provide a sponsor with additional branding opportunities such as media advertising and on-site hospitality, should increase the likelihood that more effective sponsorship processing will occur by setting the brand apart from others (Amis, Slack, and Berrett, 1999; Gwinner 1997).

Research by Ruth and Simonin (2003) suggests that companies undertaking nonexclusive sponsorships may also need to consider which other brands will be present at the event, since the presence of controversial products could promote negative attitudes toward the event, and possibly toward related sponsors. Cornwell et al. (2000) have also noted that marketing clutter at events can have a negative impact on memory for sponsors, as discussed previously. This has implications for the sponsorships managers decide to pursue and the level of sponsorship undertaken. Clearly such decisions could be informed by more research in the area.

Sponsorship Activation/Leverage

One of the keys to achieving desired consumer impact through sponsorship is to forge a link, or association, between a sponsor and the sponsored property. Mere exposure to a brand through such vehicles as on-site signage may create awareness, but awareness alone may not capture a unique position in consumers' minds. A challenge faced by many sponsors is that a large percentage of their target market may not recognize them as sponsor of a particular event. Even worse, consumers may incorrectly identify a competitor that is not a sponsor as an event sponsor (Crimmins and Horn, 1996; Johar and Pham, 1999; Pham and Johar 2001).

Collateral communication of a brand's relationship with a property is referred to as activating, or leveraging, a sponsorship. While both terms are in use, we use the term "leverage" so as to avoid any possible confusion with the term "spreading activation" found in discussions of network memory models.

Sponsorship leverage can be achieved through a variety of marketing communication tools. For example, United Parcel Service touted its Olympics sponsorship by placing signage on its delivery vehicles. Beverage marketer SoBe leveraged its title sponsorship of the Summer and Winter Gravity Games, annual extreme sports competitions, by using media advertising, regional and national sweepstakes, local radio promotions, venue signage, and on-site sampling (Brockington, 2003).

Higher levels of sponsorship leverage have been associated with perceptions of sponsorships succeeding in differentiating a brand and adding financial value to the brand (Cornwell, Roy, and Steinard, 2001). Crimmins and Horn (1996) provide a blunt assessment of sponsors that fail to invest adequately beyond payment of rights fees: "If the brand cannot afford to spend to communicate its sponsorship, then the brand cannot afford sponsorship at all" (p. 16). This implies the need to examine combined effects of sponsorships and other promotional tools.

A few studies in sponsorship have examined combined effects. Lardinoit and Derbaix (2001) considered individuals' levels of enduring involvement with basketball, television sponsorship, and field sponsorship in a $2 \times 2 \times 2$ factorial design. They found a weak positive interaction between television and field sponsorship on unaided recall under conditions of high involvement, but a negative interaction when testing for aided recall no matter the involvement level. Thus their research suggested that the typically employed strategy of combining television and field sponsorship may not be cost-effective.

McCarville, Flood, and Froats (1998) utilized a five-group study with differing cumulative exposures to sponsorship-related communications: (1) control, (2) cause sponsorship exposure, (3) cause sponsorship plus detailed sponsor information, (4) cause sponsorship, sponsor information plus coupons, and (5) cause sponsorship, sponsor information, coupons plus product sample (pizza). Individuals who received product samples gave higher ratings for product quality, consistency, and intention to purchase than those who received none. While the findings regarding a popular food among college students might be questioned for demand characteristics, the lack of variance for the other message groups suggests that more research is needed to better understand sponsorship leverage in integrated marketing programs.

In yet a third study of this type, Becker-Olsen and Simmons (2002) report two experiments examining the influence of fit as developed by collateral program activities. In their experiments participants read news clippings containing an announcement of a firm's online store with the presence or absence of information regarding the firm's sponsorship of a nonprofit organization (with high or low fit). Results showed that individuals exposed to a low-native fit condition, Alpo (brand of dog food) sponsoring the Special Olympics (athletic event for the mentally disabled), versus a high-native fit condition, Alpo sponsoring the Humane Society (charity supporting humane treatment of animals), reported less favorable thoughts and less favorable affective and behavioral responses to the firm. In the second experiment, created fit derived from program details (for example, Alpo sponsoring the Special Olympics and also donating a pet to participants and publicizing evidence that caring for pets increases the self-esteem of the mentally disabled) resulted in positive outcomes parallel to those found with native fit (p. 287).

Obviously, both the weight and the nature of leveraging activities are central to communication effects achieved in sponsorship. One logical extension of the current research on leverage is to consider thematically tied advertising. One would expect that collateral advertising that not only notes the sponsorship relationship, but as Crimmins and Horn (1996) suggest, strengthens the link creatively, will create stronger traces in memory.

SUMMARY CONCLUSIONS AND FURTHER RESEARCH

This chapter concerns itself primarily with exploration of theoretical explanations of how sponsorship works. Even though a good deal of literature is reviewed in this process, this chapter cannot be considered a comprehensive review of sponsorship research since it mainly focused on works positing a theoretical explanation of sponsorship, to the exclusion of many that did not. In addition to the centerpiece of sponsorship processing mechanics, a number of factors influencing these and the nature of sponsorship outcomes were examined. Again, we must disclaim comprehensive coverage with the goal being illustrative rather than exhaustive consideration of potential variables of interest. For example, in addition to the factors of past experience, knowledge, involvement, arousal, and social alliances; tens if not hundreds of individual and group level variables might be considered in any empirical work on sponsorship effects.

Thus, while this model of consumer-focused sponsorship-linked marketing communications could be criticized for being a sketch, it is the first to account for the theoretical progress to date and to bring together important variables such as individual (and group) factors and market and management factors in understanding their influence on sponsorship processing mechanics and related outcomes. Several research directions have already been mentioned, but additional future research areas stemming from this chapter deserve emphasis and some expansion.

Need for Experimental Studies

First, it is clear that additional well-controlled experimental studies are essential to better understand processing of sponsorship communication stimuli. As Pham and Vanhuele (1997) state, "Without a rigorous methodology for studying how consumers process advertising fragments, any conclusion about their effectiveness or ineffectiveness seems premature" (p. 408). Related to this point, dependent measures should be carefully designed to correspond to the communication issues at hand. Ecological validity needs to be reexamined. If cued recall or recognition tasks are utilized, they should parallel the recall and recognition needed by individuals to navigate in the marketplace. Extending this idea suggests that we must consider nonconscious processing more thoroughly in future research.

Implicit Memories

Additional research on implicit memories, those not available to conscious recollection, implies a need for research into the unconscious and automatic sponsorship-linked influences on consumer behaviors. Research by Bargh (2002) in social cognition finds a substantial role for nonconscious processes and, moreover, a central and modifying role of needs and goal pursuits in psychological and behavioral phenomena (p. 281). In the sponsorship context, this suggests that not only are brand names or logos processed without conscious awareness, but that within the sponsorship or its leveraging, goal pursuits (for example, health-related goals and competitive goals) might be activated. Bargh (2002, p. 282) argues that when health-related goals are activated "the person should evaluate groceries in terms of his or her health values and their implications" while "competition goal operation should cause one to evaluate status-oriented products more positively." Bargh warns that the demonstrated powerful influence of simple goal priming on nonconscious processes implies a great responsibility for researchers because of the potential for abuse.

Resolving Imbalance

We have discussed balance theory as one mechanism useful in understanding sponsorship effects. Recent theorizing by Woodside and Chebat (2001) suggests that storytelling as a methodology can help understand how consumers resolve imbalanced states. Storytelling refers to explaining the related concepts and motivations that underlie actions and events, so that the entire situation can be better understood, rather than just superficial elements of it. The authors cite an example of Barq's brand root beer sponsoring heavy metal music in order to target teenage boys. In their analysis, given that parents tend to view this music as rebelling against parental authority, the authors tell that the company must embrace parents as consumers (presumably by discontinuing the sponsorship) or the parents must start to dislike Barq's. This approach to balance analysis describes not only imbalanced relationships, but also how the main actors resolve the tension found in an imbalanced state. Further investigation is warranted.

Multiple Sponsors

We have also mentioned clutter as a potential influence on consumers' processing of sponsorship-related information. It seems that the investigation of balance theory via storytelling might also help unravel any imbalanced relationships in the case of multiple sponsors. Companies are already sensitive to combining their sponsorship activities with those of tobacco or alcohol, but additional sensitive or incongruent relationships, perhaps less obvious, could be considered with this approach. It is assumed here that harmonious relationships would be perceived by individuals as less competitive and chaotic and thus less cluttered. This could also hold implications for the concept of articulation. If various sponsors for a single event are perceived to be harmonious in their relational context, this might support memory for these sponsors within an associative memory model. One must also recognize that this approach might reduce sponsor distinctiveness and thus empirical research is needed. In short, research examining integrated marketing communications programs should be extended, again with well-controlled experiments. Further, we must ask how closely related should the various communications strategies employed in sponsorship-linked marketing be for optimal learning?

Sponsor Distinctiveness

Sponsorship has been found by managers to be useful in differentiating the brand from competitors (Cornwell, Roy, and Steinard, 2001)—the idea being brand image is enhanced through sponsorships of exciting, image defining events, making the brand stand out from others. From an associative network perspective, sponsorship is adding a unique and potentially strong link to the brand in memory. Interestingly, competitive pressures and the success of sponsorship as a communications tool find direct marketplace competitors to be direct competitors for sponsorship opportunities. For example, PepsiCo and The Coco-Cola Company divide the NASCAR sponsorship pie in the soft drink category (Pedicini, 2003) and while the nature of their sponsorship commitments are constantly in flux, sponsoring drivers, teams, and particular races, both brands hold links to the concept "sponsor of NASCAR" in the consumer's mind. This phenomenon seems even more problematic when one major competitor replaces another as official product or service. According to Henderson, Iacobucci, and Calder (1998) when sets of nodes become structurally equivalent, brand parity follows. Additional research is needed to understand information processing for brands in parity and their special need for distinctiveness when utilizing a sponsorship-linked marketing strategy.

New Approaches to Congruence

Although the value of congruency between sponsor and event is relatively well established now, this notion offers little to those sponsors having few natural links to sports, arts, and charities. Previous research has focused on examination of high and low fit and on improvement of fit via articulation. Yet another theoretical perspective on congruence, that of Mandler (1982), considers the "value" of congruity and argues that congruence "gives rise to valuations of familiarity, acceptability, and a basic sense of liking" (p. 3). The predictability of congruent relationships, however, means that they are less interesting and so they may receive less-extensive processing and therefore be less positively valued. Mandler further argues that moderate levels of incongruence result in additional processing, namely, that required to resolve the incongruence, and that when this processing is successful it too is positively valued. In other words, people find resolving moderate incongruence to be a rewarding and valued experience. Highly incongruent items may receive additional processing, but Mandler theorizes that this produces frustration and is therefore negatively valued. In summary, Mandler predicts an inverted U-shaped relationship between incongruity and valuations. His theoretical predictions have been supported in studies of the relationships between a product and a product category (Meyers-Levy and Tybout, 1989) and between new brands and companies with existing brands (Meyers-Levy, Louie, and Curren, 1994).

Jagre, Watson, and Watson (2001), in accordance with Mandler's (1982) congruity theory, have put forward several specific research propositions. They proposed that extremely low-fit sponsors will produce greater levels of recall than either high-fit or moderate-fit sponsors due to the higher level of processing required to resolve the sponsor-event incongruity. In terms of attitude, they suggested that moderate-fit sponsors will experience higher attitudinal ratings and more favorable sponsor evaluations than either high- or low-fit sponsors since, as Mandler outlined, incongruity is more interesting than congruity, but too much can lead to frustration and negative evaluations. It was further proposed that low-fit sponsors will result in lower attitudinal ratings from consumers and less favorable sponsor evaluations than either high- or moderate-fit sponsors. While these propositions may be justified in terms of Mandler's theory, empirical validation in a sponsorship context is clearly needed before firm conclusions can be drawn.

Mandler's (1982) value of congruency theory is not inconsistent with past findings in sponsorship since typical research investigates congruent and incongruent sponsor-event pairs, but does not discuss the additional processing required for resolution and the resulting positive values. With this theoretical perspective in mind, we must ask whether a lack of congruence is truly problematic from an information-processing perspective. Moreover, we must ask whether the emphasis on congruence as a central promoter or inhibitor to information processing and subsequent memory of sponsorship stimuli has overshadowed other factors of potential interest (such as a person's persuasion knowledge, discussed below).

Persuasion Knowledge in Sponsorship

Friestad and Wright (1994) developed the Persuasion Knowledge Model to explain theoretically how people develop and use persuasion knowledge to cope with persuasion attempts. Of particular importance in the sponsorship area is their "change-of-meaning principle" (p. 12) where viewing an agent (sponsor) as using a tactic during a persuasion attempt holds an influence on the persuasion episode. Sponsorship, although clearly commercially driven in recent times, still retains some philanthropic meanings in some contexts. For example, sponsorship of a race to support breast cancer research and mammogram screening is a choice of the firm and, while commercially motivated, is still seen as benefiting the community. If, however, the sponsor engages in some additional tactic aimed at leveraging the sponsorship, say attempting to sell a product to those people on a mailing list for the event, there may be a change of meaning for the sponsorship that is related to the additional selling message. Individuals may now perceive the sponsorship as a tactic and discount any previously held positive feelings toward the firm associated with its philanthropic sponsorship.

A number of papers have questioned the commercialization of sponsorships (for example, Weiner, 2000) and have investigated the perceptions of individuals, but none have considered how sponsorships and related collateral communications are perceived by individuals as persuasion attempts. This is a potentially valuable area of future research, particularly for cause-related sponsorships and community-based sponsorships that seek to develop goodwill. It seems that if concurrent or subsequent leveraging of the sponsorship involves tactics viewed as more commercial in nature than the original sponsorship, a change of meaning may be triggered and the image and goodwill developed in the consumer's mind might be revisited.

Particular Sponsorship Models

We have presented a general model of mechanisms found in consumer focused sponsorship. Marketing practitioners and researchers alike would benefit from further consideration of the relationships between information-processing mechanics of particular sponsorships in sports, arts, and causes, and desired sponsorship outcomes. For example, sponsorship of a team-based sport with a large fan base would probably be most concerned with the process of identification, whereas sponsorship of a charitable event might be more concerned with image transfer and the development of goodwill. The relationship between sponsorship type, mechanisms, and outcomes suggests even more careful consideration of sponsorships combining two of the main categories (for example, sports and causes).

Sponsorship is a fast-growing marketing tool. In line with this growth, research into sponsorship has increased substantially in recent years. In order to improve the standard of future research, critical synthesis and periodic stocktaking, such as offered in this chapter, are clearly needed. This chapter provides a model of consumer-focused sponsorship-linked marketing communications that can serve as a foundation on which future research directions can be considered and developed.

NOTE

From *Journal of Advertising,* vol. 34, no. 2 (Summer 2005): 21–42. Copyright © 2005 by American Academy of Advertising. Reprinted with permission of M.E. Sharpe, Inc. All Rights Reserved. Not for Reproduction.

REFERENCES

Aaker, David A. (1996), *Building Strong Brands,* New York: The Free Press.
Alba, Joseph W., and J. Wesley Hutchinson (1987), "Dimensions of Consumer Expertise," *Journal of Consumer Research,* 13 (March), 411–454.
Amis, John, Trevor Slack, and Tim Berrett (1999), "Sport Sponsorship as Distinctive Competence," *European Journal of Marketing,* 33 (3/4), 250–272.
Asch, Solomon E., and Marged Lindner (1963), "A Note on 'Strength of Association,'" *Journal of Psychology,* 55 (1), 199–209.
Ashforth, Blake E. and Fred Mael (1989), "Social Identity Theory and the Organization," *Academy of Management,* 14 (1), 20–39.
Bain, John D., and Michael S. Humphreys (1988), "Relational Context: Independent Cues, Meanings or Configurations?" in *Memory in Context: Context in Memory,* Graham M. Davies and Donald M. Thomson, eds., Oxford: John Wiley and Sons, 97–137.
Bargh, John A. (2002), "Losing Consciousness: Automatic Influences on Consumer Judgment, Behavior, and Motivation," *Journal of Consumer Research,* 29 (2), 280–285.
Becker-Olsen, Karen, and Carolyn J. Simmons (2002), "When Do Social Sponsorships Enhance or Dilute Equity? Fit, Message Source, and the Persistence of Effects," in *Advances in Consumer Research* (Volume 29), Susan M. Broniarczyk and Kent Nakamoto, eds., Provo, UT: Association for Consumer Research, 287–289.
Bennett, Roger (1999), "Sports Sponsorship, Spectator Recall and False Consensus," *European Journal of Marketing,* 33 (3/4), 291–313.
Bobinski, George S. Jr., and Gabriel G. Ramirez (1994), "Advertising to Investors: The Effect of Financial-Relations Advertising on Stock Volume and Price," *Journal of Advertising,* 23 (4), 13–28.
Bornstein, Robert F. (1989), "Exposure and Affect: Overview and Meta-Analysis of Research 1968–1987," *Psychological Bulletin,* 106 (2), 265–289.
Branscombe, Nyla R., and Daniel L. Wann (1991), "The Positive Social and Self Concept Consequences of Sports Team Identification," *Journal of Sport and Social Issues,* 15 (2), 115–127.

Broach, V. Carter Jr., Thomas J. Page Jr., and R. Dale Wilson (1995), "Television Programming and Its Influence on Viewers' Perceptions of Commercials: The Role of Program Arousal and Pleasantness," *Journal of Advertising*, 24 (4), 45–54.

Brockington, L. (2003), "SoBe's Deal Nabs Summer, Winter Games," *Street and Smith's Sports Business Journal*, 6 (2), 6.

Celsi, Richard L., and Jerry C. Olson (1988), "The Role of Involvement in Attention and Comprehension Processes," *Journal of Consumer Research*, 15 (2), 210–255.

Clark, John M., T. Bettina Cornwell, and Stephen W. Pruitt (2002), "Corporate Stadium Sponsorship, Signaling Theory, Agency Conflicts and Shareholder Wealth," *Journal of Advertising Research*, 42 (6), 16–32.

Cornwell, T. Bettina (1995), "Sponsorship-Linked Marketing Development," *Sport Marketing Quarterly*, 4 (4), 13–24.

Cornwell, T. Bettina (1999), "Recent Developments in International Sponsorship Research," *Sponsorship Business Review*, December (2), 36–42.

Cornwell, T. Bettina, and Leonard V. Coote (2005), "Corporate Sponsorship of a Cause: The Role of Identification in Purchase Intent," *Journal of Business Research*, 58 (3), 268–276.

Cornwell, T. Bettina, Michael S. Humphreys, Angie Maguire, and Cassandra L. Tellegen (2003), "The Role of Articulation in Sponsorship-Linked Marketing," *Proceedings of the Advertising and Consumer Psychology Conference 2003*, Lynn R. Kahle and Chung-Hyun Kim, eds., Seoul, Korea: Society for Consumer Psychology, 8–9.

Cornwell, T. Bettina, and Isabelle Maignan (1998), "An International Review of Sponsorship Research," *Journal of Advertising*, 27 (1), 1–21.

Cornwell, T. Bettina, Stephen W. Pruitt, and Robert Van Ness (2001), "An Exploratory Analysis of the Value of Winning in Motorsports: Sponsorship-Linked Marketing and Shareholder Wealth," *Journal of Advertising Research*, 41(1), 17–31.

Cornwell, T. Bettina, Donald P. Roy, and Edward A. Steinard (2001), "Exploring Managers' Perceptions of the Impact of Sponsorship on Brand Equity," *Journal of Advertising*, 30 (2), 41–51.

Cornwell, T. Bettina, George E. Relyea, Richard L. Irwin, and Isabelle Maignan (2000), "Understanding Long-Term Effects of Sports Sponsorship: Role of Experience, Involvement, Enthusiasm and Clutter," *International Journal of Sports Marketing and Sponsorship*, 2 (2), 127–143.

Crimmins, James, and Martin Horn (1996), "Sponsorship: From Management Ego Trip to Marketing Success," *Journal of Advertising Research*, 36 (4), 11–20.

Crow, Dean, and Janet Hoek (2003), "Ambush Marketing: A Critical Review and Some Practical Advice," *Marketing Bulletin* 14 (1), 1–14.

Dean, Dwane Hal (2002), "Associating the Corporation with a Charitable Event through Sponsorship: Measuring the Effects on Corporate Community Relations," *Journal of Advertising*, 31 (4), 77–87.

Duke, Charles R., and Les Carlson (1993), "A Conceptual Approach to Alternative Memory Measures for Advertising Effectiveness," *Journal of Current Issues and Research in Advertising*, 15 (2), 1–14.

Ferrand, Alain, and Monique Pages (1996), "Image Sponsoring: A Methodology to Match Event and Sponsor," *Journal of Sport Management*, 10 (3), 278–291.

Ferrand, Alain, and Monique Pages (1999), "Image Management in Sport Organizations: The Creation of Value," *European Journal of Marketing,* 33 (3/4), 387–401.

Friestad, Marian, and Peter Wright (1994), "The Persuasion Knowledge Model: How People Cope with Persuasion Attempts," *Journal of Consumer Research,* 21 (3), 1–31.

Gardner, Meryl P., and Philip J. Shuman (1987), "Sponsorship: An Important Component of the Promotions Mix," *Journal of Advertising,* 16 (1), 11–17.

Gardner, Meryl P., and Philip J. Shuman (1988), "Sponsorships and Small Businesses," *Journal of Small Business Management,* 26 (4), 44–52.

Grush, Joseph E. (1976), "Attitude Formation and Mere Exposure Phenomena: A Non-Artifactual Explanation of Empirical Findings," *Journal of Personality and Social Psychology,* 33 (3), 281–290.

Gwinner, Kevin (1997), "A Model of Image Creation and Image Transfer in Event Sponsorship," *International Marketing Review,* 14 (3), 145–158.

Gwinner, Kevin, and John Eaton (1999), "Building Brand Image through Event Sponsorship: The Role of Image Transfer," *Journal of Advertising,* 28 (4), 47–57.

Gwinner, Kevin, and Scott R. Swanson (2003), "A Model of Fan Identification: Antecedents and Sponsorship Outcomes," *Journal of Services Marketing,* 17 (3), 275–294.

Hastie, Reid (1980), "Memory for Behavioral Information That Confirms or Contradicts a Personality Impression," in *Person, Memory: The Cognitive Basis of Social Perception,* R. Hastie et al., eds., Hillsdale, NJ: Lawrence Erlbaum Associates, 155–177.

Heider, Fritz (1958), *The Psychology of Interpersonal Relations,* New York: John Wiley and Sons.

Henderson, Geraldine R., Dawn Iacobucci, and Bobby J. Calder (1998), "Brand Diagnostics: Mapping Branding Effects Using Consumer Associative Networks," *European Journal of Operational Research,* 111 (2), 306–327.

Hoek, Janet (2004), "Ambush Marketing: Research and Management Implications," in *Global Sport Sponsorship,* John Amis and T. Bettina Cornwell, eds., Oxford, UK: Berg Publishers.

IEG (2000), "Year One of IRL Title Builds Traffic, Awareness for Northern Light," *IEG Sponsorship Report,* 19 (23), 1–3.

IEG (2003), "Sponsorship Spending to Increase 8.7 Percent in 2004," *IEG Sponsorship Report,* 22 (24), 1, 4.

Jacoby, Larry L., Jeffrey P. Toth, and Andrew P. Yonelinas (1993), "Separating Conscious and Unconscious Influences of Memory: Measuring Recollection," *Journal of Experimental Psychology: General,* 122 (2), 139–154.

Jagre, Emma, John J. Watson, and John G. Watson (2001), "Sponsorship and Congruity Theory: A Theoretical Framework for Explaining Consumer Attitude and Recall of Event Sponsorship," in *Advances in Consumer Research* (Volume 28), Mary Gilly and Joan Meyers-Levy, eds., Provo, UT: Association for Consumer Research, 439–445.

Johar, Gita Venkataramani, and Michel Tuan Pham (1999), "Relatedness, Prominence and Constructive Sponsor Identification," *Journal of Marketing Research,* 36 (3), 299–312.

Keller, Kevin Lane (1993), "Conceptualizing, Measuring and Managing Customer-Based Brand Equity," *Journal of Marketing,* 57 (1), 1–22.

Keller, Kevin Lane (1998), *Strategic Brand Management,* Upper Saddle River, NJ: Prentice-Hall.

Keller, Kevin Lane (2001), "Mastering the Marketing Communications Mix: Micro and Macro Perspectives on Integrated Marketing Communication Programs," *Journal of Marketing Management,* 17 (7/8), 819–847.

Kirmani, Amna, and Peter Wright (1989), "Money Talks: Perceived Advertising Expense and Expected Product Quality," *Journal of Consumer Research,* 16 (3), 344–353.

Kroeber-Riel, Warner (1979), "Activation Research: Psychobiological Approaches in Consumer Research," *Journal of Consumer Research,* 5 (March), 240–250.

Lardinoit, Thierry, and Christian Derbaix (2001), "Sponsorship and Recall of Sponsors," *Psychology and Marketing,* 18 (2), 167–190.

Lardinoit, Thierry, and Pascale Quester (2001), "Attitudinal Effects of Combined Sponsorship and Sponsor's Prominence on Basketball in Europe," *Journal of Advertising Research,* 41 (1), 48–58.

Madrigal, Robert (2000), "The Influence of Social Alliances with Sports Teams on Intentions to Purchase Corporate Sponsors' Products," *Journal of Advertising,* 29 (4), 13–24.

Madrigal, Robert (2001), "Social Identity Effects in a Belief-Attitude-Intentions Hierarchy: Implications for Corporate Sponsorship," *Psychology and Marketing,* 18 (2), 145–165.

Mael, Fred A., and Blake E. Ashforth (1992), "Alumni and Their Alma Mater: A Partial Test of the Reformulated Model of Organizational Identification," *Journal of Organizational Behavior,* 13 (2), 103–123.

Mandler, George (1982), "The Structure of Value: Accounting for Taste," in *Affect and Cognition: The 17th Annual Carnegie Symposium,* Margaret S. Clark and Susan T. Fiske, eds., Hillsdale, NJ: Lawrence Erlbaum Associates, 3–36.

Marshall, D.W., and Cook, G. (1992), "The Corporate (Sports) Sponsor," *International Journal of Advertising,* 11, 307–324.

Mathur, Lynette Knowles, and Ike Mathur (1996), "Is Value Associated with Initiating New Advertising Agency-Client Relations?" *Journal of Advertising,* 25 (3), 1–12.

McCarville, Ronald E., Christopher M. Flood, and Tabatha A. Froats (1998), "The Effectiveness of Selected Promotions on Spectators' Assessments of a Nonprofit Sporting Event Sponsor," *Journal of Sport Management,* 12 (1), 51–62.

McCracken, Grant (1989), "Who Is the Celebrity Endorser? Cultural Foundations of the Endorsement Process," *Journal of Consumer Research,* 16 (3), 310–321.

McDaniel, Stephen R. (1999), "An Investigation of Match-up Effects in Sport Sponsorship Advertising: The Implications of Consumer Advertising Schemas," *Psychology and Marketing,* 16 (2), 163–184.

McDonald, Mark A., George R. Milne, and JinBae Hong (2002), "Motivational Factors for Evaluating Sport Spectator and Participant Markets," *Sport Marketing Quarterly,* 11 (2), 100–113.

Meyers-Levy, Joan, and Alice M. Tybout (1989), "Schema Congruity as a Basis for Product Evaluation," *Journal of Consumer Research,* 16 (June), 39–54.

Meyers-Levy, Joan, Therese A. Louie, and Mary T. Curren (1994), "How Does the Congruity of Brand Names Affect Evaluations of Brand Name Extensions?" *Journal of Applied Psychology,* 79 (1), 46–53.

Mitchell, Andrew A. (1979), "Involvement: A Potentially Important Mediator of Consumer Behavior," in *Advances in Consumer Research* (Volume 6), William L. Wilkie, ed., Ann Arbor, MI: Association for Consumer Research, 25–30

Mitchell, Andrew A. (1981), "The Dimensions of Advertising Involvement," in *Advances in Consumer Research* (Volume 8), Kent B. Monroe, ed., Ann Arbor, MI: Association for Consumer Research, 191–195.

Morris, Bob (1998), "Extreme Sport, Extreme Chic, Extreme Hype," *New York Times,* February 8, 9.1.

Mundorf, Norbert, Dolf Zillmann, and Dan Drew (1991), "Effects of Disturbing Televised Events on the Acquisition of Information From Subsequently Presented Commercials," *Journal of Advertising,* 20 (1), 46–53.

Musante, Michael, George R. Milne, and Mark A. McDonald (1999), "Sport Sponsorship: Evaluating the Sport and Brand Image Match," *International Journal of Sports Marketing and Sponsorship,* 1 (1), 32–47.

Newell, Stephen J., Kenneth V. Henderson, and Bob T. Wu (2001), "The Effects of Pleasure and Arousal on Recall of Advertisements during the Super Bowl," *Psychology and Marketing,* 18 (11), 1,135–1,153.

Nicholls, J.A.F., Sydney Roslow, and Sandipa Dublish (1999), "Brand Recall and Brand Preference at Sponsored Golf and Tennis Tournaments," *European Journal of Marketing,* 33 (3/4), 365–386.

Olson, Erik L., and Thjømøe, Hans Mathias (2003), "The Effects of Peripheral Exposure to Information on Brand Performance, *European Journal of Marketing,* 37 (1/2), 243–255.

Park, C. Whan, and Gordon W. McClung (1986), "The Effect of T.V. Program Involvement on Involvement with Commercials," in *Advances in Consumer Research* (Volume 13), Richard J. Lutz, ed., Ann Arbor, MI: Association for Consumer Research, 544–548.

Pavelchak, Mark A., John H. Antil, and James M. Munch (1988), "The Super Bowl: An Investigation into the Relationship among Program Context, Emotional Experience and Ad Recall," *Journal of Consumer Research* 15 (December), 360–367.

Pearson, Kevin (2003), "For More Sports Fans, X Marks the Hot; Culture; Inland Athletes Are among those Helping a Generation Symbol Turn into Booming Business," *The Press-Enterprise,* 10 August, A01.

Pedicini, Sandra (2003), "For Motorsports Sponsors, It's a Race to the Finish Line," *Orlando Sentinel,* 16 February.

Petty, Richard E., and John T. Cacioppo (1981), *Attitudes and Persuasion: Classic and Contemporary Approaches,* Dubuque, IA: William C. Brown.

Petty, Richard E., John T. Cacioppo, and David Schumann (1983), "Central and Peripheral Routes to Advertising Effectiveness: The Moderating Role of Involvement," *Journal of Consumer Research,* 10 (September), 135–146.

Pham, Michel Tuan (1992), "Effects of Involvement, Arousal and Pleasure on the Recognition of Sponsorship Stimuli," in *Advances in Consumer Research* (Volume 19), John F. Sherry, Jr. and Brian Sternthal, eds., Provo, UT: Association for Consumer Research, 85–93.

Pham, Michel Tuan, and Gita Venkataramani Johar (2001), "Market Prominence Biases in Sponsor Identification: Processes and Consequentiality," *Psychology and Marketing,* 18 (2), 123–143.

Pham, Michel Tuan, and Marc Vanhuele (1997), "Analyzing the Memory Impact of Advertising Fragments," *Marketing Letters,* 8 (4), 407–417.

Pope, Nigel, and Kevin E. Voges (1999), "Sponsorship and Image: A Replication and Extension," *Journal of Marketing Communications,* 5 (1), 17–28.

Pracejus, John W., and G. Douglas Olsen (2002), "The Role of Brand/Cause Fit in the Effectiveness of Cause-Related Marketing Campaigns," *Journal of Business Research,* 57 (6), 635–640.

Prior, Anat, and Shlomo Bentin (2003), "Incidental Formation of Episodic Associations: The Importance of Sentential Context," *Memory and Cognition,* 31(2), 306–316.

Quester, Pascale G. (1997), "Awareness as a Measure of Sponsorship Effectiveness: The Adelaide Formula One Grand Prix and Evidence of Incidental Ambush Effects," *Journal of Marketing Communications,* 3 (1), 1–20.

Rifon, Nora J., Sejung Marina Choi, Carrie S. Trimble, and Hairong Li (2004), "Congruence Effects in Sponsorship: The Mediating Role of Sponsor Credibility and Consumer Attribution of Sponsor Motive," *Journal of Advertising,* 33 (1), 29–42.

Roy, Donald P. (2000), *An Examination of the Influence of Perceived Brand-Event Congruence on Consumer Responses to Event Sponsorships,* Unpublished doctoral dissertation, University of Memphis, Memphis, Tennessee.

Roy, Donald P., and T. Bettina Cornwell (2004), "The Effects of Consumer Knowledge on Responses to Event Sponsorships," *Psychology and Marketing,* 21 (3), 185–207.

Ruth, Julie A., and Bernard L. Simonin (2003), "Brought to You by Brand A and Brand B: Investigating Multiple Sponsors' Influence on Consumers' Attitudes toward Sponsored Events," *Journal of Advertising,* 32 (3), 19–30.

Sandler, Dennis M., and David Shani (1989), "Olympic Sponsorship vs. 'Ambush' Marketing: Who Gets the Gold?" *Journal of Advertising Research,* 29 (4), 9–14.

Schaefer, Allen, and Bruce D. Keillor (1997), "The Effective Use of Endorsements in Advertising: The Relationship between 'Match-Up' and Involvement," *The Journal of Marketing Management,* 7 (Fall/Winter), 23–33.

Scott, Randall K., and David H. Goff (1988), "How Excitation From Prior Programming Affects Television News Recall," *Journalism Quarterly,* 65 (Fall), 615–620.

Shanklin, William L., and John R. Kuzma (1992), "Buying That Sporting Image," *Marketing Management,* 1 (Spring), 59–67.

Shimp, Terrence A., and Larry G. Gresham (1983), "An Information Processing Perspective of Recent Advertising Literature," *Current Issues and Research in Advertising,* 6 (2), 36–79.

Söderlund, Magnus (2002), "Customer Familiarity and Its Effects on Satisfaction and Behavioral Intentions," *Psychology and Marketing,* 19 (10), 861–880.

Speed, Richard, and Peter Thompson (2000), "Determinants of Sports Sponsorship Response," *Journal of the Academy of Marketing Science,* 28 (2), 226–238.

Squire, Larry R. (1987), *Memory and Brain,* Oxford: Oxford University Press.

Srull, Thomas K. (1981), "Person Memory: Some Tests of Associative Storage and Retrieval Models," *Journal of Experimental Psychology: Human Learning and Memory,* 7 (6), 440–463.

Sujan, Mita (1985), "Consumer Knowledge: Effects on Evaluation Strategies Mediating Consumer Judgments," *Journal of Consumer Research,* 12 (June), 31–46.

Tajfel, Henri, and John C. Turner (1985), "The Social Identity Theory of Intergroup Behavior," in *Psychology of Intergroup Behavior* (Volume 2), Stephen Worchel and William G. Austin, eds., Chicago: Nelson-Hall, 7–24.

Tavassoli, Nader T., Clifford J. Schultz, and Gavan J. Fitzsimmons (1995), "Program Involvement: Are Moderate Levels Best for Ad Memory and Attitude toward the Ad?" *Journal of Advertising Research,* 35 (5), 61–72.

Tripodi, John A., Martin Hirons, David Bednall, and Max Sutherland (2003), "Cognitive Evaluation: Prompts Used to Measure Sponsorship Awareness," *International Journal of Market Research,* 45 (4), 435–455.

Tulving, Endel, Daniel L. Schacter, and Heather A. Stark (1982), "Priming Effects in Word Fragment Completion Are Independent of Recognition Memory," *Journal of Experimental Psychology: Learning, Memory and Cognition,* 8 (4), 336–342.

Wann, Daniel L., and Thomas J. Dolan (1994), "Spectators' Evaluations of Rival and Fellow Fans," *Psychological Record,* 44 (3), 351–358.

Weiner, Jay (2000), "Selling World Peace at $55 Million a Pop," *Business Week,* (3701) October 10, 110.

Woodside, Arch G., and Jean-Charles Chebat (2001), "Updating Heider's Balance Theory in Consumer Behavior: A Jewish Couple Buys a German Car and Additional Buying-Consumer Transformation Stories," *Psychology and Marketing,* 18 (5), 475–495.

Zaichkowsky, Judith Lynne (1994), "The Personal Involvement Inventory: Reduction, Revision and Application to Advertising," *Journal of Advertising,* 23 (4), 59–69.

Zajonc, Robert B. (1968), "Attitudinal Effects of Mere Exposure," *Journal of Personality and Social Psychology Monograph Supplement,* 9 (Part 2), 1–27.

Zajonc, Robert B. (1980), "Feeling and Thinking Preferences Need No Inferences," *American Psychologist,* 35 (Feb), 151–175.

INDEX

About the Editors and Contributors

GENERAL EDITOR

BRUCE D. KEILLOR is coordinator of the American Marketing Association's Office for Applied Research-Direct Marketing and Professor of Marketing and International Business at The University of Akron. He is also a research fellow at Michigan State University. Dr. Keillor specializes in international marketing strategy and direct multi-channel marketing and has authored more than 60 articles published in journals worldwide. He has also contributed to numerous books. In addition to his academic credentials, Dr. Keillor has also been an active entrepreneur as co-owner of a direct-marketing software company he helped found in 1994. Dr. Keillor also has extensive executive education and consulting experience as a copartner in BBA Associates, a global marketing consulting firm.

EDITORS

DEBORAH L. OWENS, Ph.D., is Associate Professor of Marketing and International Business at The University of Akron. Dr. Owens received her Ph.D. from Kent State University in May 1997, where she majored in Marketing, with a minor in International Business. She also has a Master's degree in Business from Kent State, and a Bachelor's degree in Industrial and Systems Engineering from The Ohio State University. She spent 12 years working in the health care arena, first as a management engineer at the Ohio State University Health System, and then at Children's Hospital Medical Center in Akron, Ohio. She teaches in both the undergraduate and MBA programs, including courses in Business Research Methods, Marketing Research, Buyer Behavior, Marketing Principles, and Marketing Strategy. Her primary research interests include promotion strategies, customer satisfaction, political marketing, and cross-cultural influence on buyer behavior. She has also authored a book, *The Business Plan Project Workbook,* for the Glencoe Division of McGraw-Hill, co-authored several industrial cases, and contributed two chapters to *Direct Marketing in Action,* published in 2006 by Praeger Press. Dr. Owens has published in the *Advances in Business Marketing and Purchasing, The Case Research Journal, The Journal of Consumer Satisfaction, Dissatisfaction and Complaining Behavior,* and other scholarly journals.

DOUGLAS R. HAUSKNECHT, Ph.D. is Associate Professor of Marketing and Interim Director of the Institute for Global Business at The University of Akron. He has had articles published in the *Journal of Consumer Research, Psychology and Marketing,* the *Journal of Consumer Satisfaction/Dissatisfaction and Complaining Behavior,* and the *Journal of the Market Research Society,* among others. He graduated from the University of Florida in 1988. Since joining the faculty at The University of Akron, he has consulted with a variety of local and national organizations including the Better Business Bureau, the American Red Cross, and The Davey Tree Expert Company.

CONTRIBUTORS

CHERYL AGRANOVICH founded WellCorp, Inc., in 1995 to provide corporations with health management solutions. With a degree from Mercy College of Detroit, she got her start in the health industry as a registered nurse in an emergency room. WellCorp has grown from a base in Cleveland to a nationwide clientele, and it has twice been named one of the 99 Best Places to Work in Northeast Ohio. It is also a three-time recipient of the Weatherhead 100 fastest-growing companies in Ohio. In 2005, Agranovich was recognized as a Northeast Ohio Ernst & Young Entrepreneur of the Year and was named a Woman of Note by Crain's *Cleveland Business.* She is an advisory panel member of the Athena PowerLink and a member of the State of Ohio Board of Education Physical Fitness and Wellness Advisory Council.

MARK BEDNAR, Director of Marketing and Communication for WellCorp, Inc., develops communication strategies for the firm's clients. Mark has a B.S. in Communications from Kent State University. He has worked as an editor, manager, and page designer for the *Record-Courier* in Ravenna, Ohio; the *News-Herald* in Mentor, Ohio; and *Plastics News* in Akron, Ohio.

ROBERT BLACK has over 31 years of experience as a corporate executive and is a Registered Professional Engineer. He has a B.S. in Chemistry from Pennsylvania State University, an M.S. in Electrical Engineering from the University of Missouri, and an MBA in Finance from The University of Akron. The inventor and marketer of Clean Shower, Black is the founder of Automation, Inc. and general partner of Clean Shower, LP. He is also a part owner of Hydrochem Systems, Inc. He is a member of the American Chemical Society and holds 15 issued U.S. patents, with additional U.S. and foreign patents issued and pending.

T. BETTINA CORNWELL (Ph.D., The University of Texas) is Professor of Marketing and Cluster Leader, Marketing, in the UQ Business School at the University of Queensland, Australia. She was formerly Professor of Marketing in the Fogelman College of Business and Economics at the University of Memphis. Her research focuses on promotion and consumer behavior, especially regarding international and public policy issues. She has published articles on the topics of consumer behavior and sponsorship-linked marketing in the *Journal of Advertising, Journal of Advertising Research, Journal of the Academy of Marketing Science,* and the *Journal of Consumer Research*. With John Amis, she published *Global Sport Sponsorship* in 2006.

KEN DICKEY is co-founder of The Institute of Strategic Mapping and has an extensive business career producing superior results from average businesses. Mr. Dickey successfully implemented his process for strategic thinking as President/CEO of the multinational Cleveland Motion Controls. Prior to this, Mr. Dickey served as Senior Vice President, Sales, for Reliance/Rockwell Automation, and as General Manager for Reliance Electric Industrial Motors. Dickey is the recipient of The University of Akron Distinguished Alumni Award, and he has served on The University of Akron Strategic Planning Team, Reliance Electric Marketing Council, and the National Board of Governors-Alumni Association, The University of Akron. He holds a B.S. in Finance/Marketing from The University of Akron and an EMBA from Case Western Reserve University.

ANNEMARIE FARRELL, Ph.D., is Assistant Professor, Sports Management and Media at Ithaca College. She received her doctorate in Sport and Exercise Management from The Ohio State University, with the dissertation *Why Women Don't Watch Women's Sport: A Qualitative Analysis*. She holds an M.A., Sport and Exercise Management, from The Ohio State University, and a B.A. from Mount Holyoke College in Political Science and Sport Studies. Her work focuses on consumer behavior, spectator and fan motives, women's sports marketing, Title IX law and policy, and qualitative research methodology.

JANET FINK, Ph.D., is Assistant Professor, Sports and Exercise Management, and Program Coordinator, at The Ohio State University. She teaches courses in Sport Finance and Sport Law. Before coming to Ohio State, Dr. Fink spent two years on the sport management faculty at the University of Texas at Austin. While at the University of Texas, she taught Sport Finance, Sport Law, and Sport Sponsorship classes, and she collaborated with the athletic department to study aspects of sport consumer and athletic donor behaviors. She taught in the Columbus Public Schools and coached volleyball for a number of years before receiving her M.A. and Ph.D. from Ohio State. Dr. Fink's primary research focus is in the area of diversity management with a particular interest in the underrepresentation of females and minorities in sport leadership positions and the misrepresentation/underrepresentation of female athletes in the media. She has published, presented, and submitted several papers in various journals regarding this research, including *Quest, Journal of Sport Management,* and *JOPERD.*

ELIZABETH A. GALAMBOS is the Marketing Director for Brott Mardis & Co., a certified public accounting firm in Akron, Ohio, where she helped the firm move from scattered, partner-driven marketing activities to a comprehensive strategy that has helped position the firm as a reputable and recognized brand in the marketplace. She also works with the firm's clients as a marketing consultant to develop marketing plans and invent solutions that are suitable for limited budgets. Prior to joining the firm, she worked in journalism, radio broadcasting, and graphic design. She is also an accomplished photographer and volunteers much of her time as the PR and marketing chair for ArtCetera, a young professionals' networking organization focused on the support, appreciation, and progression of the arts in the Greater Akron community.

CHRISTOPHER GEBHARDT has been building brands and businesses for over 18 years, leveraging his unique blend of experiences and skills. He has client and agency experience in which he worked on new and established brands, employing traditional media and advertising channels as well as emerging media and technologies. Currently, he is co-CEO of 2 Degrees Ventures, which provides brand and marketing consulting services to established brands, works with private equity players to provide branding and marketing services to new ventures, and connects brands with entertainment properties and celebrities. Prior to forming 2 Degrees, he launched branded-entertainment pioneer Integrated Entertainment Partners (IEP) and then merged it into The Firm. Prior to IEP, he was senior vice president, client services director, and the executive director of emerging technology and innovation for Ogilvy & Mather. He has an undergraduate degree in accounting and is a CPA, he has an MBA from the Kellogg School of Management, and he speaks frequently at emerging marketing technology conferences and business schools on the topic of the future of marketing and advertising.

MICHAEL HARDMAN holds a B.A. in Economics from Hillsdale College and an MBA in Marketing from the University of Toledo. He has also completed supplementary postgraduate study in strategic planning at the Massachusetts Institute of Technology. He is president of the Hardman Group, a consultancy with emphases in primary research, strategic planning, and marketing communications.

ANNA MCALISTER, Lecturer in the School of Business and the School of Psychology at the University of Queensland, Australia, teaches courses in undergraduate and postgraduate consumer behavior and undergraduate research methods. Her Ph.D. thesis advanced the understanding of preschool children's social and cognitive development. She has a Bachelor of Psychological Science from the University of Queensland and a Graduate Certificate in University Teaching. Her postdoctoral research combines interests in consumer behavior and developmental psychology to investigate individual differences in children's development that can be used to explain children's understanding of advertising intent and their progress through the consumer socialization process.

STEPHEN M. MILLETT is a futurist and Leader of Technology Foresight at Social Technologies, an information and consulting company in Washington, D.C. He is retired from Battelle, where he was the manager of numerous futuring studies for corporations around the world. He led expert focus group and scenario projects in consumer product, energy, and automotive companies. He is co-author of *A Manager's Guide to Technology Forecasting and Analysis Methods* (1991). In addition, he is the author of 27 professional journal articles and a contributing editor of *Strategy & Leadership*.

LEN PAGON is President and CEO of Brulant, Inc., which fuses the creative design and Internet marketing capabilities of an interactive agency with deep technology. Some of his key areas of thought leadership and insight include the use of technology to strengthen relationships; how businesses should approach and strategize around the multi-channel marketing environment; how to ultimately attract, convert, and retain customers over time; and issues surrounding the life cycle and adoption curve of the Internet. He is also an executive committee member for the Young President's Organization, and he sits on the board of e-Mergent Marketing, a leading search-engine marketing and Web site usability firm. Finally, he is a founder and board member for PerceptIS, a technology services and outsourcing firm, and a consistent contributor to trade and national media partners including *IBD, USA Today,* and the *Wall Street Journal*.

HEIDI PARKER is a doctoral student at The Ohio State University. Her research interests center on sport consumer behavior.

ROBERT PIEKARCZYK received his MBA from Tiffin University with a concentration in Marketing. After working in new product development and market launches at Invacare, Inc., he took over as Sales and Marketing Director for the Cleveland Grand Prix. An avid sports car racer, Rob has extensive experience on the subject of event marketing from many different perspectives. In addition to his professional activities, he also teaches a course in sports marketing at Cleveland State University.

CATHERINE QUATMAN, Ph.D., received her M.A. and doctorate in Sport and Exercise Management from The Ohio State University and her undergraduate degree in Sport Administration from Edinboro University of Pennsylvania. Her research interests span a broad range of topics including organizational behavior, consumer behavior, group dynamics, and human research management. Her most recent research has focused on a rapidly developing area of social network theory and analysis to help explain how certain patterns of interaction arise and how particular relations affect individuals' and groups' behaviors. Dr. Quatman is particularly interested in extending network analytic techniques to the study of the organizational behavior in the sport sector, social cohesion on sports teams, and social contagion associated with sport consumer behavior.

PAUL QUIGLEY is a partner with Brulant, Inc. Paul has extensive experience in strategy formulation, organizational restructuring, operations, system design, system implementation, and process improvement. Prior to this, he held positions with Accenture, Consolidated Health Care Coalition (which he co-founded), Homefront Health Care, Critical Care American/Medical Care America, and Harvard Pilgrim Health Care Plan.

DONALD P. ROY (Ph.D., University of Memphis) is an Associate Professor of Marketing in the Jennings A. Jones College of Business at Middle Tennessee State University. He has published several articles on sport sponsorship and sports marketing in publications such as *Journal of Advertising, International Journal of Sports Marketing & Sponsorship, Journal of Marketing of Higher Education,* and *Sport Marketing Quarterly.* He contributed a chapter to the book *Global Sport Sponsorship* (John Amis and T. Bettina Cornwell, eds., 2005).

ANTHONY A. STERNS, Ph.D., serves as the Vice President of Research for Creative Action, LLC, a small consulting firm specializing in market research, especially creating and taking new products and services to market. The company's cognitive therapeutic intervention activity, Memory Magic, developed with funding from the National Institute on Aging, is distributed nationally. He is also the acting CEO of a start-up company, Fast Optimum, LLC, commercializing new optimization and resource allocation software technology. Dr. Sterns is an Adjunct Associate Professor at the University of Maryland University College (UMUC) and Fellow of the Institute for Life-Span Development and Gerontology at The University of Akron. He teaches graduate Management and undergraduate Psychology and Gerontology courses. He holds a Bachelor of Engineering degree in Naval Architecture and Marine Engineering from the University of Michigan, a Master's degree in Psychology, and a doctorate in Industrial Organizational Psychology from The University of Akron.

HARVEY L. STERNS, Ph.D., is Professor of Psychology and Director of the Institute for Life-Span Development and Gerontology at The University of Akron. He is also Research Professor of Gerontology at the Northeastern Ohio Universities College of Medicine. He is a faculty member in the Applied Cognitive Aging and Industrial/Organizational Psychology graduate programs. He has published extensively on cognitive intervention, work and retirement, career development, training and retraining, and maintaining professional competence. He is a licensed psychologist in Ohio and is a Fellow of the Gerontological Society of America, the American Psychological Association, American Psychological Society, Association for Gerontology in Higher Education, and the Ohio Academy of Science. He has served as President of Division 20 Adult Development and Aging of the American Psychological Association, Association for Gerontology in Higher Education, Sigma Phi Omega National Academic and Professional Society in Gerontology, and the Ohio Network of Educational Consultants in the Field Of Aging, Jewish Family Service, Akron. He is Vice President of Business Development for Creative Action, LLC.

VINCENT TALLEPIED is partner with First Ukrainian Fund, a buyout firm that operates in Ukraine. He started his career in the medical systems branch of General Electric Company. In 1992, he joined Goodyear Tire and Rubber Company and held various management positions in finance and MIS in France and at corporate headquarters in Akron, Ohio. Back in France in 1999, he founded and managed startup SantéFamille. He then joined Gemini Consulting Inc. as a manager. His main fields of expertise are strategy, business planning, and performance management. His research interests include product life cycle, fashion, consumer culture, and he has published articles on fashion and product life cycles. He graduated from ESCEM (Ecole Supérieure de Commerce et de Management). He lives in Paris with his wife and two children.

CLINTON S. WEEKS (B.A., University of Queensland, Australia) is currently a Ph.D. candidate in the Schools of Business and Psychology at the University of Queensland.